TOUGH GIRL

An Olympian's Journey

TOUGH GIRL

An Olympian's Journey

Carolyn Wood

WHITE·PINE·PRESS

Portland, Oregon

TOUGH GIRL
White Pine Press, Portland 97225
© 2016 by Carolyn Wood

Berry, Wendell. *The Unforeseen Wilderness: Kentucky's Red River Gorge*. Counterpoint Press, 2006.

"I Can't Help But Wonder (Where I'm Bound)"
Words and Music by Tom Paxton.
Copyright © 1963, 1964 BMG Ruby Songs and Reservoir Media Music
Copyright Renewed
All Rights for BMG Ruby Songs Administered by BMG Rights Management (US) LLC
All Rights Reserved Used by Permission
Reprinted by Permission of Hal Leonard Corporation
© 1996 Chrysalis One Music Publishing Group Ireland Ltd. (IMRO)
And Cherry Lane Music Publishing Co., Inc.
All Rights for Chrysalis One Music Publishing Group Ireland Ltd. (IMRO)
Administered by Chrysalis One Music (ASCAP)
All Rights for Chrysalis One Music Publishing Group Ireland Ltd. (IMRO)
Assigned to Reservoir Media Music (ASCAP)
Published by Reservoir Media Management, Inc.
All Rights Reserved
Used By Permission of ALFRED MUSIC

"In Excelsis Deo," lyrics by Patti Smith. Copyright © 1975 Linda Music. Used with permission.

"High Hopes"
Words by Sammy Cahn
Music by James Van Heusen
Copyright © 1959 (Renewed) Maraville Music Corp.
All Rights Reserved Used by Permission
Reprinted by Permission of Hal Leonard Corporation

"Rome Olympic Games 1960," © 2016 The Associated Press.

Other photos courtesy The Oregonian; Ray Jacobs, Roslyn Heights, New York; Tye Steinbach; Ralph Vincent; Multnomah Athletic Club archive; and Lynn Burke.

Some names and identifying details have been changed in this book to protect the privacy of individuals.

Editing and design by Indigo Editing & Publications

ISBN: 978-0-9977828-0-6
LCCN: 2016911754

In gratitude to my parents, Carlton and Virginia Green Wood, and for my granddaughter, Sekara Grace.

Always in big woods when you leave familiar ground and step off alone into a new place there will be, along with the feelings of curiosity and excitement, a little nagging of dread. It is the ancient fear of the unknown, and it is your first bond with the wilderness you are going into.

—WENDELL BERRY

CONTENTS

PROLOGUE: LETTING GO

2012

WE STOOD IN THE LAKE, my father and I, sixty-some years ago.

"You can't make me!" My knees locked in certainty in the water. Daddy was trying to teach me to swim, but my feet stuck on the bottom.

"You'll swim when you're ready," I remember him saying. "It'll be easy when you decide to do it."

When my partner of thirty years decided to walk away, I hung on, my knuckles white. *You can't make me quit*, I believed. "Swim to the end of the pool" is a life rule. But my rule, not hers. She left me clinging to the end of something.

If you can't stop the finale, what can you do?

You could go to bed and read for a year or dip into the bottle. You could go get that tummy tuck or lid lift and head off to the Hot Flash Dances or go online, desperately seeking Susan. I learned to knit as Rose was leaving, but that was my mother's trick, to fill a space with wool. My mom knit sweaters, blankets, and hats, stockings, leggings, scarves, and vests, little Christmas puppets that sat atop candles, as if all that yarn could fill the empty space my father left when he disappeared to gamble—and later, after he died.

Being outdoors brought me greater solace. Hiking, backpacking, treks through the Himalayas. I did them all through our two years of separation. One day a friend told me her story about selling the *Herald-Tribune* and busking in the Métro when she ran out of money in Paris. "What happened to that girl?" I asked, thinking of the audacity of youth. It was a good question to ponder now.

Where would I find that tough little girl I'd been who wouldn't put her face in the water, who chased after her brother, broke the windows in Mr. Weber's warehouse, and never cried at school—the one who played Superman and Tarzan and Sergeant Preston of the Yukon out in the backyard?

I needed to tap into the strength of that stubborn kid who wouldn't learn to swim until she had to and who wouldn't stop once she got started. A physical challenge, I reasoned, would get me back in touch with the gutsy girl I remembered once being, the tough one who resolved to work hard and ended up winning Olympic gold.

In early June after Rose's and my first or second meeting with the mediator, his meter ticking while we quibbled over property values and accounts, the end of our relationship is obvious. We aren't going to finish our journey together. I pack up the car and drive south to Yosemite for the Wilderness Volunteers project I signed up for in the winter. One morning as we climb the trail to Tiltill Valley, the team leader talks about a cycling trip he and his wife took. They wandered back roads through the South for a month with only a map and a general idea, no reservations, no plans.

What an idea: head out and explore. *Hut to hut*, I think, remembering a dream Rose and I shared years ago when we drove through the Pyrenees in France and Spain. We would return and hike, we said. To keep our backpacks light, we'd stay in those mountain refuges, *albergues*, like the thousand-year-old monastery in Roncesvalle that offered free rooms to pilgrims. Now, with our separation, that plan has been scrapped.

But the idea of a journey resonates. I want to get out of town, away from all that pain. "Hit the Road Jack." "Keep on Truckin'." "On the Road Again." The songs repeat in my mind while we climb toward the valley. I could walk across Spain by myself, without a partner. Why not?

I love hiking and backpacking, but at sixty-seven, I can't carry forty pounds anymore. I've climbed and trekked high altitude but always with a leader, in a group. Now I'm on my own. When the divorce becomes final in September, I'll need to do something, something physical and hard and alone. I need to test my endurance, to explore solitude, to lean into fear.

In the volunteer camp, I try saying it: "My next trip? Oh, I might walk the Spanish Camino." Everyone tells a long-walk story then. Back home in Portland, Powell's Books provides piles of accounts, maps, photo books, and guides to study. I take notes and begin to imagine how long it might take. The mileage—over five hundred miles—seems staggering. It will require training.

That makes sense, to return to discipline and training. After a great loss, you search for the familiar. When I lost custody of my son before he even turned two, I began running. Alone in the early mornings or the afternoons, those times when his play noises no longer filled the house, I'd walk over to the track. Later, I'd find the roads where joggers ran their miles. The rhythm of footfall and rasped breath drummed away the emptiness.

After a week of studying the Camino, I write to my now-grown son: *Thinking hard about walking the Camino de Compostela in October and November—500 miles! What do you think? Hope my hip holds out.*

The next day I buy my plane ticket.

I will walk for forty days.

I'll try to find the gutsy girl who got her feet off the bottom and learned to swim.

PART I

SWIMMERS, TO YOUR MARKS

1952–1958

Hard Lessons

1952–1953

At first my father sat on the canvas deck beside the Wauna Lake swim dock and offered a suggestion. "Just let go of the side, honey. Hold your breath, and sit down. It's easy."

Believing him, I went down into the dark, wet world, lost my footing, and scrambled to stand. My feet slipped on the slick boards, and I stumbled forward blindly as if running in a nightmare.

Now we stood in the lake together, my father and I. *You can't make me*, I thought as he stood before me in the cool water.

He smiled and took my hands, then gently pulled me toward him.

"Just put your face in, honey. On the count of three: One. Two. Three." He lifted my hands a little, forcing me down as he backed up, pulling me off my feet. I arched my back and lifted my head higher, my feet pushed toward the bottom and the slimy green boards. I was not going to put my face in that water again.

The next summer when school let out, Richard, my older brother, had his jobs—mowing lawns, picking berries, delivering to the paper route—to earn money for a new bike and fireworks. Mom said she needed to keep me busy and out of trouble. First came Vacation Bible School and then ballet lessons. But in the afternoons, when she looked out from the kitchen window, she'd see me streak down the street on the bike I wasn't supposed to be riding. Standing at her ironing board or beside the stove, she could hear our cries from the tree fort or vacant lot. When I stomped in wearing Richard's leather chaps and vest, she must have suspected I was never going to be the little doll she'd wanted. When my hands slid clumsily along the piano keys, she knew we wouldn't be playing duets. The day I flung myself on the floor after another steamy ballet lesson with Anita Pienovi, she stood in the doorway and sighed. She told me that Daddy loved dancing, but I didn't care. I hated how it made me sweat. Then she suggested swim lessons.

But learning to swim seemed as impossible as learning to fly. And just as scary. It was falling, out of control, unsafe, like riding on my brother's handlebars when he pedaled too fast going down hills. *It might be easier to swim in milk*, I thought, looking up at an Alpenrose Dairy billboard on the way to the pool.

Mom signed me up with Portland Parks Bureau, and I began swim classes downtown. The Shattuck pool, small and dank, was in the basement of an ancient elementary school on the Park Blocks, where, under the tall trees, it always seemed to be dusk. I took and failed many lessons there with a few neighbor kids.

At Wauna Lake, Mom still made me wear a life jacket, a stained, moldy-smelling canvas one made for a five-year-old. I wanted to swim, to shed that horrid jacket and be able to paddle the canoe or ride with the big kids in the motorboat. I wanted to be able to jump off the diving board in front of all the girls who sat on the dock smeared in iodine and baby oil, a concoction to deepen their tans. I just couldn't get my feet off the bottom.

At some point I finally mastered putting my head underwater. Clinging to the gutter, I could do bubbles. Up and down. Up and down. I bobbed with the best of them. I imagine myself then, head encased in the tight white cap, chin strap choking, curls bulging beneath the rubber, my eyes pulled back into a squint. We were to practice the float.

Shivering in Wauna Lake, 1952

"Step away from the edge two giant steps," the instructor, a rather harsh woman who never got into the pool, shouted at us from the deck. "Turn around. Put your arms by your ears and lie down on top of the water."

Two steps. Turn around. Arms up. So far so good. Lie down. The water came almost up to my neck, making it hard to lie down. I bent my knees a little, and the water edged toward my mouth.

"Head down and push off." Her voice pierced my cap and curls.

I grabbed a breath, squinched my eyes tight, and reached toward the gutter, fingers spread as if to push away the water. I leaned forward, trying to lift my legs. But my feet seemed encased in concrete booties, weighted to the bottom so that as my top half edged forward, my feet shuffled in slow, heavy steps, keeping me upright.

"Too close to the wall," she hollered. "Go back and try again."

Finally, forcefully, I plunged my face into the murky green and released one leg. The other remained rooted to the tile. I was almost swimming with my one-leg float.

Toward the end of the class series, she ordered us to line up and demonstrate the dead man's float for the Red Cross test. I waded out into the pool beside my friend and lay down with everyone else in the class, fingers stretched toward the too-thin gutter, my safety leg latched to the bottom.

"I did it," I shouted when several kids announced their success. "I floated!" And for a moment, I believed I had. The teacher's eyebrows rose as she looked right at me. We both knew about the foot.

What could have been so frightening? Perhaps I was too earthbound to trust the buoyancy of water. Or just too stubborn to let someone boss me around.

Over spring vacation of second grade, we drove to Chowchilla to visit Daddy's family. Richard and I shared the backseat of the new 1953 Buick we'd borrowed from Grandma Green, our territories marked by the velvet-covered, pull-down armrest between us. When we crossed the state border, Mom and Daddy sang "California, Here I Come" over and over until we all knew it by heart. Together we belted it out the windows while we drove down into the Central Valley.

On the first morning, we woke to sunshine streaming in the window. Auntie Ida, Dad's older sister, who was a warm, chuckling woman full of hugs and stories, sent us off on chores—picking oranges, gathering eggs. The sun already warmed the morning chill, and on the driveway, when I slapped my feet against the fine red dirt, the silty soil squished like talc between my toes. Later, up at their big ranch, we fed the horses and watched the calves with their mothers. The grown-ups joked about the big bull on the hill, the one with the ring in his nose. A cousin taught Richard how to drive the tractor, and after that he spent every day helping.

One afternoon Daddy drove me over to the homestead, the ranch where he and his family grew up, the house not much bigger than a Wauna

Lake cabin. We had to walk down into a pit where they got their water, a sulfur-smelling well that made me almost throw up.

"Go ahead and drink it." Daddy laughed, dipping out a cup of the water. "It's good for you. It'll make you strong." I tried a few sips.

We walked a long way from the house, through low rolling hills topped with oaks. He pointed out overgrown fields he'd worked and remnants of old fences. We scrambled up a low hilltop totally covered in moss. "It will take a hundred years to grow back," he told me as he carved my name in the moss. "You can come back every year from now until you're a hundred and seven, and your name will still be up here on the hill." I leaned against his shoulder, and he put his arm around me, pulling me closer. "One time Louis and I were up here working, and we found an Indian graveyard. Right here by the mossy knoll. We didn't want to desecrate the bones," he said, "but we had to plow the field." We sat for a while on the moss in the late sun.

We didn't spend uncommon time together, my father and I. But he had taken just me to this special place, carved my name, and shared a secret from his childhood. I loved him. Sometimes when I think about my father now, I remember that open oak knoll and the moss edging over the rocks.

When we returned to Portland, everything changed. My mother went to the hospital, and Grandma Green came to live with us. Daddy seemed far away. Richard became angry. I remember only a few fragments from that time. Instead, summer play is colored with a golden glow, a happy wash that I spread over events too scary to comprehend. Surely my father and grandmother talked; Richard probably told me things. Daddy's younger brother, Wayne, had died from brain cancer when he was still in college. Mary Young, Mom's Theta sister, had gotten breast cancer and died the summer before. Did anybody mention cancer?

Mom must have known she was going to have major surgery because before going to the hospital, she took me into her bedroom late one afternoon and stood beside me in front of the mirror. She dropped her robe to show me her breasts. "Someday, when you're a big girl, a young woman, you'll have breasts too. This is what they'll look like," she said, cupping each breast tenderly in her hand. I don't think I'd ever seen her naked before. She turned to me. "Remember that I had breasts." I looked, but all I remember is the darkened room, looking in the mirror, and then seeking out my mother's eyes.

"Can I go outside now?"

A few days later, Virginia Atkins, one of Mom's sorority sisters, picked me up at school and took me to Washington Park to play on the swings. It was cold outside, and the wooden seats wet. After that, Grandma Green had charge of us for weeks and weeks. Daddy went to work all day and visited the hospital at night. At least, he didn't come home until late most nights. Nobody said when Mom would return home. Sometimes a church friend came and spent the night with Grandma Green, but mostly it seemed like Richard, Grandma, and I were home alone.

When Mom finally did return, she lay in her bedroom, the shades pulled.

"Don't disturb your mother," Grandma Green scolded when I came home from school excited to show her my work. "Keep quiet or I'll have to get the switch," she threatened when Richard and I argued. I wanted it to be like before, but everything had changed.

Dr. Trumbold had performed a radical mastectomy: removal of the breast, the lymph nodes, and both muscles on the chest wall—a brutal operation. Once, she showed me her thigh where a huge patch of skin had been removed for a graft.

"This hurts worse than my surgery," she told me as she bathed her leg in cool water or rubbed the scar with cocoa butter. I didn't know how to help her, how to stop her hurting.

"Just go outside," Grandma ordered, shooing me away. And so I did— all summer long, playing and pretending and forgetting my fear.

We all hid our fears. My father seemed to disappear for a while. What was he feeling, facing the loss of his wife, being left alone with two children? And my brother, just graduating eighth grade—did he think about losing the one who showed her love by nagging that he wear his coat or eat his peas, who made his special dinner twice a week so he'd eat more,

Mom, Richard, Dad, and me, backyard, circa 1953

get bigger? Even Grandma, stoic and silent, gave no hint that she might lose her daughter. Instead, we all went on about our business, carrying on until one day she wasn't sick anymore.

The shades went up in her bedroom. There wasn't anything to fear. I wouldn't have to go live in a tumble-down shack in some far-off farm-land with Daddy, a fantasy he spun on every Sunday drive out in the country. I wouldn't have to mind Grandma Green or do what Richard told me. Mom was back, fussing and worrying. Richard headed off to high school and I to Mrs. Johnson's third grade.

In October Mom returned to the hospital for a second mastectomy, simple not radical this time. Before she left I heard her tell her best friend,

Georgie, "He said, 'Don't worry. It'll just even things out. You can stuff old stockings in your bra and nobody will notice,'" and she laughed a sharp, funny laugh. Then Georgie hugged her, and she started to cry.

At school I told my class we were adopting a Korean orphan—a brazen lie and a wild expression of hope that our family would grow not diminish. Nobody talked about fear or death, but joy leaked out of the house. For Mom I imagine the pain and then the waiting. Had the cancer seeds spread? Would there be another relapse? She must have noticed every lump and mole, always suspecting the worst. We were all waiting.

I struggled through yet another set of failed swim lessons at Shattuck School. Soon after the last class, Mom gave me a serious talking-to.

"You have to learn to swim, Carolyn." She looked at me so hard, I could not turn away. "I never learned. If something happened at Wauna Lake or the beach, I wouldn't be able to help you." She paused.

"Nothing will happen," I started to say.

But she went on. "I might not always be there to make sure you wear a life jacket. You have to learn for yourself."

I heard her clearly this time. She wanted me to be safe, to be able to save myself. Just in case. I needed to let go of the baby Carolyn and grow up. Mom might not always be there.

FALSE STARTS

1953–1955

FRIENDS FROM CHURCH BELONGED TO the Aero Club, and their daughter, Bonnie, took classes from "the best swim instructor in Portland." They invited me in on a guest pass to join her for private lessons with Tye Steinbach. In my hero story, I decided right then I would learn to swim, for Mom. But really, I learned because someone finally got into a warm pool with me. Not only that, but he also let us keep all the coins he threw into the pool and we found on the bottom. And when anyone swam across the width for the first time, she won a silver trophy. Gold when she swam the length. I wanted the prizes.

One afternoon I waited on the second step of the Aero Club pool in another steamy basement, my hands in my lap, elbows floating up. In the deep end, a couple of older kids teetered on a big, black inner tube, then leaned back so far that they fell off and disappeared into the depths. Bonnie and I had just finished one hundred bobs while clinging to the wall.

"Great bubbles, Carolyn! Great bubbles," Tye had praised. He was short and built like a bear with muscular, sloping shoulders, but his eyes crinkled as he teased and laughed. He spent most of his teaching time in the pool, squirting water from a clenched fist or tossing coins into the water.

I watched him take Bonnie's hands in his and pull her forward. She lay on top of the water, her bottom two blue melons. Then he stepped back, released her hands, and Bonnie lay there, bubbles rising white on either side of her cap. He tapped her head, and she stood in triumph.

I can do that, I thought. *I can.*

I reached out to Tye and caught his hands, determined to match Bonnie. When Tye released me, I floated too. Really floated! Later, we lined up shoulder to shoulder, and Tye commanded: "One. Two. Three. Dead man float." We dipped our heads, stretched out, and floated free from the bottom. Even me.

When I finally launched into the thick, warm water and into the quiet world where all I heard were my own bubbles and moans, my high-pitched screams flung into the greenness, I discovered a place where nothing could touch me. Floating, self-propelling, diving into this water world became as seductive as climbing into our backyard trees, those groves of Douglas, white, and grand firs that grew along vacant lots throughout our neighborhood in Southwest Portland, remnants of the 1920s Multnomah Athletic Club golf course that had failed during the Depression.

Once I climbed so high in a sappy white fir that the top swayed with my weight. Through the thick green branches, I glimpsed rooftops, cows in Zwaheln's field, and beyond that to Raleigh School. Unlike the murky underwater world, the scene looked etched. A recess bell buzzed across the fields and roads.

"I can see the school," I shouted down to Mary and Melinda and Stevie, my neighborhood playmates. But my mother answered instead.

"I've got cookies here. Come down."

I descended hand by foot until just before the ground, then turned and dived headfirst onto a swooping branch and glided toward earth. The branch bounced gently like a canoe on lake water. At the bottom Mom waited to scold.

"Don't do that again. It's dangerous. Look at the pitch on your shirt, in your hair."

I couldn't avoid her worry at home or in the trees. But in the pool, I could let go of house rules, escape the voices that nagged or worried or fought. In the water I could close out the incessant noise of expectation.

Tye worked with Mom in the spring while I took a new series of lessons. He taught her a simple sidestroke she could do along the wall to strengthen her ravaged chest and arm muscles. By summer, I could swim well enough for her to let me go in the shallow end of the new golf club pool by myself. She'd sit on the side dabbling her feet or in a deck chair chatting with friends. In the early evening, after most of the kids had left, we'd go in the dressing room and she'd tell me to hold the curtain tight while she changed.

"If anyone saw me, they'd be scared to death." Scars ran up to her collarbone. Her armpit sank into her ribs. Across her chest, a wide, white slab of skin stretched over bone on one side, a raw red line across the other. I held the curtain and helped her hide.

That fall Tye offered me free lessons three days a week. His daughters would be in the class and we'd be good together, he told us. We might make a relay. Mom drove me downtown every Tuesday and Thursday, and on Saturdays I went with Daddy in his truck.

By winter, Mom agreed to let me cut my hair. She hadn't cut her long curls, she told me over and over, until she left for college. "Here they are." She showed me, lifting them from the cedar chest where they lay wrapped in tissue, a handful of long chestnut curls, longer and darker than mine. No way was I keeping curls until college or even until fifth grade. My hair stayed wet and tangled too long after swimming. Nobody at the pool had long hair.

One Saturday in January—I'd just turned nine—Mom and Daddy drove me to my first swim meet at Vancouver's Memory Pool. It looked much longer than the Aero Club's eighteen-yard pool. Kids' high voices echoed from where teams sat together wearing their colors: red and white for the Multnomah Club, green and white for Columbia Athletic, blue for Aero Club.

When they called the race, "Girls ten and under 50-yard free-style preliminary," I climbed up on the starting block and repeated Tye's instructions: "Only dive when the gun goes off. Touch the wall before you turn around. Don't hang on the lane line." If I broke the rules, I'd be disqualified. From the block I looked down the long lane to the end where a woman dressed in a white skirt and blouse stood staring straight back at me. The water seemed like a mile away from up there.

"Swimmers, take your marks," a deep voice commanded. I looked over to the man holding a gun, then down at the water so far below, and climbed off the block to the tile lip just as he barked, "Get set," and fired.

I stood straight up, then flopped out into the pool and dashed to the far end. All the other girls had flown off the blocks, sleek in their red tank suits and racing caps. By the wall I'd almost caught up. Then came the turn.

Tye hadn't taught me the turn yet. Everyone flipped and set off on lap two while I hauled myself around and launched off the wall. Pounding down the lane, desperate to catch up, I must have gone fast enough to make finals, because my name appeared in the program that night on a mimeographed sheet: *10 and under 50-yard freestyle—lane 5*, right next to Gretchen Rittenour, a star from the Multnomah Club, who went to my school. After the race, my father penciled in #2 next to my name. Even at that first meet, I grasped the purpose. You race for the prize.

Driving home after the meet, Daddy told me he was really proud of how fast I'd swum.

"But I didn't win."

"No, but you were faster than any of them. You need to learn a few things." He reached out, squeezed my shoulder, and ruffled my hair.

"Yeah, like diving in. And turning. Tye never told me about those big block things."

In the spring Mom went back to the hospital to have her thyroid removed. I don't know how long she was gone or how long she convalesced. I only remember the scar that ran from ear to ear, one she covered with a silk scarf and later with thick strands of beads. Swim lessons were over for now. She needed to recover.

Sending me to Girl Scout camp gave my mother some healing time. Before I left she took me to the Scout shop in the basement of Meier & Frank to get a collapsible cup and a flashlight, then to Youngland's for a new bathing suit especially for Camp Wind Mountain. We would sleep in tents there and swim in a lake the way Richard had at Boy Scout camp.

All week we hiked the trails, ate in a mess hall, and sang "Taps" after dinner at the flag ceremony. In the tent at night, the other girls talked about their families. Some told wild, unbelievable stories. One girl's dad had a metal plate in his head from a bomb and sometimes went crazy. Another dad had two Purple Hearts. For the first time, I felt ashamed of my father. He was old, too old to have gone to war.

"My mother had cancer, and they cut off her breasts," I confessed in the dark, trying to keep up with their stories.

Instructors divided us into groups for swim classes in the lake. Red Caps stayed on the shallow shore for basic lessons; White Caps got to go out into the lake and could paddle in the canoes. I knew that I could bob and float, open my eyes underwater and count fingers, steamboat and windmill my arms—everything they would teach in the Red Caps. I'd even been in a swim meet. But at camp we had to pass a test: swim from one dock to another through black water over unknown depths to earn the white cap.

On test day I followed the girls along a walkway jutting into the lake then glanced back to the shore where the sissy girls who couldn't swim were being assigned red caps. Ahead of me on the deck, one girl after the next jumped or dived into the lake. The neighbor girl who'd carpooled with us to Shattuck pool leaped out and paddled off to the distant dock. I watched and willed myself to try, but my feet clung to the canvas, knees locked like they had at Wauna Lake years before. I returned to the shore.

I didn't mind being with the Red Caps, I told myself. We spent a lot of time just standing in the warm yellowish water, the sun on our backs. I remember the cool shrink of my skin when I'd submerge to peer at watery yellow legs and puffs of debris rising from dancing feet. I could even show off a little because I didn't mind jumping up and splashing down into the water-world below the surface. But sometimes I would gaze over the deck to the diving board where all the White Caps ran and cannonballed off into the lake. I sent one pitiful postcard to my father at the store where he worked, the Green's Market address—a photo of the lake, big girls paddling a canoe out from the lodge. *Tell Mom I'm a little homesick. P.S. I like Mom's food best!!!!!!* No mention of swim lessons or Red Caps. At night in the tent I wondered what was happening at home. Would Mom still be there when I got back?

I have questions I can't answer about that year. My mother must have been living with terror that something else would go wrong in her body. She was withdrawn at times, cross at others. When Daddy came home all full of bravado and chatter, she often met his good humor with silence. She'd lost confidence in herself, that daredevil college coed who'd once flown in an open-cockpit biplane. Up there at Camp Wind Mountain, I lost confidence too. I had wanted to do something, something that I should have been able to do, but doubt and fear held me back—doubt that I could make it and fear of what would happen if I was left out on the lake alone.

"It's Tye calling for you," Mom shouted into the backyard one day in late August, long after I'd returned from camp.

I climbed down from the tree fort, jogged to the kitchen, and took the phone. "He wants me to swim in a race," I whispered to Mom.

"Just a relay," Tye said. "You only have to swim one length, no turns."

I looked out to the back woods, where my playmates' voices rose and fell in the trees, and handed the phone back to Mom. "I don't want to go to a race," I said. "I want to play. You tell him."

Maybe if I'd had the courage to swim in the deep lake, I would have gone to the meet.

But I didn't want to give up childhood yet like my older friend Melinda had that summer, even as I felt it slipping away. She'd outgrown Tarzan and cowboys and mostly practiced the piano, read, or played with the big girls now. Mary became my sidekick—at least when she wasn't out golfing.

One afternoon, Mary and I played Indians, shirtless in our leggings. We ran the trails in the woods behind the Millers' and had just come through the Critzers' yard when we heard voices and laughter from Melinda's backyard. Using sign language to communicate, we snuck through the bushes and peered into the backyard. Melinda and two older girlfriends cartwheeled across the grass, their brown legs flying up and over.

We edged closer, invisible behind a screen of leaves, watching, scouting. Through the fence I could see Becky next door sunning on a chaise. Her five-year-old stood at the fence, fingers clutched through the wires. I put a finger to my lips. "Shhhhhhh." The little girl stared at my furious signal for silence, then yelled to her mother, "Carolyn's in the bushes."

The big girls spotted us and invited us to join them cartwheeling, but I wasn't ready to leave our forest fantasy and simply shook my head no. Indians didn't speak English. Mary and I skulked along the edge of the lawn and then sank into cross-legged seats to watch. The big girls ignored us until Melinda's cousin, Ernest, arrived.

One of the girls turned to us then. "Aren't you going to put your shirts on?" she asked.

"No, why should we?" I answered, English suddenly available. My skin prickled in a hot blush, and I stood up. The girls crowded around Ernest and asked if he could do cartwheels, their backs to Mary and me. Only Melinda glanced over her shoulder as we melted into the undergrowth and back into the forest, where I didn't feel as naked.

Something had happened over the summer that I didn't yet understand. I'd come home and plunged back into play, wanting to re-create familiar summer fantasies, but the pretend world had changed. Or I had become aware now of pretending. I wanted to transform into someone else, to be able to fly off buildings or swing from trees, but now I knew what I could not do. I could not be Superman or Tarzan or an Indian scout. My father had not gone to war. I was not even a White Cap. In that week at Camp Wind Mountain among those other girls, I'd been confronted by a new reality. I'd felt ashamed and afraid, experienced self-doubt. You had to swim from dock to dock to earn your place. You could not simply say, "Oh, I can do that," or pretend you were someone who already had. In the real world, you had to prove yourself or you didn't get the prize.

BEGINNINGS

2012

I WISH I COULD SAY that the gutsy girl I was looking for, the one I thought I'd find in my childhood recollections, had exhibited more courage. She was much like I am now, doubtful of her ability to bridge the dark chasm of loss, afraid to be left alone, ashamed of her failure to navigate deep waters.

At least I'm trying to be brave, I reassure myself. On the way to France, I stop first in Louisville to visit my son, now a professional actor, where he's preparing for *Long Day's Journey into Night*, an apt title for what lies ahead of me. I want his blessing before the long trek begins. During the day while he rehearses, worries keep me company. Does my right knee hurt? What about my left toe? Are my socks a bit too thin? Is the pack light enough? Experienced pilgrims have advised walkers to carry under eighteen pounds. This is bare-bones packing: wear one set of clothes, carry another plus a jacket, rain gear, sleeping bag, and liner. Add in hat, gloves, neck gaiter, and some essentials like ibuprofen and earplugs and the pack makes weight at sixteen pounds before adding water and lunch. Beneath the surface of preparations and plans lie deeper questions, doubts, and memories.

Ahead, Santiago de Compostela lies like that impossible dock did sixty years ago. Then, I'd made myself content with giving up without trying, lolling in the warm, shallow waters. I know better now; challenges require you to make a start followed by stroke after stroke after stroke or, in this case, step after step. More than a physical test is beginning—this time I am facing not only a journey meant to help me get unstuck, to get my feet off the bottom, but also to provide time to release old dreams, to find a stronger self and prove I can live alone.

Just as I had no idea where learning to swim a half century ago would lead, so, too, I cannot predict this journey's ending. *I will begin with a simple step and a breath and the intention to be awake, to listen, to notice, and to let go. I will practice paying attention to thoughts and feelings without judging or clinging.* All this I write in my journal on the plane speeding toward Paris, a new journey, for the first time in decades without Rose, though her presence visits my dreams and memories fill my thoughts.

The doorbell rang late, long after the party had started. Outside Rose stood, her hands jammed in the pockets of a navy-blue car coat, her cheeks blazing, her black hair already streaked with white at thirty. "Am I too late?" she might have asked as she glanced in at the gathering a friend and I had orchestrated, to which we'd invited every woman we found interesting or attractive in hopes of meeting someone new, a code meaning a girlfriend. Rose had just returned from a cycling trip in Canada's Gulf Islands, and she stayed late into the night telling stories of riding ferries and sleeping in remote boater campgrounds. *This one is interesting*, I thought.

But months passed before I heard from her again, in August when I was working at the family fish market cleaning salmon, trying to earn airfare to Chicago to help a love interest move into her new home.

"Hey, would you like to go see an art exhibit at the museum?" she asked. "Or to a drive-in movie?" She caught me with that line and the laugh that followed.

"I'm sort of busy until the end of September," I said. "Call again."

But I was the one who called her from the Other Side of Midnight, a lesbian bar, late the night I returned from Illinois. "I'm free," I told her.

That wasn't entirely true, of course. I had a four-year-old son I'd lost in a painful custody battle two years before, but he only spent time with me on Tuesdays, overnight every Friday, and on Saturdays until five o'clock. I had a field placement and graduate school about to begin, my second year of social work school. And I wasn't a bit free of the pain from the loss of my baby boy, although I tamped it down the way I'd held my sexuality in check for over twenty-five years.

I didn't know how to be a lesbian in 1976 when I was ripped out of the closet in a two-week custody trial and lost what at the time felt like everything of value in my life. For a year I drank a lot of beer, hung out in Tasha's until it closed and then in the Rising Moon, women's bars down on skid row Burnside, looking for someone to lead me into the lesbian world. I took women's studies classes at Portland State, ate platters of brown rice and beans at Mountain Moving Cafe while listening to wo-myn's groups who came up from the Bay Area to play. I did all I could not to feel the incredible loss of my son. And even in 1978, I was still learning how to be a lesbian, how to navigate the women's world where radicals and feminists had been out for years. Rose was a part of that world, had been since the early seventies. She'd pumped gas, painted houses, played softball on the Lavender Menace, and had scads of girl-friends over the years.

On an early date in October, we hiked up Beacon Rock in the Columbia River Gorge, picnicked on bright-green Anjou pears, cheese, and crackers. On the drive back to Portland, we stopped along the Sandy River. She wanted to ask something before she got involved. Did I like to travel? She said she knew that I had a kid, and she didn't want to be held back by children. As the oldest girl in a Catholic family of nine, she'd waited all through her childhood for the youngest to be old enough for the family to go to Disneyland. It never happened, she told me, because there was always a new baby. She finally went with girlfriends after she got to college.

Yes, I told her, I traveled. By the time I was thirty, I'd journeyed all over the country to swim meets, flown to Europe three times, and spent thirty days hiking through Oregon on the Pacific Crest Trail. I'd backpacked the Olympic Peninsula, the Wallowa Mountains, Strawberry Mountain, and Mount Hood's Timberline Trail, had trudged along the Rogue and Deschutes Rivers. I had traveled.

On our first trip together, we went to British Columbia, where she led me through the ferry docks and hillside climbs out of ports on Salt Spring, Pender, and Galiano, small islands that lie between Vancouver Island and the mainland. I rode a clunky old borrowed bike and stuffed my gear in plastic bags inside thrift-store panniers. We camped out, swam in sun-warmed inlets, and sprawled on white-shell beaches, old middens, to watch the long northern sunsets. We'd make that trip more times over the years, once with ten-year-old Michael pedaling to keep up, once after the Vancouver Gay Games where I competed in swimming and track. I'd found a fellow adventurer, I thought, someone who'd backpack and explore the world with me.

The first morning in France, I wake in the dark of a hotel in Bayonne dreaming of Rose—an angry, distrustful dream—and struggle to shake myself awake. Later, my inner voice begins with, *Remember when you asked if I traveled?* as the train runs through the morning dusk following the River Nive to Saint-Jean-Pied-de-Port, the traditional starting point of the Camino de Santiago.

When the train stops and I begin to walk, I notice the village looks the same as it did fourteen years ago when Rose and I drove through on our way from Lourdes to Spain, the same red-roofed and shuttered stone buildings and the cobbled streets leading down to the river before climbing up into the Pyrenees. On foot, the hill is steeper than I remember it looking through that windshield. I'm glad to stop after only seven miles at the refuge in Orisson. The first night seventeen pilgrims gather around a long supper table, sitting alone to-gether, each contemplating a transition—a new marriage, a retirement, a reconnection of mother and daughter, the beginning of a sabbatical, the death of a parent, divorce.

The next morning a Korean woman, her daughter, and I sit in the dark, the moon a sliver and Venus clear in the east, waiting for light, waiting to begin the climb up to the summit, across the border, and down into Spain following Charlemagne's retreat path after his defeat in Pamplona. It's after eight when we start hiking into the brief, pink sunrise and up to Col de Lepoeder. Hills rise steep and bare but for gorse and browned bracken fern. Sheep graze or walk in lines, their bells chiming up the canyons. High on an outcropping, two griffon vultures gaze out over the valleys, which are filling with clouds. Now and again horses appear, some with bells on their necks, motionless like the small herds of white cows we pass, heavy hoofed and indifferent to us pilgrims. Clouds swell in cumulous balloons to the west and spread to mist in the east. Once, next to the path, two squat, big-bellied ponies appear through the mist, one spotted like the prehistoric cave painting Rose and I saw in Pech Merle so many years before. Thoughts of her accompany me as I trudge on alone.

From the frontier, the trail descends down, down, down through a steep, rocky, leaf-strewn beech forest. When it comes out of the woods, there stands the ancient Gothic Collegiate Church of Roncesvalles, the white stone hostel and church that Rose and I saw from the road as we drove through in 1998, the year of her fiftieth birthday. Memories arise and form like the clouds over the pass. I try to remember my goal to let them dissipate as if they were weather. But questions keep rising to take their place: *How long will she dwell in my thoughts? How long will she affect my emotions, my sense of self, my future? What does it mean to feel guilt and shame? When will I release the thought that I'm not good enough?*

GETTING TOUGH

1955–1956

THE FAILURES AND EMBARRASSMENTS OF summer quickly disappeared when swim lessons turned to training in the fall. A new swimmer my age joined the team, a boy from Florida: Don Schollander. His mother, Martha Dent, had been a double for Maureen O'Sullivan in the Tarzan movies. In a thick Southern drawl, she instructed us to call her "Marthadent, all one word." She knew Johnny Weissmuller, the Olympic swimmer who had played Tarzan, and had lots of advice about everything, especially swimming. She and my mom became close friends, Donnie and I combative training partners. We both had big brothers, fussing mothers, and speed.

That fall Tye taught us how to do flip turns, freestyle, and backstroke. We raced each other swimming widths to practice our flips—one hundred always the goal. We sprinted back and forth, back and forth, flipping and counting, stopping only to argue:

"Was that fifty-six?"

"No, we're at sixty."

"No, we're not."

Then one of us would shove off again, determined to get to one hundred first.

Sometimes Tye set us up against his older swimmers. He would give us a head start—a dive and two strokes, maybe—and then sic one of his twelve- or fourteen-year-olds on us. We'd thrash down and back, swimming for our lives. Sometimes we'd throw in a big inner tube, the one kids fought to control during play time, and teeter-totter it until huge waves swamped the little eighteen-yard pool and someone yelled for us to stop. Sometimes we'd just mess around in the deep end, diving to the bottom or trying to talk underwater.

Once, alone, I tried to set a record flipping the tube over and over without losing my seat. I held tight to the sides and leaned it into a rollover, then pulled it upright to catch a breath before rolling over again. Before I got to even fifty flips, the lifeguard blew her whistle and motioned me to the side. "Your mother thinks you're drowning," she murmured, her eyes rolling. I knew that look. My brother rolled his eyes a lot too. I looked over to the pool door, where my mother worriedly peered in, and pushed off the side to flip the tube a few more times. Drowning! Ha!

I could do almost anything in the water now. Given another chance at camp, I'd earn a white cap.

Mom drove me downtown three days a week, and usually Dad picked me up on his way home from work. A few times, though, he didn't show up. The first time it happened, I waited and waited on the Aero Club steps watching cars drive by, afraid to leave my spot in case he came and I wasn't there. I felt panicky, not knowing what to do. After a long time, I hurried inside and down to the pool to ask Tye if I could use the phone.

"He didn't come," I told Mother when she answered. "What am I supposed to do?" She said she'd call the store to see if anyone knew where he was. Then she told me to stay inside, up in the lobby, until she could get there. After that, when he didn't show up in a half hour or so, I'd call Mom to pick me up. It didn't happen very often, but I dreaded that it might every time he arrived a little late, sure that he had forgotten me. Mistrust squeezed in beside anger while I waited.

Before, I had only been vaguely aware that my parents sometimes had conflicts. When Dad missed dinner or called home to say he needed to work late, I didn't care. Some nights I woke to my parents' voices, my mother weeping, her voice loud and pleading, my father's a mumble.

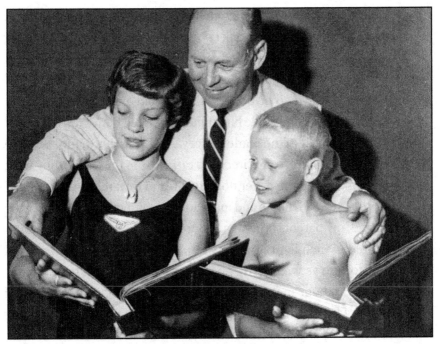

Donnie Schollander and me with Tye Steinbach, 1956

Now I paid more attention. One morning I saw him carry blankets back to the bedroom from the davenport in the living room. When he came in the kitchen, he dug in his pocket and pulled out two silver dollars for me. "They're from the olden days," he said. "They're lucky."

My mother stomped past. "They're from the track."

When Dad didn't arrive for dinner one night, Mom put the plates back in the oven and called me to the car. "We're going to the golf club to see if he's there." She drove slowly through the parking lot searching for the green pickup.

"Why would he be here at night?" I asked. "You can't golf in the dark."

"There's a men's room in the back, for cards and slots. Your father can't keep away from those machines. " Her voice was taut like wire, and it scared me.

We didn't find the truck. But as we drove home along Bertha-Beaverton Highway, I thought I saw it outside the Tillicum tavern.

I didn't say anything, even though when he came home all full of jabber, I sided with Mom and wouldn't talk to him for a while. I didn't like feeling pulled between them. It reminded me of how I'd felt at camp, afraid of being stranded alone in the dark water between two swim docks.

Sometimes I felt mad at both of them. Mad at Mom because she didn't stand up to him and make him mind, didn't tell him, "You have to..." And mad at Dad because he made her cry. And at Richard, too, because he made her worry. Those sad times, I'd rather be in the pool trying to sit on the bottom, letting the water float me up and turn me in its currents.

By winter Tye had Donnie and me ready for competition, and once the meets started, my parents united in support. Mom gave Dad a stopwatch for Christmas, which kept him busy at meets. He timed and recorded every split for me as well as my opponents. When I won or broke records, his excitement matched mine. Maybe it gave him a glimpse of the old days when he had coached high school sports. He liked jock talk and the company of other swim-team parents; Mom had her pal, Marthadent. Together Mom and Dad drove me to all the meets, which tumbled one after the other that year beginning in January: Oregon AAU Championships, MAC Age Group Invitational, Journal Juniors, the Oregon Open in The Dalles, Livermore AquaRodeo, Silver Lake in Everett, and finally, at the end of the summer, the Junior Olympics.

The biggest meet of the summer came in July, the AquaRodeo in California, where Santa Clara Swim Club dominated the way the MAC did in the Northwest. After we left early in the morning, I stretched out to sleep on the floor of our old '53 Buick. Somewhere down the road, we met Donnie and Marthadent, who followed us all the way. We stopped for lunch at the Klamath Falls Creamery and spent the night in Dunsmuir, where we swam out the kinks in the city's outdoor pool. Even after I-5 was finished in the late sixties, we would follow this same route. It was the road my father had driven from his ranch in Madera to school in Corvallis in the 1920s and then to court my mom in Portland in the early 1930s when he was teaching and coaching in the San Joaquin Valley. They retold the same stories as we drove along: "Here's where the radiator blew." "Remember how hot it was in Redding?" "Is that the lake where Wayne...?" They reminisced while I read comic books in the back or played Battleship with Don or fought over cards until he was sent back to his car.

Because I had set a state record and Donnie hadn't, Tye loaned me the special Aero Club sweat suit: royal-blue satin with red-and-white trim—*Like a boxer's robe*, I thought. It was two sizes too big, and the temperature was over ninety degrees in the Central Valley, but I wore it with a sailor's cap and a tough look, one that I'd noticed on the good Santa Clara swimmers. Ten-and-under races at Livermore were one length, twenty-five meters, and I whirled through them, winning two silver medals and a bronze. Dad had brought his 16mm Kodak, and we came home with movies of my starts and finishes and of Donnie and me racing in the El Rancho Motel pool.

After the meet we left the Schollanders and drove on to visit Dad's brothers and sisters, nieces and nephews. Everywhere, in little public pools and big ones, Dad had me show off. He'd explain to everyone that I had more races coming up, telling them as well as me that I had to stay in shape. Once when he came too close with the camera poolside, I punched out at him, embarrassed that he was filming me. Being alone with my parents for so long began to feel itchy and irritating. I wanted to push them away sometimes, their attentions too hot. I loved my parents, but I hadn't learned yet to distance myself, to separate, to make a private space they couldn't penetrate. Just as I hadn't learned how to ignore the tension I sensed between them sometimes, the hostile silences or the midnight scenes that Richard escaped with his jobs and car and upstairs room. I needed to get tough.

On our drive home, we stopped again in Dunsmuir. In the big outdoor pool in the early evening, Dad bet that he could still beat me in a race across the pool. No head start. No gimme. We stood side by side, and he called out, "Ready, set, go." When I out touched him, it felt like I could beat anyone.

Before the Livermore meet, Tye announced that he would be moving away in September to open a new swim center in McMinnville. We all wondered where we would go to train. Marthadent and Mom talked and planned. Once at dinner Mom said to Dad that the store paid his partner's Columbia Athletic Club dues as a business expense. She thought it only fair that it pay our dues at another club. "Otherwise, how can we afford it?" she asked him. I didn't know how much it would cost to join a club, but I knew they would find a way to keep me swimming. They had to. I was getting good.

On Labor Day weekend, we left home early to drive out to Jantzen Beach, a long drive from our house down Canyon Road, through town, over the bridge, and out Interstate Avenue almost to the Columbia River. Tye said it would be cold out there, to bundle up, so I wore my old cotton sweats under the satin ones, brought Richard's Boy Scout sleeping bag, and wrapped a big beach towel around my neck. We parked outside the dance pavilion next to the gigantic wood-framed roller coaster. Swimmers streamed by in their sweats carrying bags of gear—swimmers from the MAC and Columbia Athletic Club, the Northeast Y, and the Jewish Community Center, kids from Salem, The Dalles, and Eugene. It was a big meet.

I'd been to Jantzen Beach once before. Mom had told me it wasn't like it had been when she was a girl. It had changed for the worse. There was no real beach there, though I kept looking for it as we followed the paved path that led past rose gardens and carnival rides, past the fun house, the laughing lady, the bumper cars, the Ferris wheel, and two airplanes on a pole. The "beach," piles of sand that had once edged the pools, was long gone.

Other swimmers ran past us and up to the rides to see when they opened, but I was more interested in seeing the pool. At practice Tye had reminded Donnie and me that this would be our last race as ten-year-olds, our last race for him. He told us that we could set some records because the pool was fast. I didn't know what he meant really. *How are pools fast?* I thought *we* were supposed to be fast.

Journal Junior competitors from various Portland teams, Jantzen Beach, 1956

After walking the long, winding paths, Mom and I finally came to an enormous white stucco building, the bathhouse. *Women to the Right, Men to the Left—Swimmers Only*, the sign read.

Mom took my gear and promised to meet me out by the pool. I entered the massive building and followed a couple of girls wearing red sweats through the maze of lockers to a door opening onto a footbath. It was too wide to jump. I watched the girls roll up their sweats and run on tiptoes through the freezing water. They laughed that it was good preparation for the pool. I guessed that meant the pool would be icy too.

Outside, my ankles aching with cold, I hurried across the concrete deck that surrounded the two fifty-five-yard pools, trying to keep up with the older girls. We traipsed along the wide, shallow pool where already some kids were in, running and jumping through knee-deep water. *Maybe it's warm*, I hoped, *or they wouldn't be in there*. Once past the shallow pool, I spotted Mom and Marthadent Schollander behind

31

a fence. I hurried over, and Mom tossed me my bag as Marthadent shouted through the fence for me to get in and warm up. Instead, I looked around for Tye. It seemed way too cold to get in and warm up.

The meet followed the usual protocol I'd learned over the summer: listen to the loudspeaker for race announcements, check in with the clerk of the course, sit on benches or chairs or stand in shivering clusters of competitors until your heat was called. This meet, however, went by fastest times only—no prelims, no finals. One chance to win. My first race was number eight on the docket: 55-yard freestyle.

Tye pulled me aside right before the playing of "The Star-Spangled Banner," a squeaky rendition broadcast through loudspeakers on top of the diving platform. With his hand on the back of my neck, he gave me final instructions to go all out, not to slow down, not to look around, just to go, go, go until I hit the end.

"Now get in that sleeping bag, stay warm, and get yourself mad," he said. "Work up some steam."

My sweats were already a little wet, but the bag felt warm. I pulled it up over my head. "Get mad," he'd said. I thought about my brother. He'd hit my arm hard the day before, and that made me mad. "I hate you." I tested it out inside my sleeping bag. "I hate you. Hell. Damn. Crap. Balls." I recited the words Richard said that always got him in trouble. "Helldamncrapballs. Crap. Crap. Crapcrapcrap." *I'm getting mad*, I thought. And then I heard the call: "On deck: 55-yard freestyle boys ten and under. Up next: girls 55-yard freestyle."

Tye walked me to the clerk. "You can do this, champ. Follow that black line and don't look at anything else until you hit the wall." He thumped the back of my head.

I sat on the bench waiting with the other girls for the boys to finish. The pool looked as long as a lake from the shallow end to the far-off wall under the ten-meter diving tower. White-clad timers, huddled in threes around each of the eight lanes, seemed small and far away. There were no starting blocks at Jantzen, only the cement deck a foot or two above the waterline. A whistle and a call, and we walked to our assigned lanes. I glanced at the girl beside me. I'd beaten her before, more than once. She was laughing and teasing the girl to her left. I focused on the far-off wall. *Hell, damn, crap, balls,* I intoned one more time. *I hate you.*

"Swimmers, take your marks," the starter commanded. My legs tensed as my toes gripped the deck. "Get settttt," and I squatted, arms back, palms up, face forward, staring at the end, exactly as Tye had instructed. And then the gun. The cold water shocked for an instant before I was driving up and out of the starting glide, my arms whirling in classic windmill, legs pounding. *Follow the line, follow the line,* I heard in my head. *Don't look around, go for the wall.* The green water suddenly deepened and darkened under the diving area. *Just gogogo,* I heard Tye in my head. *Just gogo.* And I smacked the wall hard. I looked left and watched Noel Gabie reach out and touch.

I broke two national records that meet, and Donnie set a state record. Tye beamed and told us that we'd given him the best going-away present.

"Didn't I tell you? You kids have got it." He pulled us into a bear hug, his big arms holding us warm.

I would miss Tye and the cozy Aero Club pool, but I didn't dwell on it. He'd taught me how to psych up, and I'd won races, set records. I could even beat my dad. I was tough now, so I pushed away thoughts of missing Tye like I did the uncertainty of where we'd be training and who we'd be racing for the next season. At ten, you don't anticipate a sense of loss or imagine nostalgia for what you will leave behind. If there was any more money talk at home, I didn't hear it. Dad had been so involved all summer that I'd put away my worries about him ever forgetting me. A ten-year-old looks ahead to what's next. In September that would always be school.

On Saturday after the meet, my picture appeared in the *Oregon Journal* with a headline and an article where they called me "Miss Wood." School started a few days later, and some of the kids in Mrs. Maletis's sixth-grade class mentioned the photo. When someone started to tease about "Miss Wood," I snapped back, "Crap!"

Tough on the Trail

2012

Goddammit, I snap to myself when the annoying, loud-talking, know-it-all Brit takes the bunk next to mine and begins to broadcast his opinions throughout the dorm. All day I've marched well ahead of the yammering groups who have already aligned themselves on the Camino. Here they all are, ready to scope out the bar scene in this rain-soaked waypost. *Shutthefuckup* pounds in my head.

Do I have the patience and endurance to complete this trip? I wonder. My shins ache from walking sixteen miles on pavement through Pamplona, a toe throbs from the downhills, and my right knee has begun to niggle. I roll out my sleeping bag on the bunk and stuff tomorrow's socks and snacks in the ready bag for the morning while complaints roar in my head. All the hikes in Forest Park, the round-trip walks from home to the Multnomah Club, and the backpacking in the North Cascades did not prepare me for six hours of continuous hiking day after day after day. Being retired from teaching and living alone the past year were lousy preparation for dorm life.

Within a few more days, the Camino cough begins, a dry, raspy night hack that becomes a sore throat by morning, and itchy red bugbites cover one leg. Oh! the lamentations of the road: constipation, bleeding hemorrhoids, kneecaps stabbing with pain, dehydration, nausea, not to mention rain. *You need to get tough*, I tell myself, as Tye told me long ago. But this walk is not a sprint, and brief bursts of "helldamncrapballs" are not going to get me down the road.

When an athlete loses a race or sustains an injury or even quits for a while, the return is called a comeback. Along the Camino, I planned to practice letting go so I could stage a comeback, a return to happiness, but it's not as easy as I hoped. I have no guide, no coach, no mentor. No one blows a whistle to start the race. No one gives a pep talk, sets the pace, or holds out her hand to pull me along. Throughout the hours of walking each day, conversations, questions, thoughts, and memories seep into my mind and play in convoluted loops. I need a strategy to quiet my mind. For long, repetitive swim workouts and for seven-hour treks, I invented coping techniques—counting laps or steps, singing a song to the rhythm of stroke or footfall, watching cracks on the pool's bottom come and go or clouds drift up a river gorge or gather along the horizon.

In the evenings here, after moving forward all day long on the Camino, the simple accumulation of fatigue creates a kind of numbness and stills the mind, as do the elemental, repetitive tasks of arriving, setting out the bedroll, washing, laundering socks and underwear, finding a place for them to dry, getting food for the next day, finding dinner or cooking, setting out the night's essentials beside the morning's clothes, always the same clothes.

Despite long days of walking, mostly alone, I find little time for contemplation. I might start with a plan to be attentive to sounds and hear hunters' shotguns popping from a distant hill and a dog's far-off bark, and suddenly I'll be off on a memory of Rose's mother's dog, Charlie, who we kept for a year when she moved to a retirement home. An inner monologue overwhelms my intention as thoughts and recriminations mushroom until all I can hear are my own complaints.

One day when my mind became clogged, I picked up a stone and cradled it in my palm, my aim to carry it as long as the perseverating thoughts persisted. *When you're ready to set those thoughts aside, you may put down the rock. No hurry. Carry it as far as you like. You'll know when you're ready.* I sounded like my father at Wauna Lake assuring me I'd swim when I was ready. Sure enough, the suggestion to lug a rock along with my thoughts untethered them; I noticed the stone, felt its heft, noted its color. When I was free from brooding, I set it down beside the trail. Now, all along the way, when my mind begins to sing the same old sad songs, I bend and lift, carry and think, notice and release. It's a tactile version of the meditation technique of labeling thoughts *thinking* as a way of relaxing their grip. Heaps of stones move west along the path. I'm in hard training carrying those stones, developing a new kind of tough.

An ever-changing band of pilgrims walks the trails and roads, sometimes side by side, sometimes ahead or behind. Within a week most of the people from the first days are gone. Mr. Talk-a-Lot, the Brit, has disappeared, and the chummy party pilgrims along with him. New people fill the bunks, our dinner conversations focused on the body and its ailments: blisters, aches, sprains, flu, colds, bites, sweat, shivers, fatigue, food, the feel of the road, the weight of the mud. By bedtime most nights, we are worn down and ready for sleep before the mandatory lights out, silenced by exhaustion. It quiets inner voices too.

But in Burgos I spend two days listening to a child's fears. The little girl who swam in her first meet but was afraid to dive from a starting block and didn't know how to do a flip turn—the one who refused to go to another meet that summer—has reappeared, and now she is questioning whether she can go on. On the second night in Burgos, still deeply tired and conflicted, I drag myself into town to fill time before the restaurants open. Vendors stand roasting chestnuts under pillared trees; an accordion busker entertains as Rasta-haired street folks juggle sticks and bubbles in the plaza. Beside the castle gate, a violinist plays songs from long ago, and old men sing along as they stroll beside the river, arm in arm with their wives.

Inside the only restaurant I find serving dinner at seven, I order the pilgrim menu: garlic soup, stuffed mushrooms, and canned peaches for dessert. I confess to my only companion, my journal, that I wonder if I can continue. *Of course I know I can,* I write, *and I know I can quit. Which will I choose? And why? Do I go on just because I said would? Because I want to prove that I can? Do I go on because I find joy or at least some pleasure in the process? Right now I feel a foggy dread of being cold, sick, tired, unwanted, a burden. The dark and the rain and the loneliness all day, the long, silent walk through the empty red fields and harvested vines reflect my feelings. Tom Paxton's lyrics "It's a long and dusty road. It's a hot and a heavy load" echo with my steps. "Can't help but wonder where I'm bound." It's hard to remember my purpose, my motivation. Why am I doing this? Why is so much self-punishment chosen?*

Through the kitchen-door window I watch two women, the cook and a waitress, talk, nudging shoulders and laughing. Fútbol players race silently back and forth across the TV screen above the bar. I look up just as an old man steps through the outer door and the young waiter hurries across the room, takes his arm, and leads him to a table. The tender gesture loosens tears, and I bend back to my soup, startled.

By the time dessert arrives, another pilgrim, young and alone, enters and sits down at the table next to mine. He has the Camino look, somewhat lost, eyes a bit glazed. He's wearing flip-flops over heavily bandaged feet. I have to ask. "Blisters," he says. "Boots too small, but I'll make it." In our exchange, that small effort to ask and to listen, something shifts a bit.

The little girl who followed Tye's orders to "get tough" only knew how to harden up for battles, to take hits, to suffer pain by getting mad. But I am learning now that to be tough enough to stay the long course, to listen all the way to the end of the story, to let emotions rise and express, requires elasticity rather than steel. I finish my journal entry that night:

Today's lessons:
The rain stops; weather moves on.
I can take care of myself.
A tired, sick body will go on.

TWO WORLDS

1956–1957

"HANG WITH THE COOL KIDS, WOODSIE," my brother had told me just before school started again. His girlfriend agreed. She said it was important how you looked at school and helped me choose what to wear on the first day of sixth grade—a new, pink, full skirt that looked like one of hers. Grandma Green had made me several cotton skirts, and she was sewing my first wool-checked straight skirt for when the weather got colder. Once Richard's girlfriend suggested I comb my hair in a ducktail. She thought it'd look cute; I thought I looked like Elvis when she brushed my hair back and swept it up in a tail. Immediately, I wanted Mom to tell the hairdresser to cut it shorter next time. That would be cool.

Now, inside Mrs. Maletis's room at Raleigh School, familiar classmates had already claimed their desks. I stood in the doorway unsure which row to pick. Gretchen Rittenour, an age-group star from the Multnomah Club, passed by on her way to a different classroom. She'd won the breaststroke for eleven- and twelve-year-olds in the weekend meet. I wished she were in this class. Maybe we'd be on the same team after the MAC tryouts at the end of the month.

I found a place near the front and settled in. The starched petticoats under my skirt scratched my legs, and already the room felt hot. In the next row, Mary Lynn and Patty were laughing about something.

Patty's face turned red. I wondered if they were talking about me. Did I look cool enough? We all had on similar pastel cotton skirts and freshly ironed blouses. More kids hurried into the room and found seats.

Almost all the desks were filled when a new student appeared at the door with her mother. She looked like Hans Brinker's sister or an illustration from *Heidi*. Mrs. Maletis introduced her as Gretchen Young, who had moved from Portland to Raleigh, and directed her to an empty desk across from mine.

"Portland? Are you in the right grade?" I scoffed. She looked about eight years old—skinny, wide blue eyes, long blonde braids tied with ribbons, a puff-sleeved blouse, short, pleated skirt with suspenders, and long white kneesocks. She definitely did not look cool. I liked it that Mary Lynn and Patty laughed at my comment and for the moment I'd diverted attention away from my own self-consciousness. The new girl took her seat and shyly smiled. When Mrs. Maletis chided me for being unwelcoming, I tucked my chin and muttered, "Balls," under my breath. My mean year had begun.

Sarcasm and anger came quickly that year, as if I were channeling my brother, who at sixteen stormed in and out of the house in a rage much of the time, slamming up from the dinner table, yelling at Mom to leave him alone. For three years, ever since he'd been working at the store, he'd kept silent about Dad's gambling. Maybe it made him mad at them both, like I had felt when Mom took me searching for Dad's truck. But really, I didn't know why he was so mad all the time any more than I knew why everything seemed so dramatic to me that year. My emotions rioted, and I tried to cool them with sarcasm. It deflected others and protected my own secret fears and uncertainties at school. I didn't need it in swimming because there I knew my place. Soon, I hoped, I'd be on the team at the Multnomah Club.

The Multnomah Athletic Club stood on the hill leading up to Southwest Vista Avenue and Portland Heights. In 1956 it rose three stories, covered in Virginia creeper and topped with red tiles. A tight circular

Multnomah Athletic Club entrance, midcentury

drive framed the entrance. The back porch opened out on Multnomah Stadium, where in June Rose Festival floats struggled up the ramp at the start of the Rose Parade, all summer the Portland Beavers slugged baseballs around, and in the fall the stands filled for the University of Oregon–UW football game. The Club was the place where old Portland families came to dine, play cards, exercise, and compete—or to gossip, tryst, make deals, and gamble.

Mom and I had only been in the Multnomah Club two times before the afternoon of swim team tryouts, once for a meet that winter and two years earlier to buy a special racing cap like the ones the MAC girls wore. Today I felt nervous walking into the old ivy-covered building where the same lady as before sat at a high desk, two red-jacketed bell-boys beside her.

As before, she leaned forward from her platform and reached her hand over a wide desk holding a printout of every member's name, pushpin poised for check-in, and asked my mother how she could help her.

Two years earlier, we hadn't known where we were going. When Mom told her we were there to buy a bathing cap for racing, the lady had frowned. "Oh, for swim team?" But before Mom could answer, the white-haired lady turned toward a man coming in through the spinning glass doors and greeted him with a smile, pushed the pin into the board, and then turned back to Mom. "Downstairs," she directed us. "Stand 2." She motioned toward the hall beyond the lobby as if shooing us away. Mom didn't seem concerned by the scary lady. She pulled me along by the hand, and I remember my shoes clicking on the marble floor. It felt like we were in the downtown bank, the one where Grandma went, or the library, a place where we weren't supposed to talk out loud.

What did she mean, Stand 2? I wondered.

We wandered through the hall until we found stairs and clattered down to where two swinging doors led onto the swim pool balcony. No Stand 2. Down the next flight, Mom spotted a sign for the ladies' locker room. Inside she asked again, and an attendant led us to a tiny room with a wide window-counter in the far corner of the lockers. Stand 2.

We stood there for what seemed like an hour waiting for someone to come. Then three girls in red bathing suits pushed in beside us. One picked up a bell and rang it loudly. "Hurry up!" she yelled into the window-like opening. A man in a white shirt poked his head around the corner. Mom had let the girls go ahead of us that day.

Even then I had sensed the mystery, the privilege, though I didn't have words for those concepts. The Club was a place where people I didn't know belonged, at least not people from my neighborhood. It was for Portland people, whose dads were doctors or dentists or lawyers or architects. People who bought lobster and crab legs from my dad's store or brought in their ducks and pheasants to be dressed during hunting season. People whose kids seemed to win most of the races. We didn't belong. But I wanted to. I wanted to be good enough someday.

Now my chance was here, on a day in late September, a few weeks after school started. Mom and I stopped on the balcony and looked down at the pool. It seemed twice the size of Aero's: six lanes, twenty-five yards, a deep end with a one- and a three-meter diving board, and a balcony that ran the length of one side and across the shallow end. On the north wall hung a billboard-sized color photo of Maureen Murphy. She had recently qualified for the 1956 Olympic team in backstroke and was headed to the Melbourne Games that winter. I'd be swimming in the same pool as Mo Murphy. *Maybe she's down there now*, I thought as I leaned over the balcony hoping to recognize someone below. All I saw were dozens of kids kicking laps, up and back in the pool, laughing as they leaned on kickboards. A couple of boys ran along the side yelling at the swimmers.

Donnie and I passed our tryout, and we both made the team. We started practicing with Phil Hansel five days a week, but within weeks, this coach—the one our parents had so carefully chosen—left for Texas. Jack Pobochenko, MAC's swim instructor, took over the workouts until they hired a new coach. It didn't matter to me. Jack seemed friendly, like Tye, and the workouts weren't very hard. I could easily keep up with the girls on the B team, where I'd been placed. So many kids swam for the MAC that they had A, B, and C boys and girls teams.

Our Aero Club twosome merged into a whole world of swimming families: the McKelligans; the Eggens; the Rittenours, Pattersons, and Sieberts, all cousins; the Huffschmidts; the Boyds; the Walshes; the Everetts; the Gabies; the Gardners. Once you left the quiet lobby and ran downstairs, you entered a kingdom of kids. I loved the noisy, rough-and-tumble world. Mo Murphy wasn't the only star either. There were all the other champions whose pictures appeared meet after meet in the *Journal* and the *Oregonian*: Lou Lily, J. D. Brown, Carol McKelligan, Joe Santry.

Dad took me to Caplan's Sports again to get new sweat clothes in the MAC colors—red pants and a white sweatshirt. Donnie and I couldn't wear the Winged M Club emblem, be on a relay, or have our points count for the Club because AAU rules made athletes swim "unattached" for one year after leaving one club for another. But we could wear red suits at meets, and everyone would know we were on the team.

By October we shared a carpool with the Rittenours and Sieberts and Gretchen Young, the new girl I'd made fun of but who now was a friend.

We'd discuss the latest episode of *Spin and Marty* or argue whether the Dodgers or Yankees would win the World Series, forgetting school on the winding drive up Scholls Ferry Road and down Canyon Road to the Club. When I shucked my clothes in the locker room and pulled on my suit, I felt like the real me. Thumping along lap after lap wore me out, and the water washed away all my anger and uncertainty for a while.

Once I'd made the team, the world split in half between school and the Club, each with its own rules and codes, its own measures of success. All that year I felt a desperate pressure to excel. Swimming was easy. Academic expectations—math, reading, book reports, poetry recitations, music, South American history—required study. Keeping up with academic rivals—Gretchen, for instance—required 100 percent on tests, longer and longer poem recitations, perfect penmanship. Social alliances at school became ever more complicated. And then there was my hopeless desire to be noticed and liked by Mrs. Maletis.

I felt like I had when I was eight and had my first crush on the lifeguard at Portland Golf Club. All that summer I'd bobbed and jumped up and down in the shallow end trying to get Marlis Claussen's attention. I didn't care about hiding my feelings then. A neighbor friend and I would "play college," where she'd be Marlis and I'd pretend to be a football player dating her, a fantasy on days too hot for riding bikes or playing Tarzan, when we'd sit in the shade and spin out a story.

But now I had a crush that needed to be kept secret, from myself as much as from others. I wanted to show Mrs. Maletis how smart I was, but instead I said mean things about her, made jokes, passed notes. I wore an I-don't-care mask and started to roll my eyes in disgust at some of her assignments and comments. I acted out to hide my infatuation.

In one unit we studied South America, and she assigned us to memorize every country and its capital. I'd been drilling for days, trying to visualize the map while I swam, but I'd always forget one or two countries. On the night before the test, I came home from swim practice, my eyes swollen and red from the chlorine. Halos surrounded the lights, and my eyes itched and ached.

Daddy quizzed me, patiently feeding me hints when I forgot a country or a capital. After I had a crying fit, Mom left the living room to go watch TV with my grandmother. Late that night I burst into tears again.

"I can't remember. I can't remember," I repeated as I hurled a pillow off the sofa. "Gretchen will get a hundred, and I'll get a B. Mrs. Maletis said we had to know them all." I feared I'd not meet Mrs. Maletis's expectations and that I'd not be as good as Gretchen.

Dad calmly told me that I'd remember them all in the morning after I'd had a good night's sleep. He closed the book, stood up, and promised that he'd read me all the countries and all the capitals when I was in bed just before I fell asleep. He said I'd dream them and then call them up the next day during the test. I didn't see how that would work, but he was often right about school things and sports. He'd been a teacher once, and a coach.

Through all my turmoil and emotions that year, my father stayed steady. If he came home late or went to the track, I don't remember now. He got us into the Club, he drove the carpool home on his nights, and if schoolwork seemed impossible, his gentle reassurance comforted me. I could forgive him the times he had left me stranded or Mom in tears. Once the winter meets started again, he and Mom became official AAU timers with their own white uniforms. We were all part of the team.

There's lots of luck in sports. There's your lucky suit and your lucky sweats, your lucky lane. I got lucky with coaches. I had the best first coach, Tye, who nurtured and praised and honed speed, speed, sprint. Even better luck came with Jim Campbell.

"MAC Signs Campbell—Swim Coach Confirmed," the *Oregon Journal* headline read in November 1956. Jim Campbell, a competitive rower and later a college basketball coach, had served five years in the Army Air Corps as a gunner. "He is known as an aggressive coach who places prime importance on physical condition," the article concluded. After the war he'd worked and coached at Walter Reed in Washington, DC, where he trained two Olympians for the 1952 Games and another for the 1956 Games. His swimmers had initiated the dolphin kick in the butterfly, a new stroke since the early 1950s. He would bring the secrets of that stroke, and much more, to us.

The whole team sat waiting in the bleachers set up at the shallow end of the pool. Jim didn't say anything at first; he merely paced like he was trying to find words. And then he started: "You can be a champion if you're willing to work hard. Or you can be a loafer or a quitter. It's up to you." He paused again and looked at us practically one by one. "Guts, ladies and gentlemen, guts are the difference between a champ and a chump." He paced back and forth again, his black hair tousled, his face red and wrinkled as if from too many hours outdoors. He had on what he would wear to every practice and meet for the next year and a half: rumpled khaki pants, navy-blue sweatshirt, dirty white sneakers—no socks. "Guts," he repeated. "Now let's see what you can do."

We jumped into line in fleets of six or seven behind the lane markers across the pool.

"Let's see who's fastest. Hut," he shouted, and we dived and sprinted a length. "Up! Up! Get up!" came his shouts from the far end, and we hauled ourselves out and set up for another sprint. Somebody might have started up the ladder, but he yelled, "Stop!" and made her do five haul-outs in punishment. "No loafers on this team," he barked. "No ladders! Use your bodies. Guts!"

We didn't stop the whole practice, it seemed. Red-faced, panting— sweating, really—we dived, sprinted, and hauled out for almost an hour. Some kids skipped a lap and lay out on the deck; others got slower and slower, changing to breaststroke. When someone stopped and set his feet down at the shallow end, Jim roared, "Swim to the end of the pool. Don't be a quitter." Sometime during this first test while he paced back and forth on the pool deck, he shouted out again, "Let's see who has guts. Let's see who's a champ. Who can work it up a notch?"

In my head I shouted back, *I can. I can. I can.*

I never wondered how you got guts, but I knew I had them. I'd learned a lot from my older brother: how to take a punch, an Indian burn, the

Chinese chest-thumping torture. How to light a match. How to swear to keep a secret, tell, and suffer the consequences. How to say "uncle" but still not give up. It all took guts.

Maybe this day or another, Jim began to place us in fleets of similar speeds so that we raced each other. Then he started the catch-up trick—like Tye had done.

"Wood—get up. Lilley. Eggen. Boyd." They were all three or four years older. "Let's get some speed going now. Wood—go on the first *hut*. And don't let them catch you."

At the end of practice, standing out on the end of the diving board, he smiled. "Good work." That was all. I believed he was looking at me. I scooted into the locker room ecstatic. I had guts.

First Jim caught our attention with racing; then he introduced calisthenics to our daily workouts—sit-ups, squat-thrusts, deck kicking, and jump-ups—to strengthen and to wind us before setting us off on sprints. By the end of Christmas vacation that year, many of the big kids had quit or moved to teams where workouts were not so intense. If calisthenics were Jim's first training tool, wind sprints became the second weapon in his arsenal. After the squat-thrusts and sit-ups and push-ups, he'd set us up for ten one-length sprints.

"No breath, ladies and gentlemen. I see anyone take a breath, you *all* start over. Understand? Hut!" He set us off before anyone could question him. The first length flashed by. Up and out, we waited for the next fleet and the next to thrash down the pool.

"Hut." And we flew out again. By the fifth or sixth, my lungs felt hot and stretched, and I moaned underwater. On the eighth, someone took a breath.

"This is my team," Jim yelled from the board. "You don't decide when to breathe. I do. Start over. Ten twenty-fives. No breath."

Without enough air, it's hard to sprint, so we slowed down. But if you went too slow, the group behind might catch up, clawing your legs, pulling you back. It became a delicate balance of exertion and control. An effective technique to teach guts.

Guts are the difference between a champ and a chump, I'd chant with each stroke, my lungs aching, my arms heavy and hot.

"Don't cheat," we'd mutter down the line. "Don't cheat; he'll see you."

We did eighteen twenty-fives without breath that first time, and almost every time after that, since someone, usually the same someone, always broke down and tried to snatch a breath unseen. But Jim could see all. Our lungs expanded, our confidence grew—the loafers quit the team.

Jim had a third weapon that he used only for a while: the Harness. Somewhere in town, maybe at the original G. I. Joe's out by Delta Park, he got hold of two or three old Air Force seat belts—wide canvas harnesses that he attached to pieces of inner tubes he'd cut into lengths, tied together, and secured onto the balcony railing above the shallow end. Two at a time, we'd strap ourselves into the Harness, walk out to the edge of the shallow end where it dropped off, and on his "hut," dive and sprint toward the deep end, stretching the rubber tubing only to be pulled backward if we sloughed off. We sprinted until he whistled—an endless amount of time, but *ah, the relief!* when it came and we could lie back and breathe, the strap gently pulling us toward the shallow end.

Every time we came in to practice and saw the team before us in the Harness, we'd groan. *Who will be tortured today?* we wondered. Jim had me breathing to my off side, trying to correct a head bob I'd developed. That meant I swallowed gallons of water every practice, even more when I was battling the Harness. One night as we were lining up for warm-ups, Jim had J. D. Brown, one of the high school boys, show us a "real sprint" on the Harness. He set off, stretching the black tubing out almost twenty yards, it seemed. Someone next to me hit my arm and nodded toward the tubing—a tiny tear.

"What if he breaks it?" we whispered. "What'll Jim do?"

But J. D. didn't break it that day. Every time the Harness came out, we waited to see who might bust it open. We each tried to be the one. We talked about it in the locker room, out of Jim's earshot. We took bets on who would and when. Jim didn't use the Harness every practice, but

MAC swimmers between races, MAC Invitational, 1957

when he did, especially with the older boys team, we'd all crowd in to watch. The tiny rip had grown almost halfway across the rubber, but Jim seemed oblivious. The night J. D. Brown broke free, catapulting himself all the way to the deep end, the whole team cheered. Jim stopped practice, took him down to Stand 2, and bought him a milkshake. The Harness disappeared from practice. It had served its purpose.

Jim wasn't the only one who worked me hard that year. Throughout sixth grade Mrs. Maletis had us memorizing and reciting poems every week. And she drilled us on penmanship. I had a pretty good memory and a lot of muscular strength and speed, but not great fine motor skill. She gave us sheets of lined paper where we drew circles, perfect circles touching the top and bottom lines, over and over again. Then we'd draw slanted lines, barely touching the top and bottom, up and down, up and down across the page. Mrs. Maletis would wander around the room, bending down to look at our warm-ups, complimenting, suggesting, smiling. Gretchen Young's exercise sheet looked like a typewriter had covered it—every circle, every line perfect.

One day I'd filled about fifteen lines with what seemed to me almost perfect circles and some pretty good slanted lines. Mrs. Maletis walked up our row, looked over Patty's shoulder, and nodded approval, then placed a comforting hand on Wayne's head, encouraging him to finish at least one line. Passing by Gretchen's desk, she smiled and nodded, a knowing look exchanged between them. I was finishing a row of slanting lines when she stopped at my desk.

"Carolyn, your writing makes me seasick," she laughed.

I turned away quickly and looked back at my paper, then joined Mary Lynn and Patty, who had heard and were laughing too. In my head behind my blush, I swore. *If this makes you seasick, just wait. I'll really make you sick.* I didn't care if I'd get a minus in penmanship forever after.

I hated Mrs. Maletis even as I tried to show her that I was every bit as good as Gretchen or Patty or Mary Lynn. I anonymously left jokes on her desk from *Mad* magazine, ones that made fun of teachers. I laced my classroom comments with "What a load of crap" and mimicked kids to get laughs. One recess she asked me to stay after to talk to her.

"I know you are leaving these." She held up the cartoons. "They make me feel bad. Do you have anything to say?"

I looked at her, my face frozen.

"You say mean things to your classmates. Words hurt, Carolyn. I don't want to hear 'balls' or 'crap' anymore. It's not ladylike, and it's not nice." She waited. "Do you know what they mean?"

I nodded slightly. *It's not ladylike* sounded like my mother.

"What do they mean?" she persisted.

"Balls are things you play with. Crap is a word. There's a swimmer in

Australia named Lorraine Crapp." My cheeks were on fire, and I wanted out of there.

"Go out and play. But think about what I said."

I didn't want to think about what she said any more than I wanted to hear what the locker ladies said or my mother when she scolded. I ran out onto the playground. When someone asked what she wanted, I yelled, "Oh, crap! Vocabulary words."

By midwinter 1957, Jim sorted us into groups by ability, not age, and I became part of the senior team—with access to the coveted team room, a sanctuary for only the big kids' team. A tall window opened up to an ivy-covered fire escape high above Multnomah Stadium from which we could watch concerts or see the Rose Festival or just climb out and be bad. Opposite the window on the far wall, a wide, laddered rack sloped up over a radiator, which always seemed to be on. From the rungs hung dozens of tank suits drying or dried, old, faded nylon suits, runs going up the butts and leg elastic stretched out. These were girls' training suits kept separate from their racing suits, I learned. I only had one suit.

Mirrors hung along the long wall opposite a coatrack and a beat-up old sofa. It was not a room for modesty or secrets. A back door led down into the shower room, a long tiled room with six-foot slabs of black-and-white marble separating the six or seven stalls, each with massive showerheads that pounded out hot water. The team room's other door opened into the women's locker room—banks of mirrors and lockers, a shadowy curtained area with sunlamps and massage tables, a carpeted lounge where ladies sometimes sat in satin slips, their hair towel-wrapped, smoking cigarettes while they leafed through magazines. The locker ladies—tiny, menacing, ancient women—occupied the cage, an inner sanctum separated from the locker room by a wide counter and metal grating. They were charged with protecting ladies' valuables and harassing the swim team kids, or so we believed.

We thought we were entitled to run wild through the locker room. Their job was to catch and control us. It did not take long before I became as wild and as inconsiderate as the young girls who had rattled the bell in Stand 2 when Mom and I first came to the Club to buy a cap. Now I really belonged on the team.

Toward the end of sixth grade, we played softball in PE, jockeying for spots on the best team. I liked playing catcher, taking fast pitches, hollering taunts at batters, swinging like Mantle, sometimes even switch-hitting. I did not play catch at recess like I used to with Sheila or Rod, the smart boy who threw like a girl. Rod had found a math friend, and Sheila, with her straight hair blunt-cut across her forehead and her slouchy, stomping walk, acted too much like a boy. She was even more sarcastic than I was and seemed angry most of the time. She made me nervous that she might say something to embarrass me. I stayed away from her and tried to keep up with the cool kids.

Someone started a Slam Book, a spiral stenographer's notebook with pages of personal questions: favorite singers, favorite colleges, favorite songs, best friends, boyfriend, girlfriend. Soon we all had one that we secretly slipped from desk to desk, then quickly thumbed through in panicky searches for a name. At recess or on the bus came the questions and challenges.

"Is Jan your boyfriend? Mary Lynn likes him too."

"How can you like Elvis? He's such a greaser."

"Why does Walt want to go to Stanford? Where is it?"

Every night I listened to Dick Novak's *Rhythm Room* radio show on KPOJ. You could get a request form at Stacey's Cleaners. I asked Mom to take in some clothes so I could dedicate a song, then for nights lay awake listening to the requests. Finally it happened. "Here's Fats Domino singing 'Blueberry Hill': for Jan from Carolyn."

The next day at school, someone ran up. "I heard your request last night. Do you really like him?"

I didn't know if I liked him or not. *Should I?* These personal intrigues mixed with my anxiety about skirts and shoes, geography tests and poem recitations, piano lessons and music recitals, penmanship and vocabulary.

Trying to be cool had become too complicated at school. The swimming world felt so much simpler: work hard, swim fast, goof off in the locker room.

Two Worlds and More

2012

For a few days at the beginning of the Camino, I shared the road with Monica and Gordon, Canadian artists about to begin a yearlong sabbatical in Berlin. They stopped every hour and aimed their cameras toward what lay ahead, then turned and photographed the road behind, and finally focused on something right beside them—a silvered branch, a feather on the trail, a three-legged horse. The images would become source material for a series of paintings for Monica, an experimental performance piece for Gordon. Several evenings we ate together and told stories from the day's walk. Then our conversations would veer off to talk of films and books and art and politics.

Now, alone, I ache with loss. I can make myself sick conjuring up all I miss.

I've lost so much weight, my pants slip off my hips and pool at my feet if I don't cinch the belt, but after the rest in Burgos, I definitely feel stronger and more supple walking. The Camino is entering another world now, much the way Oregon divides a few miles east of the Cascades, changing from green to dun. Ahead lies the Meseta, a high, vast plain, mainly treeless and windblown, devoid of farms, vineyards, or villages—the land of Don Quixote.

Today a north wind blows so strongly that I reel along the path. Ahead blue-black storm cells drop rain, but in the hour or more I struggle forward, they vanish and instead, fantastic clouds scud across the sky. Strange cones that look like breasts, some tiered with newly planted pines, others topped with flat nipples of rock, punctuate the wide and muted vista. Time seems to fly away with the wind or disappear like the rain. I can't tell if I've walked an hour or three or if I am only starting out. For long spells, nothing appears on the horizon, the browned land stretching flat in all directions from the road, not a tree to interrupt the line. Then a speck begins to bob against the sky with each footfall. The speck becomes a rectangle that rises from the horizon, its top forming a triangle, and then two arched windows, still so far away that it is no bigger than my little fingernail, and after another half hour or hour, the speck finally resolves into a church, one of a few buildings in an adobe *pueblo* crumbling beside the road. I could be in a film—*The Passenger* or *Meek's Cutoff*. Where is my partner to share this insight?

Pick up another rock, Carolyn, and carry it for a while.

When we met, Rose and I occupied worlds as different as the Meseta from the Pyrenees, and each of us was doing reconnaissance in alien territory to learn the rules and the measures for success. She wanted out of the "lesbian ghetto," as she called the life of her twenties, just as I wanted in. Her stories of friends and lovers animated that previously imagined and forbidden world. And her Irish-Canadian Catholic family fulfilled my longings for heritage. I could offer a house in the suburbs, sorority sister training, and seven years of teaching experience just as she was starting her career in education. We'd go to a gay bar on a Saturday night and take my mother to the symphony on a Sunday.

In the morning on the Meseta, ice rims the puddles and outlines twigs in white. By the time I've covered five or six miles, I've eaten my chocolate ration and a handful of nuts, and have been humming tunelessly in rhythm with my feet when the hum shifts to a Patti Smith anthem, and I holler into the empty cold: "Jesus died for somebody's sins but not mine." A memory of a long-ago Saturday morning arises, the stereo blasting in the living room, Michael running the vacuum into chair legs, I following with a dust rag, Rose cleaning up the kitchen.

Michael had already been bridging two worlds for four years when Rose moved in with me. He was six years old. Every Friday he left his father's flannel-gray, buttoned-up world at the top of Council Crest where dinners passed in seeming silence down to our messy, eclectic, music-filled home. Friday nights we might listen to the radical feminist talk show *Bread and Roses* on KBOO Community Radio before going out to an old movie at the Guild, a Miss Marple with Margaret Rutherford or an art film at Cinema 21, *Eraserhead* perhaps, or a lecture by Doctor Demento or a performance piece of the Girl Artists. We took him to see their *Split Shift Cafe*, an installation so realistic that after watching for a half hour, he asked when we were going to eat.

Tonight before dinner, I watch a French group sitting at a wooden table in the albergue. They lean in toward each other, their voices rising and falling until someone slaps the table for emphasis and they all rear back in an explosion of laughter. I think of Michael telling me how our house always seemed lively and youthful with its heated, animated conversations ripping around the table. Once when he was ten, he and Rose argued whether a spoon or a fork was the better utensil for eating stew, an impassioned debate that may have veered toward phrases like *phallic symbol* or *male privilege*, as it sometimes did. Other nights he'd sit at his kitchen desk, drawing elaborate sagas of knights and dragons or underwater explorers or apocalyptic space wars, multichaptered epics, the pages taped together, the story drawn in weekly installments Friday after Friday, and he'd eavesdrop as Rose and I debriefed the week, our difficult students, our coworkers, our friends' breakups, the party list for a potluck.

While the French tell their stories, a German sits drinking his beer alone, and in the corner by the fire, a young Swiss woman hunches over a sketchbook drawing. She's making a picture book for her students, she tells me, to show them what lies along the trail. I watch her hand as she draws her pen along the paper and a cow takes form.

"Here, make a scribble, and I'll turn it into a picture," Rose used to tell Michael as they sat side by side on the couch when she'd take a break from drawing, Nina Simone or Joan Armatrading singing through the sound system. She'd become an animator and drew in black ink on 16mm clear leader, the cheapest medium for a poor but aspiring artist. Film spooled across her desk as she drew while looking through a magnifying lamp. Tiny horses galloped along frame by frame. It took years to complete a single film. She, too, lived in two worlds then, educator by day and artist by night and weekend, the landscapes as different as the Meseta and the mountains.

The next morning I trudge alone along an ancient Roman road. Monica and Gordon are long gone. Somewhere far ahead, a warm room awaits. Someone I know or will come to know might already be there. Behind me the Swiss girl still draws in her sketchbook and Michael and Rose sit doodling on the couch. I reach down to pick up a stone, my breath a white puff.

Private

1957–1958

I NEVER TALKED ABOUT MY father's gambling at school or at the Club. It wasn't a secret, exactly. Just like my mother's feelings that she'd become a freak because of her surgeries, I simply didn't mention it. By seventh grade I barely noticed my parents, or only saw them in side-glances, out of the corner of my eye sitting beside them in the car or scurrying past them in the kitchen. We only came together on Saturday nights and those Sundays when we all went to church or watched *The Ed Sullivan Show* with Grandma Green. After Richard left for college, I moved into his room upstairs where I could hide out. I craved privacy.

All that summer some of us played phone games to pass time in the afternoons when we visited each other's houses, calling random numbers and asking for Susie or Katy or Peg, and then after calling five or six times, we called one more time: "Hi, this is Peg. Have there been any calls for me?" What a riot, we thought. One girl in our group began to fill my mind. We kidded around at the Club and teased each other in groups; we spent hours at night on the telephone. Sometimes we'd just call each other and talk about nothing. If the line was busy, we'd call the operator and ask her to break through, claiming it was "an emergency call." I couldn't stop thinking about her.

One night right after school started, I sat on my parents' bed, the phone on my lap. I was supposed to be practicing a speech. In fact, I had dialed Halley's phone number thirty-eight times only to hang up when her brother or mother answered.

If she doesn't answer the next time, I'll quit, I promised myself. *Just one more time.* I willed her to answer.

Calling Halley wasn't a prank, though. It was an obsession. I loved the rush I got when she looked my way, caught my eye and smiled, talked to me. I had to hear her voice.

Just two more times.

"What are you doing in there?" Mom called from the kitchen. "I don't hear you practicing. Are you still on the phone?"

I hated her checking up on me. I felt guilty, as if she knew who I was really calling.

"I'm trying to check on homework," I lied through the closed door. *Two more times, and then I'll quit.*

The next day at practice, Halley caught my arm just as I was going into the pool. She told me somebody had called her house about a hundred times the night before. Her dad was going to have the caller traced, he was so mad. It sounded like she was warning me.

"Weird," I said, pulling away, blushing. "Who'd call you?" I tried to sound sarcastic. "Some creep with a crush?" I hurried on to the pool. The cold water cooled my face and my thoughts. *No more calls, Carolyn. No more. She knows. Everybody will know. Stop,* I ordered. *Stop now, stop now, stop now.* I pounded down the pool.

Crushes on any female I actually knew—lifeguards, teachers, girls—disappeared that year. I willed them away and pushed them deep underwater. Instead, I bought movie magazines with photos of Debbie Reynolds, Doris Day, Leslie Caron and created elaborate stories where we each played a role. For a while I developed a wicked crush on a dancer on *American Bandstand* and hurried home to watch the show upstairs alone. I was pretty sure nobody else felt like I did—not at school or down at the Club.

Raleigh grade school rally squad, 1958

I had no vocabulary for what I only vaguely suspected, but I knew to keep it a secret. At school we all knew the boys who were called sissies, but they were too sweet to tease. I wasn't a sissy. I just didn't have any interest in pairing up or flirting the way my classmates did. Boys were only good to race, to beat, and to sneak around with at the Club. Boyish girls were more problematic, a little too much like me. I avoided them at school and teased everybody else.

In those days we attended church on the Park Blocks downtown with a liberal minister and an open-minded congregation, at least for the mid-1950s. Mom had attended all her life. One Sunday as we sat in our usual pew in the balcony while Dad ushered downstairs, Arleta Kennerly, who worked at the Portland Art Museum, stopped to peer in at the doorway then motioned her friend to follow her. They sat two rows in front of us, Miss Kennerly straight and tall, her friend short and round. Miss Kennerly tilted toward her friend to listen.

"Those two cromos," my mom whispered in a tone I didn't recognize.

I scanned her face. What did that mean? Was she mad at them? "What?" I whispered back.

"She's like Shelley Walsh's brother. Arty." Mom's friend Betty called Mr. James the hairdresser "arty" too, and I could tell that was a bad thing to be. Mom straightened her knit skirt over her knees and pulled out the hymnal.

I watched the ladies. They didn't look very arty, whatever that meant.

Mom had another term for women who didn't marry or conform to her standards of femininity, and this one she hadn't made up: *mannish*. Tomboys had to be careful not to grow up mannish. Mrs. Wolfe was mannish because she played too much golf. Arleta Kennerly was arty, but her companion looked mannish in her brown tweed suit. Mary would probably become mannish. And Sheila Herman already was.

I knew Mom worried about me. She and Grandma had worked to feminize me. They'd given me dolls and pretty clothes when I was little. Ballet lessons at Anita Pienovi's studio started and ended one summer. In second grade piano lessons began. Grandma had tried to teach me to sew.

"Just a few basic stitches is all. Your mother could do cross-stitch, hemming, and buttonhole before she was six," she told me while I sat scowling on her sofa.

"I don't care. I don't want to." I jammed the needle through the cloth and caught my finger. My stitches lurched along the edge in seesaw lengths. "I hate this, I hate it!"

Grandma looked up, her blue eyes holding me tight. "You're not trying."

Of course I wasn't trying. I wasn't going to get trapped indoors with them. I would never give in to femininity.

By the beginning of seventh grade I knew over a hundred dirty jokes. I could rattle them off one after the other. Some of the big kids on the team added to my supply, while boys at school offered more. We traded jokes at recess, and they passed along tales that I'd take back to swim team of Japanese torture techniques and horror stories about ants eating out brains.

Once during a meet in McMinnville, our whole relay almost missed the race because we were holed up in our Buick, windows blocked with towels, sharing joke after joke after joke. Some were the simple book-title jokes like *Under the Bleachers* by I. C. Butts or *Red River Valley* by K. O. Tex. The more sexual jokes took forever to tell because someone always needed an explanation:

"What do you mean, 'He put his thing...?'"

His thing got used a lot in the team room. "Did you see *his thing* today when...?" I wasn't particularly interested in guys' things. At the Club, swimming hard and winning races occupied my thoughts. At home I could have other fantasies. That was safest. But getting my period and what that would mean in the pool worried me.

Sometime after a classmate had gotten her period in sixth grade, Mom gave me a book about becoming a woman. She showed me a drawer in the bathroom with a box of Kotex hidden under a hand towel. "This is for when you become a woman," she told me. I remembered an earlier occasion down at the church years before. Bonnie Sulmonetti and I had been exploring back rooms while our moms worked in the kitchen. In the women's restroom behind Fellowship Hall, Bonnie put a nickel in the sanitary napkin machine. I'd never really noticed the big white box before, but Bonnie, who was older, wanted me to see the napkin. It arrived in a cardboard box with two safety pins.

Bonnie hid it behind her back when a church lady came in, and then we ran out.

"What is this?" I asked Bonnie, fingering the thick cotton pad.

She just laughed and told me I'd find out.

When I did get my period in seventh grade, I wore two Kotexes to school and carried two more with me. On our class field trip to Salem, I still bled through the double pads.

"I have to use Tampax," I told Mom. "Everyone on the team uses them. I'll bleed into the pool if I don't."

"You're so young," Mom said. "I don't think it's safe."

But the next week, she told me she'd talked to Marthadent Schollander, who was a certified health teacher. Marthadent had assured her that I would be fine once she explained everything to me.

Mom hadn't had a period since she was thirty-five. After my birth she'd had a hysterectomy. I'd heard the story a million times. It always started with "You're my miracle baby." Because she'd had fibroids—as big as grapefruits, the story went—I was born cesarean. When they took me out, the umbilical cord was wound twice around my neck. "If you'd been natural birth, you'd be dead. Isn't that a miracle?" her story always ended.

I met Marthadent in a corner of the Club lobby. She'd brought a small box of Tampax and took one out to unwrap it. I looked around, but nobody seemed to notice us.

"Take this cardboard tube in one hand. It helps to wet it a little. It'll slide in easier."

Wet it?

"Then find your opening, your vagina."

My mind skittered, and I tried not to laugh. *Pay attention*, I commanded.

"Just insert it and push the plunger. You might have to try a couple of times." She handed me the box. "You can do it." She patted my arm as she stood up. "Just practice. You'll have lots of chances."

Now I really was like the big kids. And I wasn't going to have blood dripping down my legs or trailing behind me in the pool.

"Back in the saddle again," Pam sang as she shrugged off her coat in the team room.

Linda looked up from her homework. "I've got *the curse* too. And cramps."

I heard the lament often. Someone was always getting *the curse* or cramps. Sometimes they used it as an excuse to get out of practice. Jim would just nod and suggest that they do dryland training. Linda didn't really like swimming. She was a diver. And she was a fountain of knowledge about sex.

"Boys love it when you press your breasts against their back. It drives them wild." Linda had really big breasts. "When you do *it*, you need to teach the guy about your magic button."

"What?"

"Mom told us. She had to teach Dad. It's a special place down there that makes *it* feel really good. *It* makes you get wet. You know."

I had no idea what she was talking about, but I thought it might relate to wetting the tampon tube. I didn't want to think about pressing breasts into boys or getting wet.

You can't hide your body in a tank suit. I didn't even try. But other things—fear, desire, ignorance—I concealed. I was twelve years old swimming on a team with older kids. Someone always came in the team room with news or gossip or a dirty joke. I listened and learned when to join in. But I also learned how much to share, when to be silent, and how to change the subject or redirect embarrassing questions. Some things you keep secret.

SECRETS

2012

BEFORE SUNRISE ON A MOONLESS morning, the intermittent trail hard to follow through ferns bent low with last night's rain, I stumble along behind my headlamp. Ten minutes gone and the path peters out. *Dammit, I'm on the wrong route. I've missed the markers.* I scan the brush for an opening and feel exasperation and a touch of fear, that panic I'd felt when my brother used to trap me under the covers, a need to rip my way out. From somewhere above and to my left, a faint light approaches. "The trail is up here," a Spaniard I'd seen in the albergue calls, and he waits for me to scramble up to him before he hikes on. We walk together in companionable silence until the sun rises and the trail markers, those blue scallop shells with yellow arrows, can be easily seen.

I was lost in the dark, I think, now feeling slightly chagrinned. It will make a funny story tonight, how I confidently took off into the dark only to get lost in the bushes. I don't need to be ashamed or fear any consequences. It isn't a secret. No one on the Camino is going to care—no one holds expectations one way or the other.

My mind wanders while I walk, remembering when I was little and how many secrets I'd tried to keep. "Don't tell," my brother commanded every time he hit me. "Don't tell," Melinda warned when we rode our bikes into forbidden territory. I didn't tell my parents that my brother smoked or about being scolded by Mrs. Maletis. Some were easy secrets to keep, some not.

Other secrets I hid so well, I didn't know where they were buried. What did I fear through all those years? That I'd be caught out as deviant, queer, so different from my peers that no one would like me? Or was I afraid that I'd disappoint everyone's expectation of who I should be? Of course I feared rejection. Of course I feared disappointing my family. Of course I feared losing love. To be found out would end life as I knew it, as it was supposed to be lived. I'd be like one of those "cromos" my mother disdained. In college I converted to Catholicism partly because it offered protection and support. I could defend my virginity with piety. I could be a nun. What a delusion! One night when I said I wanted to study in the sorority house instead of going out, my boyfriend at the time snarled, "What are you, a lezzie?" I felt a shot of panic and slammed down the phone.

No, I'm not a lezzie, I lied to myself then and for the next several years. Finally, to prove it to myself and others, I married, hoping to fulfill expectations, still saying no to what I knew to be true. *No* always came easy if I was scared. When a man with a knife demanded money, I shouted, "No!" as if my fierce reaction would banish him. The six-inch slash across my thigh is evidence that you can't stop what's going to happen with a *no*. I could not stop coming out eventually.

Thoughts get away from you when you walk along hour after hour. Thoughts will travel places you'd long ago forgotten or wanted to forget. I had started off the morning in darkness, strayed off track, had a little fright, and suddenly it was noon and I was back in time feeling the stab of shame. It wasn't much further to go to remember that when Rose told me she needed some space, I didn't tell my friends. *No*, I thought. *We'll work this out.* When she moved half her things to her new studio, the news felt too painful to report. When everything disappeared while I was visiting Michael in New York, there was no stopping the end.

That evening in an ancient hospice open to villagers and pilgrims, a group of local women sit knitting around a table. As they work I imagine their conversation echoing ours back home—first the reports of weddings; babies; kids who found jobs, finally; a recipe that worked, another that didn't; and then the real business: details of a mother's fall, a husband's bum knee, a neighbor's stroke, worries for a father's deepening dementia. All of it subtext for what nobody admits: our own fears for the future.

Since the first night in Orisson when everyone shared a reason for walking, I have rarely heard discussions of motive. We chat informally in the afternoons while doing laundry or in the evenings while heating soup—reports on trail disasters, someone's toes, another's ankle, who is taking the bus, who is giving up. I listen for clues. I know that the old Quebecois, in remission from cancer, wears Depend at night. He told me in his broken English how hard they are to find in shops so far from the cities. The man with his dog, which isn't allowed in the albergues, gets up early each morning to drive his car ahead to the next stop so the dog will have somewhere to sleep, then rides a bus back to our beginning point to walk with his pet—that man's son committed suicide. We all walk with understood purpose.

I lie on my bunk in the darkened room and think about my other treks—Kilimanjaro, the Annapurna Sanctuary, Bhutan—ones where sixty-somethings like me needed to prove we were strong enough, fit enough, able enough, tough enough. We'd chosen something rigorous and demanding, as if by completing it we were saying: "Nope, not old yet. La-la-la-la-la." We'd gasp on the ascents and congratulate ourselves at the summit. "Yep, aced that test." But then and now, we all know there is a pass somewhere ahead that we won't be able to cross. On the Camino, nobody mentions the memorial markers we pass along the way. But we notice them. Those of us on the other side of sixty know where the road ends, we understand the metaphor. It's not a secret.

SUMMER IDYLLS

1958

JIM'S NEWS THAT HE WAS leaving to be head coach at the University of Pennsylvania shocked the team that spring. How could he abandon us after we'd learned to be disciplined and to swim our guts out? I loved him too much to call him a quitter, but I felt disappointed. Some of the older kids planned to follow him east that summer to train. I wanted to, but Mom wouldn't hear of it.

"You're twelve years old. I'm not letting you go anyplace." And that was that. I didn't put up much of a fight. Going all the way across the country seemed too much to imagine. Besides, I'd miss the summer meets swimming at the top of my age group.

Jim stayed in Portland until after the first summer meet: Journal Juniors on Memorial weekend at Jantzen Beach. I broke some national age-group records, as I had two years earlier at Tye's final meet. Because of my records and Jim's departure, the *Journal* photographed us together. We posed with Jim kneeling on the deck beside me on the pool ladder. Before the photographer snapped the picture, Jim pushed my knee in, angling my body toward the camera.

"Keep your legs together, kid. You don't want to show it all." He raised his eyebrows and smiled. "You know?" I remembered the picture of Mo Murphy coming out of the pool, the photo cut at her waist, and

Carol McKelligan on the diving board, her knee pulled into her chest, her body slightly turned away. I nodded. I wished he would stay.

George Pasero, the *Journal*'s sportswriter, wrote a whole column on Jim and the swimmers he was leaving behind. Pasero's headline read: "Carolyn Wood Said Olympic Hope." He quoted Jim, "'She has already broken many of Molly Botkin's records and even some of Chris von Saltza's marks.'" My little pipe dream of following Mo Murphy to the Olympics suddenly carried outside expectations. A reporter had printed it. Jim believed that I had "it," whatever "it" was—speed, desire, guts.

At school the next day during seventh-grade chorus practice, Miss Shriver announced to the class that she'd read in the paper "our alto" might be going to the Olympics. My cheeks burned, and I immediately despised her for drawing attention to my deep voice even as I felt a puff of pride. Would school ever end? Thoughts of summer, with its long days of practices and competitions, brought a sense of relief even if Jim wouldn't be there to coach us.

Some kids swam competitively because their older brothers or sisters did. Some had parents who wanted them out of the house and some who wanted them to work hard and win. Some hated to train but loved to race. Others enjoyed the camaraderie of the team. I loved everything about *swimming*, the word that encompassed teams, training, racing, age groups, carpools, long course, short course, horseplay, and pranks, medals, trophies, time trials, records, and pictures in the paper.

I liked to train—the daily pattern of warm-ups, repeats, exhaustion, cooldowns, rest. I liked the slow buildup of distance in the fall, weaving up and down lanes to avoid head-on crashes and to escape tailgaters, the aerobic tests of winter, the tapering toward important meets. The meets themselves didn't scare me or make me nervous. They were like big circus events, a new act coming up every few minutes: the roiling crowd of kids from eight to eighteen straining to hear the loudspeaker announcements, hoping not to miss their races, the gun, the cheers, the lane counters for events longer than four laps, the coaches' whistles, the happy chaos of preliminaries, and then the posting of results, looking

Coach Jim Campbell and me at Jantzen Beach, 1958

to find your name and time, looking to find your main competitors, looking to see if you made finals and which lane you'd have that night.

When my last prelim ended, Mom would leave her timer's post in lane one and drive me home to eat, to sleep. Even that quiet time I loved, not really thinking about the races but aware and calm, getting ready inside. Then came the drama of the finals. Fewer kids splashed through warm-ups. Teams sat together wearing their colors, and even those not in the finals watched and cheered as the pre-race rituals began: the national anthem played on a phonograph and the call for the first event. I learned to pay attention, to know the order of events, when to get up and begin loosening, when to use the toilet for the last time, when to come to the blocks. I loved racing, just as I had loved running to make my bed first or speeding to clean my plate when Mom set up competition with Richard. Always the goal to be first. And if I wasn't first, I liked believing that next time I would be.

Because we had no head coach, we worked out twice a day at the Club instead of outdoors in Lake Oswego, where we had trained with Jim the summer before. The swimming teacher who replaced him wasn't a disciplinarian, and we took advantage. Our training lost its intensity and became a playful interlude that summer. Some of us who took tennis lessons from Mr. Tauscher stayed at the Club all day, milling around between workouts with too much time to kill and too few places to be. Club rules kept us off the main floor where the grown-ups came to dine or to play bridge in the dark living room. Men wandered the back hallways toward the billiard room or the hidden card rooms far in the back. The third floor housed short-term lodgers, old fat men who reeked of smoke and sometimes used the pool during workouts, bobbing up and down in lane one while we veered to avoid them.

Verne Perry's office was up there too. You did not want Mr. Perry to notice you. As manager, he ran the Club with authority. We thought he hired and fired employees, accepted or rejected members, and disciplined out-of-control kids. We'd heard him yell after a running child in the lobby, and the locker ladies had threatened us with his punishments anytime we got too rowdy in the locker room.

The third floor was definitely off limits, as were the outer wings of the Club that housed wrestling rooms, a rifle range, and men-only areas, like Joe Loprinzi's weight-lifting room hidden behind swinging doors beyond the pool. So besides the outdoor tennis courts and the pool, the only places safe for bored and wandering kids were the squash courts in the basement or the basketball and badminton courts on the second floor.

One day after tennis class, a boy on the team told us about a hidden attic he'd found above the gym. It was full of old stuff, he said: boxing bags and Christmas decorations, furniture, maybe some archery bows or rifles. We had hours before our next practice. Seven or eight of us followed him up the back stairs to the gym and then up a circular ladder to the running track that ran above the ball courts. Sure enough, in the ceiling at one corner was a trapdoor with a chair placed under it. Our leader climbed onto the chair, reached his hands up into the opening, and jumped as if hauling himself out of the pool, then reached down and pulled us up one by one, all but the few who chickened out. They offered to stand guard as we disappeared into the ceiling.

The attic ran the full length of the gym, and from the far end, a tiny square of light shone where another trapdoor opened above the track.

"We need a flashlight," I complained from the back as we crashed through the equipment and rummage, laughing and pushing, the darkness scary and exciting. One by one, each kid disappeared through the far hole and thumped down onto the track. By the time Patsy and I got to the doorway, it seemed strangely quiet. I crouched, spread my hands on the opening, and slowly lowered myself as far as my arms could reach, and then let go.

On the gym floor, a woman stood looking up at me, her arms crossed.

Patsy called from the attic, "Where is everybody?" then she, too, dropped almost on top of me.

"Mr. Perry wants to see you in his office." Her voice spoke Big Trouble. "Follow me."

Mr. Perry's office, it turned out, lay beneath the attic floor. He sat us down and reminded us this was an adult membership club, that these shenanigans would not be tolerated.

"If I hear of either of you getting in trouble again, I will suspend your membership for two months." I sat paralyzed, dragged into the horror of being suspended, of missing workouts or meets. But Patsy offered up both an apology and a protestation of innocence.

"We didn't know it was off limits, Mr. Perry. We were just up on the track practicing. We're really sorry." He nodded us out, and we raced back to the locker room relieved.

"We're really sorry," I repeated in singsong as we raced down the stairs. Patsy, the youngest of ten from a Northeast Portland Irish Catholic family, played jazz piano, sang harmony to any song, told hysterical stories about the omnipotence and brutality of her Madeleine School nuns, and would laugh at anything anywhere, even underwater. I appreciated her skill at getting away with things. As usual in those years, I expressed my admiration by teasing.

In late July we traveled to California in a MAC car caravan—three or four cars putting along together—to the Livermore AquaRodeo. Once more, my mom and dad loaded up the Buick for the two-day haul south, this time with Patsy and her mother. Donnie, his brother, and his mom followed right behind us. All along the road, we played games. Sometimes Patsy's mom rode in another car, and Donnie or another teammate would join us in the backseat. We played rounds of Battleship until we were sick of it. When we tired of playing G-H-O-S-T, a spelling game, we sang along with the radio. I caught Patsy cheating at cards more than once until we all quit and Don went back to his car. By the time we drove through the Central Valley, it was 105 degrees, the heat blasting back from the open front windows and searing our eyes.

"We're almost there," Dad shouted from the front as we bickered between ourselves. "I bet the El Rancho pool is waiting for you girls."

I suggested we put on our suits in the car, but Patsy worried that someone might see us. It might be a sin. I dug through my duffel, pulled out a big striped towel, and rolled up my window to catch it tight. Patsy blocked her window, too, but then squatted on the floorboards to hide under her sweatshirt. My parents chatted in the front seat. Patsy's mom still rode with the Schollanders.

MAC swimmers Patsy Walsh, Judith Rees, and me, Livermore AquaRodeo, 1958

As soon as Dad parked at the motel, Patsy and I tore from the car and into the pool. We were paddling around, cooling off, when a blue wood-paneled station wagon turned into the parking lot. In front we could see the driver and passenger, but when the back doors opened, my idol stepped out—Chris von Saltza. She held practically every age-group record in freestyle and backstroke from 50 to 400 yards and set American records every time she swam. I'd seen her up close that winter at the MAC Classic and in Seattle where she'd set an American short-course record.

Patsy and I stood gaping in the shallow pool as Chris and her sister disappeared into the room next to the one I shared with my parents. Patsy suggested we listen in on them, so we pressed bathroom glasses between the wall and our ears as we'd seen people do on television, but all we could hear was the tink of glass on plaster.

At the meet I studied Chris, how she sat, surrounded in silence before each race. She kept on all her sweats until she checked in, then just her sweat-top until she got on the blocks. I mimicked her technique of shaking out her arms and legs before the start. When her Santa Clara relay won, she got on the stand last, behind everyone, then draped her arms over them to receive her medal. I did the same when our relay won minutes later in the eleven-and-twelve age group.

Dad brought his 16mm camera to film my races. I begged him to take movies of Chris so I could remember exactly how she raced. When we got home and had the film developed, I watched, rewound, watched again and again Chris's start, her turn, her stroke, and her casual acceptance of awards. This was the way to be a champion—calm, deliberate, explosive, and then gracious.

On Sunday morning Dad came back to our motel room from his morning coffee and cigarette, his hands behind his back. "Which hand?" he asked, and I pointed to the left. His arm swung forward with a magazine rolled tight. There on the cover of *Sports Illustrated* was a full-color photo of Chris. On the cover! Inside were more photos and a long article with the heading: "I like to beat 'em." In early July 1958, Chris, at fourteen, had set an American record in the 400-meter freestyle. The *SI* article opened, "I have to break the record; it's been in all the papers. If I don't, I'll feel like a fool," her coach reported her telling him. Of course, she smashed the record.

I could be a junior Chris. We both liked to "beat 'em," and the Portland papers had predicted things about me too. Jim had said I was an "Olympic hope." At the pool in the morning, I studied the national, state, and pool records listed for eleven- and twelve-year-olds on the heat sheets. Chris's name appeared on some of the records, Molly Botkin's on others. I'd have to go for records *and* beat the younger sister of Chris's archrival, Sylvia Ruuska, if I wanted to be like Chris.

Swimmers hunkered down in the school gym next to the pool—circles of sleeping bags and towels. In the shaded stands, our parents waited for the brief moments of our races, our thirty-second bursts sandwiched

Chris von Saltza and me at the El Rancho Motel in Livermore, California, 1958

between hours of waiting. In the gym I watched the Santa Clara kids from my bag. Sometimes Chris joined in a card game, but more often she lay stretched out reading or sleeping. Little kids, ten-and-under boys mostly, swirled around the edges of the gym, voices high and taunting with tag or loud arguments over cheating. I had withdrawn from Crazy Eights when it got too rowdy and lay on my bag thinking about the upcoming race.

I would false-start on purpose, I decided, to get the feel of the water after the hours in the gym. Chris did that before her races. On the second start, I'd hold steady, loose but holding, and then be first off the block. Dad told me I had a quick start. I'd swim the first length with only one breath, right before the turn, flip, and then pull hard back to the finish. *Only two breaths on the second lap. I can do that.* I wanted to feel that tumbling forward fall that came with driving speed from legs and arms, a forward momentum made desperate without air until the smash into the wall. Lying there alone on my bag, the gym dim and its sounds receding, I could feel it all.

I broke three age-group records and missed one of Chris's by a tenth of a second. I was as fast as Chris had been at twelve. In my dreams I saw myself on track to be like her, going beyond age-group records and setting senior American records someday.

Chris and her family checked out early on Sunday morning before they left for the pool. After they drove off, I waited a few minutes and then tested the door to their room. It was unlocked, and I pushed it open, but the drawn curtains made it dark and empty feeling. I ran to get Patsy and we returned together, peering at the unmade beds, the tea bags and candy wrappers in the wastebasket. In the closet, we found a pair of flip-flops. I knew they were Chris's because I'd seen her wearing them. Patsy thought we should each take one, but I worried they might be her lucky flip-flops.

"We should take them back to her," I said. "I know where she sits in the gym. Then we can ask for her autograph."

We planned how we'd approach her, who would get her attention, who would hand over the shoes.

"But what if she asks where we found them? What'll we say? 'Oh, we were just snooping in your room?'"

Patsy, using her storytelling skills, suggested we tell Chris that the maid had asked us if they were our shoes, and we'd told her no but that we'd give them to the girl who left them.

"You say it," I insisted. "I'll get her attention, and then you explain if she asks. And then I'm going to ask if she'll sign the *Sports Illustrated*."

Patsy agreed.

When Chris looked up from her Hearts game, I started. "Chris? Are these yours?" I held out the worn pink flip-flops.

"Yeah." She looked confused. "But I left them.... Where did you?"

I waited for Patsy to explain. But Patsy had disappeared, already far across the gym running toward the safe circle of MAC swimmers, laughing.

"The maid," I stammered, backing up, forgetting for an instant the real reason I'd approached her. I dropped the flip-flops and held out the *Sports Illustrated*. "Would you sign this?"

She took the magazine and pen I offered. On the cover photo, she wrote across her shoulder: *Chris von Saltza*, and under that, *Santa Clara Swim Club*.

When we got home, I carefully took the magazine apart, keeping only the article on Chris, which I wrapped in Saran Wrap then enclosed in a plastic sleeve to keep beside my bed. Another copy of the cover went into a frame, on top of the picture of Jesus that hung above the light switch. I began writing my signature *C* with a loop exactly like hers.

The season that began with loss and sadness over Jim's departure had turned into an idyllic summer. But as August wound down, we began to wonder who our new coach would be. Rumors rippled across the water, and our parents gossiped at potlucks. When we returned to the Club in late September after our three weeks off, Walt Schlueter met us. He'd come from Fort Lauderdale and before that Chicago, where he'd coached sprint freestylers who'd been on the 1948, 1952, and 1956 Olympic teams. We might have lost a beloved coach who had taught us about guts, but Mr. Schlueter would bring completely new practice methods: weight lifting and isometrics, stroke technique, interval training. Summer vacation was over.

PART II

GET SET

1958–1960

VENI, VIDI, VICI

1958–1959

"CALL ME COACH," MR. SCHLUETER told us in our first team meeting that September. "I'm here to coach, not be your friend." Coach wore Izod shirts, drove a Triumph, listened to jazz, and smoked. He wasn't rumply and warm like Jim, but remote and cool. A technician. A moody technician, who seemed dark and scary, but the man I wanted to impress now with my guts and speed.

Once practices began he required us to come in a half hour early and report to a basement area set up with barbells and dumbbells for curl-ups, triceps extensions, military press, bench press, and squats. We lifted a full circuit that he and Joe Loprinzi, the Club's conditioning expert, had set up. Later they installed pulleys across the back wall of the pool balcony, and we practiced our strokes lying on tilted benches, pulling ten or fifteen pounds with each arm. After weight training we'd run down to the pool, dive in, and whirl over the surface on the first lap, our arms slicing the water like wires.

Coach obtained film of the Australian swimmers who'd won almost every event in the Melbourne Games. At home I'd watched Dad's movies of Chris von Saltza and copied her stroke, but these new films showed underwater shots. Coach pointed out how the Aussies' hands caught the water. "It's kind of a key hole: enter, catch, slip out, and then push hard." He rerolled the film several times, explaining. We watched what I imagined were secret films of the greatest 1956 Olympians: Dawn Fraser, Murray Rose, Lorraine Crapp. I wondered if Santa Clara had a copy of these films.

In the pool we practiced widths, imitating the Australians. I could feel the power of the push, and already Chris's high-elbow recovery felt natural. By the end of October, we all had adopted the new stroke; now we began to accumulate yardage in practice. Forget Jim's sprints. We did repeat four hundreds or eight-hundred-yard kicks, back-to-back individual medleys (IMs), then recorded our daily yardage on charts Coach set up, distances unimaginable months before.

Workouts ran over an hour now, plus more time for dryland training. I was at the Club from three thirty or four until after seven. I'd made eighth-grade rally squad in the fall, bought the pleated skirt and blue sweater, the Raleigh Panthers emblem sewn across the chest, but I never attended a single game. As swim practice demanded all my after-school time, life became centered at the Club.

Right after Christmas two new swimmers joined the team. Nancy Kanaby, a twenty-year-old, had trained with Coach in Chicago and then Florida before following him to Portland. Lynn Burke, who was almost sixteen, came from New York, where her dad had coached her at the Flushing Y. They told us they wanted to be on a strong team with an elite coach in a place where they'd get more competition, because they were aiming for the Olympics. They would share an apartment on Burnside, a derelict street that ran up from the river, not far from the Club. Nancy planned to enroll at Portland State; Lynn would be a junior at St. Mary's Academy downtown. Nancy, thin and gawky with short, straight hair, didn't look like much of a swimmer, but Lynn did—tall, blonde, and freckled all over. She reminded me of Chris, but way more outgoing. She said her name was "Lin Boik."

"What?"

"Linboik. Boik. Ya know. Irish. Boik."

"Spell it," I said.

"B-u-r-k-e." She raised her hand and drew the letters in the air.

"Burke? BIRK? I never heard of it. You're kidding."

"Listen. Ah ya nuts? Dere's a zillion Boiks on Lawn Guyland." She laughed.

"What about Flushing? Is that a joke?"

Really, I thought she was making it all up. I'd never met anyone so exotic. She came from New York, where she'd gone to Catholic school, ate pizza for lunch, rode the subway into Manhattan, and swam backstroke faster than anyone on the East Coast. She thought she'd find cowboys and sagebrush in Portland, she told us.

"I knew I'd love it because I'm part Indian. Cherokee. My grandfather was full blood," she told me one weekend when she slept over. Upstairs in the den, Lynn stabbed our fingers with a needle and we became blood sisters, an Indian thing to promise loyalty, she told me. I believed her. She was almost sixteen, part Indian, a New Yorker. She swept me into her orbit.

I didn't fall in love with Lynn. I didn't have a crush on her. I just recognized myself in her like no one I'd ever known. She loved to have fun, to tell stories and to mimic, to think up pranks and egg people on. But she also loved to work hard. She had ambition, confidence, and talent. She was the big sister I'd never had. She could tease without being mean. She would challenge me to beat her and not care if I did. She was irreverent but not cynical. She had dreams so big that she'd left home to make them come true. Her plan: win nationals and make the Pan Am Team in backstroke. After that she'd make the Olympic team. Anything Lynn did, I wanted to do too.

She told me everything Coach told her, that we'd have the best medley relay in the country, that we could even win nationals. We could beat Santa Clara. "You'll be the butterflyer," she said, "and I'll go backstroke." One time when she came over to our house, she wrote on the little blackboard in the kitchen *veni, vidi, vici*. "When we go to Rome next year, this is our motto."

During the vacation, Coach started interval training, another Australian technique. We began with the usual warm-up of four hundred yards kicking, four hundred yards pulling, and four hundred yards individual medley—then the repeats. At first we swam ten or twenty fifties on the minute, but by the end of vacation, we were doing fifty fifties on the minute. He installed a huge clock with a sweeping second hand right next to the picture of Mo Murphy. We started off in fleets every minute so that we had only twenty or thirty seconds of rest before starting again. If you swam faster, you got more rest. If you slowed down, you got less. The pool sloshed with waves generated by several kids in each lane starting, swimming, finishing, a perpetual motion machine for almost an hour.

The intervals continued after we went back to school and throughout the winter, repetitious preparation for the indoor season. Once in a while, we might work on starts or have a time trail, some variation from the repeats. On weekends we'd linger after practice to shave our legs in the showers or to talk about upcoming meets. We could hang out for an hour or more until someone's mom came looking for her.

One Saturday after the morning practice, Lynn and I stood in a shower stall, hot water pouring onto our upstretched hands, fingers withered, toes pruned. Our conversation went something like this:

"Wanna go to a movie with Nancy and me?" she asked.

"Can't. I have to practice for a recital."

"What about tomorrow?"

"Can't. Church." We turned to let the water pound our shoulders. In the next stall, Patsy and Noel did the same. And next to them Bonnie and Carol.

Someone down the way proposed an adventure. "Let's flood the showers!"

Lynn looked at me. "What?"

"Get some towels."

The shower room exploded with industry. We gathered twenty or thirty towels from the bin and piled them on each of the seven shower drains and in the two sinks, then turned on the faucets full blast. At first we just stood in the long tiled corridor and watched the water rise and spill over the six-inch sills, spreading out along the floor and clouding the air with steam. Then we raced from stall to stall, checked the towel plugs, rearranged, added, and packed the little dams that were creating our lake.

Someone called to plug the door to the pool, and Carol heaped more towels against it. When the entire shower room shimmered in three or four inches of water, we began our slides: a running start with a dive-and-slide or a daring off-the-steps dive. I slathered soap up and down the front of my tank suit, up and down like paraffin on sled runners, then splashed through the ankle-deep water to the tile steps that led up to the locker room.

"Watch," I called to Lynn. From the second step, I dived belly first across the warm, wet-washed tiles, gliding past almost four stalls, water splashing up on either side like the wake from a boat. I scrambled up to catch Lynn's eye. *Yes. She liked it.*

Now the race was on, for distance, for splashes. We were penguins in our black and soap-white suits.

"Good one," someone yelled.

"Shhh," Patsy warned, but our voices echoed as we screamed and hollered, hurling challenges.

"I can beat that," I shouted, right when the locker lady appeared on the steps.

"What do you think you're doing?" she shrieked at me as I stood ankle deep, soap in hand, staring stunned across the shower-room lake.

Patsy disappeared into a shower stall. Carol backed into the toilet, pulling Lynn with her, both probably crouching on the toilet seat. Noel hid behind a curtain. I alone faced this tiny, gray-haired harpy who kept repeating, "What are you doing? I asked you, what are you doing?"

I had no answer. *Keep calm. Don't tell.* But I remembered Mr. Perry's threat.

I followed her up to the cage and hunched in the doorway while she called Coach. By the time he came to check the flood, all appeared normal—the lake drained, the towels disappeared, every girl gone. There was no evidence of a crime, no reason for anyone to get in trouble.

"You're a brat, Woody," Lynn told me later. "And you don't rat."

Blood sister, I thought. *I'm loyal, like Tonto.*

Lynn wasn't a tomboy, but she was a prankster who every now and then liked to cut loose or encourage someone else to. Anything she dared me, I'd do. I wanted to keep up with her, to impress her as I had my brother and my backyard playmates when I was little. In those years before swimming, I'd had my share of Big Trouble, which often started with a dare.

One late afternoon when I was around eight and my neighbor, Melinda, ten, we'd snuck into Mr. Weber's warehouse, a slumping red building in the field behind my house. We'd crawled in under a pile of lumber and through the rotted floorboards to its dusty interior. Wood leaned against one wall; a rusted thrasher lay collapsed behind a tractor on the oil-stained floor. We poked through the wooden shelves that held cans of rusted nails and screws, buckets, old boxes, junk. Low light filtered through the grimy multipaned windows that muffled outdoor sounds.

After a short time inside, Melinda whispered that Mr. Weber might be coming and we should get out. My stomach contracted then, my bare arms prickled, and we fled. Outside, we circled the building to see if anyone else was nearby. On the far side we noticed a splintered pane, something that we had not caused.

"What if we really broke one?" I asked.

"I bet you won't do it," she dared.

Her challenge sounded familiar, like one my brother might make. Back then he could control me with a simple, "I dare you to..." "I dare you to eat these potato bugs." "I bet you can't hold your breath till I count to sixty." I answered his every "I bet you can't" with "Oh, yes I can."

When I paused, Melinda double-dared me. That required action. I picked up a clod, looked around, then turned and hurled it at the window. The glass shattered, a split second passed, and it crashed into the building. We ran and dropped to our stomachs in the tall grass, listening, but all we heard were birds and the wind. We waited. Nothing.

"Now you do it," I prodded.

Melinda giggled, reached for a clod, crouched and ran closer, pulled back her arm, and threw. Another pock, shatter, crash. This time we listened but didn't run. There were four or five windows left, and we pegged them all one after the other.

In her bedroom afterward, Melinda made me swear an oath never to tell no matter what anyone said. I easily agreed, experienced in promising my brother things I'd never tell but often did. By the time I got home, I felt a little sick, and later that night, I made a tearful confession.

That time when I was eight, I had ratted, not yet loyal, not like now at thirteen with Lynn and my teammates. I'd never tell on them. Back then Mom had scolded and made me write a letter of apology to Mr. Weber.

"What were you thinking, Carolyn?" she asked.

"She dared me," I answered.

Mom shook her head, sat me down at her desk, and helped me word my confession. After we wrote it out in pencil, I copied it in ink. Writing and rewriting, addressing the envelope, licking the stamp, and pounding it onto the corner had felt good. The radio show continued, Mom returned to her knitting, and Daddy, deep in his armchair, ashtray balanced beside him, looked up from the sports page. "You don't have to take every dare, kiddo."

Back then I had never thought that you might choose to skip a dare. I knew nothing of behavioral subtleties and self-determination. When you have a brother seven years older than you, you spend a lot of time trying to keep up or to get away. It doesn't feel like a choice. You *have* to tug your sled after him to Gable Hill even when your mother forbids you to go down the steep slope with the jump at the bottom. Something *makes* you pedal as fast as you can on your little blue bike only to watch him disappear around the corner hurling some taunt over his shoulder. He might climb up into the tree fort, which you were *never* to approach, and bombard you with stinging pinecones, or get a BB gun for Christmas that you could not touch, or dare you to suck slugs. He might run you down and knuckle your head if he caught you on the steps to his room.

But if you're the kind of girl who doesn't want to be left behind or cooped up indoors, who wants to run with the boys and play cowboys and war, who wants to win the snowball fights or climb to the tops of the trees, then chasing after your brother or running to escape him feels like your destiny. Of course, now I didn't care about chasing after Richard. I wanted to keep up with Lynn. I would be her loyal sidekick. *Blood sister.*

Lynn didn't swim the first meet of the season in January. But I broke Nancy Merki's twenty-year-old record in the 100-yard freestyle—1:01.9. In February George Pasero wrote in his *Journal* column that Coach believed I'd be the first Oregon female to "crack the minute for the 100 freestyle. She's ahead of the times of California's great Chris von Saltza for her age," he wrote. Dad brought the paper home to show me, but Lynn made the biggest deal of it. She told me that I was going to beat von Saltza and that our relay would out-race Santa Clara as soon as she was eligible. "We're gonna be national champions," she said.

Before the next meet, Coach called a few of us into his office. On a small MAC card, he had typed: *Dear Carol, I hope that these are your splits in the MAC Invitational.*

Carolyn, I wanted to correct him. Why didn't he have my name right yet?

Below that he'd written out the lap-by-lap splits I should do in order to swim a 0:58 in the 100 free and a 1:05 in the 100 butterfly. I looked at the times for the freestyle: 0:27.0 for the first fifty and 0:31.7 for the second. Just like our fifties on the minute. I could do it. It seemed so easy when it was broken down like that. For butterfly all I had to do was a 0:30.5 and a 0:35.3 and I'd go 1:05.8—a record. He signed it, *Good luck, Coach.*

I swam a 0:59.0! Another new record. Coach knew exactly what we had to do to swim personal bests. Lynn set a record in the 100 backstroke, and our photos appeared in the Monday *Oregonian.*

"We're done with age-group, Woody. Now we go after the big stuff." She meant she wanted American records and I should be chasing Chris von Saltza. Big stuff. I had to keep up.

When the Far Western Championships came in March, though, Chris wasn't there. She had mononucleosis. She'd miss the indoor season, her dad told the papers, but he hoped she'd be recovered by summer and ready for outdoor nationals and the Pan American Games. He said she had been too exhausted "to win the battle against mono." It sounded like some frightening disease that could overwhelm you.

Lynn broke two American backstroke records at the meet. She could see ahead to nationals and the Pan Am Trials, but I needed to improve if our relay was ever going to beat Santa Clara. Losing by a tenth of a second in the freestyle and finishing fourth in butterfly wouldn't help the team. I'd done so well in one meet only to slip backward in the next.

Sunday night I felt too tired to sleep, and my legs ached, as they often did after big meets. Dad rubbed them down with wintergreen oil and told me not to worry, to look at the trend: still growing and still getting faster. "You can't win them all," he said. But I didn't want to listen to him. I wanted to keep up with Lynn, whose advice now carried more weight.

"We gotta work hard, Woody. Two years to the Olympics. Veni! Vidi! Vici!"

CAMARADERIE

2012

MY BOOTS BITE INTO THE gravel on the long trail that cuts across the hip of a low slope. Already my odometer reads past ten thousand steps. If I look behind, I can see the path stretch half a mile before curving behind a brown rise. Below and off toward the south, an abandoned building squats under the high gray cloud cover, its windows black holes. Ahead the track stretches as far as the horizon. Only the wind blowing off the side slope seems to move until I spot a figure, then two, coming toward me. The taller is a pilgrim, with a backpack and staff, his face creased and weather reddened. A black dog follows closely on his heels. "Are you coming from Santiago?" I ask. "I'm going to Roma," he answers, with the Camino-demented smile I have begun to recognize, not unlike the grin of marathon runners at the end of races. "Roma, to see *el papa*," he says as he passes by, slowing but not stopping.

This hike is a solitary endeavor, much like swimming had been. We passed like two swimmers sharing a lane, both intent on our efforts. I think about how I prepped for this long trek, walking miles through Forest Park along the Wildwood Trail, driving up the Gorge to hike the steep paths, mostly setting out alone but always encountering someone coming or going my way, someone to greet before hiking on. I think about my years of workouts splashing up and back in pool lanes, stroke by stroke, lap by lap. We measured out our lives in yards in those days. On the Camino we measure in steps and miles. Rose had measured hers out in 16mm and 35mm film frames.

Making art is a solitary exercise too. Rose's animation, drawn frame by frame by frame, thousands by thousands, reminded me of doing laps or accumulating steps, each session of drawing building toward a final film years in the making. I admired her discipline, respected her sacrifices, understood her seriousness of purpose. I knew it in my bones. We were good at training together, comrades, like Lynn and I had been out at Jantzen Beach, each in her own lane—Rose in her studio drawing, I in my office reading books for class or paper after paper from students.

I understood imagining a goal and choosing to go after it. Lots of people—athletes, artists, students—talked about what they wanted to do, but only a few followed through. The few years I coached swimming, I remember feeling bewildered by kids who came to practice but never worked hard. They wanted to "get good," they said, but the words never became action. At art school, Rose met people with good ideas who wanted to tell you all about them but who never started the work. By contrast, pilgrims still on the Camino after twenty days, after thirty or more, have a seriousness of purpose. I think of a young woman I met along the way, a Parisian, not strong, not healthy, but determined. She came in past dusk, two or three hours after most of us, pleased to have made the distance, intent on completing as much of the path as possible, step by step. The pilgrim with the dog would arrive in Rome by Christmas.

When I was swimming, after the long water-imposed silence of a workout, we'd head to the showers and the team room, a gathering together to complain, to laugh, to play, and then we'd head home to our families, a meal, and sleep. On the Camino we share a similar bond; we've experienced the same adversity during the day that my teammates and I had after a cold workout at Jantzen Beach or endless intervals down at the Club. A day's walk ends in a warm room with friendly companions and often a shared meal. I've begun to reclaim the comfortable rhythm of solitary work broken by the coming together to eat and to talk, even among strangers who do not always speak the same language. I wonder if I will find this camaraderie again when I return home. I grieve for my lost companion, for our life together.

Last night in a small village, the pilgrims ate around a table crowded into the kitchen. After our last bites, everyone headed to bed, and we were tucked into our bunks by nine o'clock. I slipped into my silk cocoon, stretched out in my bag, pulled the neck gaiter over my eyes and ears, and rolled on my side. Sleep has come quickly every night despite the beds—whether plastic-covered foam or sagging cotton mattress, whether old iron bedstead or new creaking steel. I find sweet comfort among the ever-shifting bands of pilgrims in the bunk rooms, the warm, whooshing of breath and bed rustle, snores and whispers, my own breath and heartbeat all muted by my earplugs as if I were underwater. I'm reminded of the Anglo-Saxon story of the sparrow flying into the warm and fire-lit mead hall where it finds brief comfort before flying out again into the darkness. In the morning I awake long before dawn, dress and pack in under fifteen minutes, fresh and ready to begin again, out into another dark morning, curious for the new day.

When I walk into León late in the afternoon, sun breaks through the clouds. Inside the Cathedral, kaleidoscopic patterns of blue and red stream over the visitors. The soaring walls seem made of colored glass and light like Sainte-Chapelle or Chartres in France. Among the crowds I suddenly spot Monica and Gordon, the Canadian artists, their faces turned up toward the multicolored rose windows. *I'm not alone,* I think with a warm rush and set out across the nave to intercept them. I haven't seen them for over a week, since the day they walked with me to Burgos when I'd felt so sick. So much has happened since then. We can have dinner together and share our stories, I hope.

13

BEST INTERESTS

1959

MY MOTHER HAD OUTLASTED HER illnesses, but she transferred her worries onto me. Every day she'd ask, "How are you feeling, honey? Are you tired? Do you think you should go to practice tonight?" She adjusted mealtimes and menus to accommodate workouts and meets. She issued warnings about which foods to avoid and which to eat, about how much sleep I should get. She became my personal trainer. How often I heard: "It's good for you." Almost as often as: "It's bad for you." If I didn't heed her advice, she predicted dire outcomes. Her concern sometimes felt oppressive.

Back when I was eleven and new at the MAC, the girls team had a sleepover on New Year's Eve at an older girl's house. At the party, Patsy and I danced to "Jailhouse Rock" and howled our harmonies with "Wake Up Little Susie," the big girls egging us on. My hair slicked back in a ducktail, my collar pulled up and jeans rolled, I mimicked Elvis like I'd practiced in front of the mirror at home. But right at midnight Dad picked me up, right when they were playing the number one song of the year. It was Mom's doing. She made me come home at midnight because, she said, we'd all stay awake and be silly, and the next day or so I'd have a cold and then have to miss practice. It would not be worth it, she insisted.

"They think I'm a baby," I said when I got in the car. "It's not fair. Everybody else gets to stay."

"Well, your mother knows what's best."

He was right, of course. Mother knew what was good for me, and she wanted to help me be the best. As I got older and ever more independent, our wills began to clash in her other area of expertise, clothing and fashion. In seventh grade when the Grant girls on the team started wearing "bear coats," Korean War wool-fleece jacket liners, I begged Mom to drive me out to G. I. Joe's, the Army-Navy surplus store on Interstate near Jantzen Beach.

When she balked, I started naming Grant girls who owned bear coats. Mom had been in the first graduating class from Grant High, one of Portland's premier schools, and still felt a strong loyalty. Grant girls carried cachet. Finally, she gave in to their sense of style and my arguments, and we drove out after a Saturday practice. Mom had second thoughts as we hunted through the warehouse for the right section, and she suggested that maybe I'd rather have a new Sunday coat for Easter. I refused the bribe. I wanted a white bear coat.

I ended up with two coats, an olive drab one and a white one. We'd ravaged the surplus bins. I liked it when Mom tackled a project for me even if it took a lot of pleading to win her over. Grandma Green sewed on rickrack, and I wore the coat over cutoffs and tights, like a Grant girl, well into my high school years.

Grandma Green had earned her living as a high-fashion seamstress when she first came to Portland at the turn of the century. She'd designed and sewn all Mom's college clothes by copying dresses she saw in store windows or from Vogue Patterns. But that was long ago. Neither of them seemed to know what was cool now. If I had to wear a dress to the MAC awards ceremony, I wanted a Lanz. All the California girls had Lanzes, and so did Gretchen. But when we shopped at the Dark Horse, Charles F. Berg's new Beaverton boutique, the prices shocked Mom. She pulled one dress off the rack, held it up, and declared that my grandmother could make one just like it.

I'd been wearing skirts and dresses Grandma Green made since I was a baby. Mom knitted everything from my baby snowsuits to cable-knit sweaters. But now I wanted real clothes: Berg's blouses with my name embroidered on them, Pendleton skirts, Jantzen sweaters, and Lanz dresses. Plus Capezios. Mom flipped through the racks, checking prices. Finally, she suggested that we might find something when they had a sale.

I didn't really want a dress. I'd rather wear one of my brother's shirts under an old Jantzen V-neck sweater with jeans or Bermudas, my uniform for going down to the Club for practice. When Richard had left for college, his bedroom and all the stuff he left behind became mine: madras shirts, a white zip-up sweater with charcoal and pink ribbing, a thin pink suede belt, and a blue plaid White Stag jacket. Wearing his clothes made me feel cool and tough.

Besides, dresses never seemed to fit right on me. Skirts always felt too tight on my waist, dresses too snug on my shoulders and under my arms. Everything squeezed, itched, and eventually made me sweat. Only the no-waist sharkskin sailor dress felt decent; it could almost be a uniform with its red-and-blue piping. But for eighth-grade graduation, Grandma Green *would* make a new dress.

I had little patience for the multiple fittings, and our testy exchanges always started with her ordering me to stand still. She might reach up from pinning the hem and pinch the fabric plus some of my skin, and I'd jerk away with a screech. The scene would continue as she poked and pulled, adjusting the cloth, then commanded me, "Stand still," "Now turn," then "Not that far." When I complained that she was pinning the waist too tight, she answered with fashion facts: "The bodice *is* tight. That's the pattern." Mom watched from the doorway and then observed that everything I wore would not always be comfortable.

"Then I won't wear it," I told her.

She hadn't always been so particular. When I was younger, she let me wear her riding boots with my jeans and Richard's leather chaps and vest. She'd tuck my curls into the cowboy hat before sending me out. Once she took me to the boys department downtown in the Penney's basement to pick out any flannel shirt I wanted. Before Jim had left, Donnie and I got matching red plaid shorts for the Livermore meet. Now Mom and I didn't fight outright, but a struggle had deepened over how I looked, what I should and should not wear.

"Sit up straight," she'd whisper in church. "Don't walk like a lumberjack," she'd call down the hall.

"Don't look at me."

I was sensitive to her criticism even as I ignored it. I knew how I was supposed to look and behave as a girl. If you are going to pass in the straight female world as a repressed gay athlete, you pay close attention. By eighth grade the school world provided clear expectations for dress, behavior, even voice tone. It wasn't hard to pick up the social cues and to copy appropriate expressions. We policed each other there, creating a constant state of self-consciousness. At school, clothes served as costumes for disguise and protection. Going home or to practice always felt like an escape, a return to the world where I could really be me.

But now home exerted those same expectations. Mom wanted me to *look nice*, to *walk like a lady*. When Richard came home, he teased me about my *ape arms*. I wasn't really that big, maybe a couple of inches taller than Donnie and most of the boys my age. My shoulders were broad, but beside Lynn I felt small. She stood five foot nine, almost as tall as Chris von Saltza, and her arms were definitely longer than mine. She wore a school uniform and never had to worry about clothes, and on weekends she could wear anything and nobody at home criticized her.

Even though Mom prided herself on all her home economics skills, her expertise in nutrition accelerated when she was diagnosed with high cholesterol and high blood pressure in 1958. Immediately she began researching ways to control both through diet. A Raleigh PTA friend suggested Dr. Swank's new book on low-fat diet, and suddenly we switched to skim milk, no butter, lots of whole grains, leafy greens, dried fruit, and tons of fish from our store. Her focus expanded to include an athlete's diet as swimming took on importance.

Lucky Lynn, whose parents lived so far away, benefited from Mom's home cooking.

Throughout the winter Lynn spent occasional weekends with us to escape the little apartment she shared with Nancy and to have some home life. Mom loved having an extra daughter, someone to fuss over and feed. Everything lightened up when Lynn arrived. Mom baked fresh health food cookies for us every Friday, oatmeal-raisin jammed full of wheat germ, sunflower seeds, and blackstrap molasses. She fixed T-bone steaks, leg of lamb, calf's liver and bacon, salmon from our store. Whatever Lynn ordered, Mom served. But always fish on Fridays—because she was Catholic.

One weekend Mom had something *special* for us when we came back from Friday night's workout: Nutri-Bio vitamins. She showed us a box with yellow and green packets of vitamins and minerals as she explained how you have to have the exact right combinations to do you any good. Art Linkletter had spoken at the Nutri-Bio meeting. "Remember him?" she asked me. "He's convinced these will keep you healthy and young."

"We are young."

Mom ignored our jokes and placed three tablets, one green and two yellow, on a saucer for each of us. Then she started making a protein milkshake. Into the Osterizer went a cut-up banana, milk, five or six ice cubes, and two heaping scoops of protein powder. She flicked the switch and stood, hand on one hip, as she watched it whirl, crunching the ice, mixing the protein shake that would build up our muscles. It didn't taste bad exactly, just kind of powdery. Health food cookies were definitely better. When we got home after Saturday-morning practice, Mom had another "treat." From the fridge she pulled out a Pyrex dish filled with sickly yellow-green Jell-O. Lynn looked stunned.

"It's Irish moss in lemon Jell-O. It's packed with vitamins and minerals and protein. Try it. It's good for you." We gagged a bit down and escaped upstairs laughing.

Inspired, Mom diversified her kitchen experiments, becoming an expert in blending all kinds of extra muscle-building, stamina-building, blood-building, youth-maintaining, cholesterol-lowering supplements into our food. For a while we ate homemade chapatis after she read a book about Hunzaland, where people lived to be over a hundred because they ate a particular grain. She sold Nutri-Bio to the team, and soon everyone was on supplements.

We needed all the strength and energy we could get when, in late March, Coach started twice-a-day workouts on Tuesdays and Thursdays. Santa Clara, Berkley Y—all the California teams were doing daily doubles to increase distance. The first morning was kind of fun. Dad woke me at five thirty, and I pulled on my suit and sweats, stumbled after him to his truck, and we drove the long dark Canyon Road down to the Club, not a single car coming up the hill and only a few going to town. It reminded me of our early starts for long summer car trips, but this one ended in under ten minutes. Dad came in with me on his way to Early Birds, the men's morning workout group.

Down at the pool, Lynn and Nancy, Dick, David and Bonnie, Donnie, Judy, Noel, Kenny and Graham all waited sleepy eyed for Coach's instruction. After that first double, morning workouts were not fun. I didn't like picking out clothes the night before and jamming into them after practice or eating breakfast in the car. I'd forget my homework and have to call Mom to bring it to school. And I got so tired. Mr. Heugel, our science teacher, droned on and on in the afternoons. We were studying clouds. Cumulus. If only I were sleeping on a big bank of cumulus.

Mom filled me full of wheat germ and protein, but over the next several weeks, I'd stay home and sleep, nursing repeated sore throats. Just when I'd start back training daily doubles, I'd get slammed again. Finally she took me to Dr. Baker.

He looked down my throat and then fingered my neck under the jaw. He thought it could be tonsillitis, but my glands were so swollen that he ordered a blood test then sent me home with the advice to chew Aspergum when my throat felt too sore, and to get lots of sleep. Three

Lynn and me drinking my mom's protein milkshakes, 1959

days later came the diagnosis: mononucleosis. It was a sign. I had mono like my idol, Chris.

The excitement did not last. The early symptoms changed to a fiery pain in my throat. One night I woke whimpering, trying to call for help. I couldn't breathe, couldn't swallow. That night Dad sat up with me, propping pillows behind by back, wringing out washcloths he spread over my aching eyes. Mom made a concoction of honey, butter, and lemon; Dad spooned it in whenever I woke. In the morning my fever broke, but everything still hurt. My neck bulged where the glands stuck out, and there were lumps under my arms.

"You look like a chipmunk with the mumps." Mom tried to cheer me up, but I didn't appreciate her efforts. For a while the world outside my bedroom receded like a hazy horizon. Our minister, Dr. Brown, came to visit once, and Charlene, a classmate, brought assignments and school gossip. But mostly I slept, waking to plod through a few math problems or social studies worksheets before fading away.

I didn't miss being at school those weeks at home. Nothing pulled from there: neither games nor classes, parties nor friends. When I felt a little better, I longed to be at the Club. Lynn called every week with news and encouragement. One time she told a story about how they'd been down in the showers and the locker lady got after them.

"Patsy yelled, 'Carolyn, you better not run away,' and then the locker lady said, 'I'm calling Mr. Perry, Carolyn. I know what you're doing down there.' It's hysterical. You're getting in trouble, and you're not even here. Whadda rep ya got," Lynn said.

It did not seem as funny as she and Patsy thought. Still, I wanted to be there.

When my blood test finally came back normal and I begged to go to the Club, Mom asserted her usual warning: *If you know what's good for you...*

She made me promise I'd just watch from the balcony and not run around, and reminded me that Dr. von Saltza had told us that Chris had carefully come back slowly.

"You need to think about school," Mom said.

"No, I don't. School's almost over anyway."

"School is first priority, Carolyn."

"No, it's not. Nothing happens at school." After being home for a month, I felt adamant that school was only about talk: who was going out with who and what happened at somebody's party or who would get to do the bulletin board. First priority, I didn't say to my mom, was Lynn and the team and nationals and getting in shape and beating Santa Clara.

Her first priority, she often told us, was to love her kids. To her that meant keeping us safe and fostering our success—whether academic, athletic, or social—giving us an edge, sometimes by pointing out what might stand in the way. Richard heard everything as criticism, but I listened to her advice, ignoring some and fighting others, but always sure that she'd do anything to help me. Her attentions seemed normal: worries about my health, special meals, hours of driving to and from practice, weekends spent at steamy pools. I never doubted that she and my father loved me. Back then I thought all parents were like mine, toting kids around to sports, coaxing them to study music, encouraging good grades.

Mom and I worked out a system for me to go to school every morning then come home to rest and do homework, leaving enough time to watch *American Bandstand*. In late May I swam again for the first time in almost six weeks. Mom felt sure that the health food had hastened my recovery.

Costumes

2012

THE STEEP, ROCKY TRACK DESCENDS into a cold medieval town squeezed along two sides of a river at the base of a tall rock face. I've walked so fast through the rain that I've arrived before the albergue has opened. From a seat on a bench under the eaves, I watch the young women across the street who stand in the schoolyard smoking cigarettes and waiting for preschool to let out for lunch. Older kids from another building scurry along in clusters. Two young teens hunch their backs, stiffen their arms, and walk zombie-like toward me, moaning, and then pass by in a collapse of giggles. *Odd*, I think. But when I watch two other pilgrims descend the hill into town, rain capes flapping over their high-hunched backpacks, their poles stretching out mechanically, I get the joke. We look like mummies, zombies, the living dead as we stagger along the desolate roadways and down into ancient towns wearing our Camino costumes.

It is almost Halloween, and back home my front porch will be dark this year, no pumpkins or masks or scary music, no dressing up to startle the trick-or-treaters. Rose's annual jack-o'-lantern with a witch flying on her broom across a candlelit sky will not be there. The house is empty. My thoughts fly around like litter caught in an eddy while I wait for the albergue to open.

From the time he was little, Michael would dig around in the costume box every time he came over. One weekend he'd be a cowboy in the same leather chaps and vest I'd worn when I was little, and before me my brother had worn them. Another week he'd wear the witch costume my grandmother had made when I was six. We'd walk to a nearby pancake house to buy the morning *Oregonian*, check the high school game scores, and share a waffle. When he was older, he and Rose would sometimes don pads and helmets and shin guards on Saturday afternoons and go after each other with *batakas*, thick foam bats, in a form of costumed fencing. Maybe it's no surprise that he loved theater and became an actor.

For a few years in the 1980s, dressing up for Halloween could entertain us all for weeks. One year when he was into building medieval castles and playing with knights, Rose helped him make a papier-mâché helmet and a shield out of cardboard. She painted Richard the Lionhearted's crest on it and sewed him a tunic out of silver-metallic material. Maybe that was the year she went to our friends' costume party as Jeanne d'Arc, with burned ropes around her wrists and singed tights over scabbed and bloody shins. I was punker Exene in all black: hair, sweater, miniskirt, and stiletto heels with a bright-red lipsticked gash across my whitened face. The next year she came in an ermine-collared robe and a neck brace as Princess Stéphanie of Monaco and I as Death. *We were so inappropriate and irreverent,* I scold myself and laugh, remembering the year I dressed as a nun, Sister Severe, and smacked hands at random with a ruler I kept tucked up my sleeve.

Images from the 1990 documentary *Paris is Burning* surface, scenes of those impudent and wild gay and transgender men who gathered together in drag families to perform in elaborate costume balls. They costumed up to compete by category: schoolboys, Ivy Leaguers, Wall Street bankers, jocks, schoolgirls, call girls, models, and stars. The winners were the ones who nailed the details. *Like Rose's charred and bloody legs,* I think, as I watch another zombie hiker lurch down the hill and into town. *Like me in a wedding dress.* My thoughts touch briefly on that image and skitter away.

The bench feels cold, my jacket clammy, and I wonder when the albergue will open. Inside it will be warmer. In another moment I am back with the movie and costumes, all those men in drag, most of them now dead from AIDS. So much pain and wit and energy spent making oneself someone "other." We gays were good at it, dressing up for our roles, putting on clothes as costumes to pass in the straight world.

I'd given up fighting with my mother about clothes in high school. I might have envied Lynn for wearing a St. Mary's uniform, but we had our own basic uniform at Beaverton High: plaid skirt, Peter-Pan collared blouse, cardigan sweater, and loafers. Every year it changed a bit, but it was easy to spot the trends, to nail the necessary details. We had a dress code in college too—no pants on campus ever. Or maybe that was a sorority rule. Either way, by the time I graduated, my professional wardrobe was well stocked. Women teachers in the Beaverton District, where I started teaching English in 1967, had a dress code that lasted even after Woodstock and Vortex and the hippie revolution. Most of my paycheck those first years teaching went to Charles F. Berg, Nordstrom, and I. Magnin.

Up in the attic, some of the old dresses and skirts from the 1960s are stored in plastic garment bags beside my mother's wedding gown, my grandmother's furs, my son's baby clothes. It's a regular costume shop up there, like the one out on Long Island where I went with Michael one summer. He was being fitted for an acting job on a TV show. Racks of police jackets, pants, blazers, shirts, and ties hung in the warehouse like clothes in a dry cleaner. Shelves held hundreds of shoes, hats, and helmets. *You could make yourself into anyone with access to those goods*, I thought, *if you were content with living a lie. If you were a phony.*

In junior English at Beaverton, I taught *The Catcher in the Rye* and led our discussions about phonies. I challenged the kids to think about the masks they wore, the costumes they assumed, the ways they betrayed who they were or what they believed in order to be popular, to fit in, to please parents or coaches or teachers. I was preaching to myself, really, aware at some level of my own self-deception, my phoniness, but pressing forward like I had that summer when I knew I wasn't an Indian scout any more, I wasn't Tarzan, but I still wanted to believe I was normal, not "other," in 1972 when I married.

Ultimately no Pendleton skirts, Lanz dresses, or hostess gowns could hide who I was. My wedding veil and a pink-and-orange plaid pantsuit, my going-away outfit, are still up in the attic. The marriage lasted only as long as it took to conceive a child and celebrate his first birthday before I asked for a divorce. I was in love with a woman. We weren't lesbians, we said. We'd never label ourselves. We were simply two people who loved each other. But the wave of women's rights and gay liberation arrived before papers could be filed. She did not want to hide a secret, live a lie, she told me. She wanted to be gay and proud, and she'd found someone else to be with. All my costumes and disguises could no longer protect me. The divorce went forward. In 1976 Washington County, no matter what dress I wore during that two-week custody trial or what child psychology experts testified, I was not going to be granted custody of a two-year-old, not if I was a lesbian at that time, had ever been a lesbian, or planned to be a lesbian—a condition considered too dangerous for motherhood. I might as well have been a zombie.

On a few Halloweens after Michael left for college, Rose and I joined a group of artists and producers from an animation studio in Portland in raucous, costumed parades that snaked in and out of restaurants and shops along Northwest Portland streets. One year we dressed as Siamese twins, squeezed together inside an immense black knit skirt, which she'd enlarged by adding a stretch panel, and an altered XXXXXL V-neck sweater. We walked in step wearing identical black-rimmed, thick-lensed, distorting glasses, blind to almost everything but our bodies walking side by side, shoulder to shoulder. The last time we participated, the theme was Bedlam. The studio was in trouble or had folded or changed owners. I wore a filthy muslin smock, smeared my hair with mud, and did not speak a word all night. It was a sad and lonely role.

More rain-wrapped pilgrims stagger toward the albergue to join the small group now waiting on the porch. We can hear voices inside, a teakettle's whistle, then footsteps and the latch pulled back. Two Spanish women and a Dutchman, volunteer hosts, welcome us with fresh sliced melon and hot tea. We shuck off our boots, stow our poles, and hang our jackets and capes—our costumes—to dry. Someone has unwrapped a chocolate bar and laid it out on the table.

HIGH HOPES

1959

IN LATE SPRING LYNN'S FATHER came to visit and stayed for a week. He not only watched practices, which were usually off-limits to parents, but he also strode the deck, stopwatch in hand or tucked in the left breast pocket of his white short-sleeved shirt. He was a tall, red-faced, thin-haired Irishman with a big laugh and a boisterous confidence that Portland fathers never showed. Like his daughter, Bob Burke teased and told wild stories. Sometimes his accent made him hard to understand, but he'd laugh and tousle my hair, and I'd laugh along. He called me "brat" and "Wood, " never Carolyn. I felt part of his clan. Once he pulled me aside. "You've got speed, Wood. And you've got spirit. You and Lynnie make a great team." Then he socked me on the arm and pushed me back to the pool.

One night my parents invited Bob and Lynn over for dinner. The house roared with stories and laughter. Dad and Bob talked baseball and swimming, Mom gave her Nutri-Bio pitch, and Lynn spun a tale about a hurricane out at Miller Place, their summer home. Bob seasoned his stories with celebrity: his cousin knew Mickey Mantle and Whitey Ford; Helen, Lynn's mother, had danced with Lucille Ball when they were aspiring showgirls. The Burkes' world glittered with embellishments. Lynn claimed Long Island had the best strawberries in the world, and Dad bet on Oregon Hoods. After they left it felt like Peter Pan and Tinker Bell had flown through the house sprinkling magic dust, everyone happy. We'd see Bob again at nationals in Redding, and Helen would visit soon. Our family had grown.

Lynn's mom had jet-black hair, shoulders broader than a football player's, her pocketbook slung over one shoulder no matter where she went, and always a cigarette, usually balanced on her lower lip. She spoke in a loud, brash voice with sweeping hand gestures. "You're a rip, Cahroline. A real rip. You're a little devil," she'd say, her black eyes twinkling, daring a saucy retort. "You and Lynnie, you're trouble." Beside these long-legged, wild-tongued New Yorkers, Coach Schlueter seemed a dour Pilgrim, my parents bland as pudding.

The Burkes, who let their sixteen-year-old daughter travel three thousand miles from home to swim in Portland, Oregon, were much like mine, ones who gave up weekends and vacations and morning sleep to get their kids to workouts and meets, devoted parents who recognized a daughter's talent and drive and knew that the window for world-class competition was narrow—before Title IX, a mere slit. For most girls swimming on club teams, competition ended with high school graduation—in one year for Lynn, four for me. Our parents were giving us the best chances to compete.

Coach arranged for the whole team, all ages and speeds, to train mornings at Jantzen Beach once school let out. The senior team he hammered with daily-double, long-course workouts as we rushed toward the women's national championships in Redding, California. Coach had high hopes we'd be contenders there in the medley relay. We'd not be going to Livermore this year or most other age-group meets because the focus now was on senior races and ultimately the Pan American Games Trials for Lynn. Coach drove us hard, and Lynn pulled us along in her wake.

The summer fell into a predictable routine. Mom woke me at six thirty, and I gagged down orange juice with Irish moss and lumpy protein powder whipped into it. In the car I'd scour out the taste with toast and honey. Sometimes we met our carpool up at Sylvan, other times down at the Club. Then, car packed with kids, radio tuned to KISN, we'd cross the Willamette River and drive north past the flashy motels, the Paul Bunyan statue, and finally to the Columbia River and the amusement park. All along Interstate Avenue, we'd belt the chorus of "The Battle of New Orleans" when it came on the radio or sing along "high apple pie, in the sky hopes" to Frank Sinatra's "High Hopes." What had been a novelty for the Journal Juniors and the Junior Olympics in previous years became a daily-double routine for us.

The gigantic wood-framed roller coaster that rose over the banks of the Columbia at Jantzen Beach awed Lynn the first time she saw it. "Gawd, look at that! It's just like the one at Coney Island." More than once she told the story about a time kids were daring each other to stand up, and a guy stood right at the top of the climb and before he could sit down, his head hit the crossbar of the downslope tunnel. Decapitated him. Lynn would pause as if we needed time to imagine the scene. Then she'd continue: "His girlfriend didn't even know until they came into the light." Lynn, like her dad, loved storytelling.

I was never going on the roller coaster. I hated the feeling in my stomach whenever I fell or jumped or dropped. I remembered the time Richard had pitched me off his handlebars chin first on the pavement. No one could make me ride the roller coaster or jump off the high dive. It took me a dozen tries to go down the big slides in the fun house.

Every morning at Jantzen, we shambled through the park along weedy rose-lined paths and arcade fronts needing paint into the hulking locker room and through the still-freezing footbath. The two huge pools stretched silver blue in the early morning light. A low fog shimmered over the surface and then erupted into steam plumes when the little kids, those younger or slower than the senior team, plunged into the shallow pool.

Beyond lay the championship pool, fifty-five yards long, twenty yards wide. A tall rectangular diving structure—built from four-by-sixes, much like the roller coaster—rose above the deep end with platforms at five and ten meters. Beside the tower were two springboards, a one-meter and a three-meter. Jantzen Beach had the only long-course pool in the Portland area in 1959, the only Olympic-size pool.

The first morning we stood in a semicircle, huddled together, our towels hugged around our shoulders, knees bent together trying to find some warmth. It wasn't raining, but it was windy and cold. Coach told us that we would begin by building a base that would carry us through the big meets of the summer. *Big meets* echoed in my head. Nationals! We were going to nationals. He talked on while we shivered, telling us that in long-course we needed to lengthen our strokes, that there would be no resting on turns, and finally he set us off with an 800 swim, then 400 IM pull, 400 IM kick, 400 IM swim. That would warm us up.

The boys sprang into the middle lanes, then Lynn, Nancy, and Noel took off. I threw my towel behind the boards, ran along the concrete deck, and stretched into a wild dive, sprinting to catch Lynn and Nancy. Repeat hundreds followed the warm-up and then a cooldown. The water wasn't cold after we started, just the air. Every time I turned to breathe, a cold wind hit my left ear. On the kickboards my hair felt frozen. About halfway through that first hour, my eyes started to burn. Lynn's were red rimmed and swollen. Donnie's looked like he'd been in a boxing match.

"Too much chlorine," I moaned. "My eyes are killing me."

"It's a public pool. They have to overdo it," Coach said.

I tried closing my eyes for a few strokes, but that had its dangers. I crashed into Patsy on a turn, and one time I started in lane two and ended up over in six. At the end of an hour and a half, we climbed out like pink-eyed rats. On the drive home, buildings blurred and the sunshine stung.

At home I ate a big breakfast and fell into bed to sleep for hours. After lunch Mom drove me back to the pool, a long, hot, noisy afternoon drive. Not many visitors were at the park. Scruffy kids and grown-ups who didn't look like my parents' friends crowded around cotton candy vendors and waited in line for the rides. Only a few families sat by the shallow pool, and some older boys in tight suits dived off the platform and showed off with cannon balls. We had a couple of lanes roped off to one side where we trained, only the senior team in the afternoon. Coach prescribed the strokes and distances. Because I would be the butterflyer on the relay at nationals, he made me do one set of fly for every one I did freestyle—all on the minute. He needed my speed, he said. But I didn't feel very speedy that afternoon. I swam next to Lynn, wishing I could do backstroke instead, because backstrokers could breathe anytime they wanted. By the fourth or fifth repetition, my arms dragged across the water and caught the pool waves. My back ached and my lungs, too, and I snuck a few frog kicks, trying to get momentum.

"Don't breathe every stroke, Wood. Alternate," Coach hollered out instructions from the deck.

Lynn knew how to motivate and encouraged me to keep up with her. "Don't let a backstroker beat you, Woody," she said. My arms gained weight with each stroke, and by the end of the lap, I could barely clear them. *Push. Push. Beat Lynn*, I chanted to myself. *They need my speed.* When we finally finished the first set, my face burned, and I flipped on my back gasping for air. No matter how many repeats we did, butterfly never got easy—except the first one. But I didn't quit.

All summer I pushed past the voice in my head that complained, *I can't do it. I can't go anymore.* I kept going, encouraging myself with another voice that said, *Come on, push. Come on*, until the wall finally found me, the set ended, the practice was over. When those moments arrived and I hadn't surrendered to the *I can't do it*, I felt calm and sure and sweet in my fatigue. Through long, hard training, I discovered an inner strength and, with it, confidence. No matter the challenge—waves, wind, breathlessness, fatigue—if I held steady and swam into it, through it, I would prevail. In time, I'd face other kinds of pain well beyond the pool, and the lesson served. It's good to know how to override the voices that fool you into quitting.

The summer took on a rhythm: wake, drive, swim, drive, eat, sleep, wake, drive, swim, drive, eat, sleep. Weekends we had only one practice, and sometimes Mom would take me to the Canyon Drive-In on Saturday night and we'd watch the movie from our old Buick. Dad often "worked" on weekends now that the dogs were running—unless there was a swim meet. When Lynn came along for *Gidget*, she dragged me back and forth to the snack bar half the night so we could spy on kids making out in the cars.

In early July Coach began treating us with Visine before practice. We'd line up, tilt our faces, and he'd draw each eye open with his fingers and squeeze in a stinging drop. "This will help with the chlorine," he promised. It might have worked. Mom had me rinse with clear water when I got home. Maybe that worked too. Sleeping for a couple of hours helped the most.

Every few weeks we'd have time trials. Coach was assessing who'd be going to nationals, who'd be on the relay. He arranged a couple of American record attempts, too, not in meets but at exhibitions, one in front of the Oregon Sportswriters and Sportscasters Association. The paper ran our relay's photograph with a big headline: "MAC Swimmers Set Two American Records." All summer I'd been trying to keep up with Lynn. On the relay, my split was a 1:04.4—Lynn's 1:04.7.

"You had a dive," Lynn reminded me when she saw the article.

"Still. I beat you." We bickered the way siblings might.

Coach told the reporters, "They can win in the national outdoor meet. Just wait and see." The next week we had a couple of lines in *Sports Illustrated*. Coach wanted to put Santa Clara on notice, he said. If we all dropped our times, we could do it.

Hopes high, we drove to Redding in a caravan like we had on our old trips to Livermore. Lynn's dad flew out from New York and drove down with Coach and Nancy. Other teammates traveled with their parents. Even Bob Johannesen, the Club's assistant manager, came to support the team that might win a title.

At our first warm-up, I spotted Chris von Saltza among the Santa Clara swimmers right away, and then Sylvia Ruuska, who I recognized from her photos in the *San Francisco Chronicle*. I'd discovered the *Chronicle* with its green sports pages along with the *Examiner* in the Multnomah Club library, a dark wood-paneled room at the back of the first floor where a tall grandfather clock chimed every fifteen minutes. A white marble statue of two naked men wrestling and another of a discus thrower sat silently on pedestals. Newspapers from New York, Seattle, San Francisco, and Los Angeles hung from a wooden rack along with the *Oregonian* and the *Journal*. Every weekend and every Monday I'd check the sports pages in case there was news about Chris or other Bay Area swimmers. Nobody ever seemed to be in the library in the late afternoons, so it was easy to hide scissors under my PeeChee and homework and cut out results and important pictures. My scrapbook brimmed with articles and photos of my California rivals and their times.

"There's Carin Cone." Lynn pointed to a small blonde across the pool. She stood listening to her coach, Phil Hansel, who'd been at the MAC my first week there in 1956. "That's who I have to beat."

"She's not very big."

"And she's old. Nineteen."

Carin Cone, like Nancy Ramey from Seattle, had been on the 1956 US Olympic team with Mo Murphy. Cone and Ramey had won silver medals in Melbourne and aimed to win the gold in Rome at their second Olympics. Magazines and papers chronicled their hopes and dreams. But before Rome came the 1959 Pan American Games at the end of the summer in Chicago. Lynn's goal was to make that team.

On race day, though, Lynn refused to swim the 200-meter backstroke final. In the parking lot of our motel, she cried while her father and Coach tried to talk with her. She stood doubled over sobbing. "I've got cramps. I've got cramps, and I can't even stand up. I can't swim." Her preliminary time had been way off her best, and she'd barely qualified for the finals. Even though her dad had flown all the way from New York to see her swim, she scratched from the race.

"Will you be okay for the relay?" I asked as she closed the door to her room.

"JesusMaryJoseph. Women," Bob Burke muttered.

How could you not swim at nationals, especially if you made finals? It didn't make sense. I'd swim with a broken arm if I made finals. Mom tried to explain Lynn's decision when we were back in our room. "Sometimes pain can overwhelm you. Or maybe it's psychological."

I didn't make finals in either butterfly or freestyle, and our relay finished a disappointing fourth. Becky Collins from Indiana set a world record in the butterfly and upset Olympian Nancy Ramey. Two days after her cramps, Lynn came back to finish second in the 100 backstroke, almost beating Carin Cone. She would make the Pan Am Team for sure—if she didn't get her period. Of course, Chris won every freestyle event she swam—100, 200, and 400 meters.

On the long, lazy drive back to Portland, my parents traded driving while I nodded off in the back. Sometimes I'd wake and listen to their chatter. After meets, as they did after potlucks and parties, they'd talk about who had been there and what so-and-so had said. They marveled at the world records they'd seen and the parents they'd met from Florida, Pennsylvania, and Texas. They wondered about the Burkes, how they could afford to send Lynn to Portland to live and to fly out to visit her from so far away. As their voices rose and fell, mixed with the radio when we came within a station's range, my thoughts wandered.

Before we left Redding, Coach had asked us how we liked the high level of competition we'd found at nationals. Now lying stretched on the backseat, I considered his question. Best had been seeing all those famous swimmers. That and getting ready for the trip. Before we left for Redding, Lynn had suggested we get matching PJs, so Mom had taken us to Lerner's, where we bought pink-striped shorty pajamas. We made lists of what we'd take to wear at the pool, at the motel, at the awards ceremony, if there was one. In Redding I wore moccasins from the Oregon Centennial, and we got matching cowboy hats at a Western store. Planning ahead with Lynn had made the trip fun and taken away worries about how we'd do. Now it was over, and we hadn't matched up very well to the competition. But even though I hadn't made finals, I didn't feel discouraged. I'd just had mono. I was only thirteen.

For eighth-grade graduation, my parents had given me a turquoise metal Samsonite suitcase exactly like Lynn's. Grandma Green added

American record-setting medley relay: Lynn Burke, me, Bonnie Boyd, Nancy Kanaby, 1959

a matching overnight case, which I had filled with two starched petticoats rolled and stuffed into nylons, a packing trick the older girls used, to go with a full skirt outfit that I never wore. Weary from the effort and excitement of the week, I drifted in and out of thoughts about races and relays, clothes and Olympians. The world of national champions and Olympic stars had come within reach. Moments before the car rocked me to sleep, I called up to the front, "Thanks for the luggage. I'm going to use it lots."

FIRST TRIALS

1959

SOON AFTER WE GOT BACK from nationals, Coach called a meeting of senior swimmers and their parents. Some of our times in Redding had met the qualifying standards for the trials, he told us. Mr. Johannesen had advocated for us. The Club would sponsor four girls for the Pan Am Trials: Lynn. Noel. Nancy. And me. We were leaving Portland on August 3.

I bounced in my chair. We were flying in an airplane to the trials! Hardly anyone I knew had ever been on a big plane. Lynn pounded me on the back as Coach settled us down with details. We'd spend the night in Chicago at the Sheraton hotel where he had previously coached. Nancy, who'd swum for him there, described the pool to us: mosaic tiles and marble, a gigantic fountain, and located on the fourteenth floor. I tried to imagine a pool in the sky but couldn't picture it. In Portland, pools were always in basements or outdoors. After a night in Chicago, we'd take a small plane to East Lansing, Michigan.

"But where will they stay?" I could hear worry in my mom's voice.

All swimmers would be in the college dorms, Coach told her. We'd eat in the cafeteria, and the Club would give each of us five dollars per day food allowance.

"I'll take care of her, Mrs. Wood," Lynn said. "Don't worry."

My mom blinked. Dad reached over and patted my shoulder and then Noel's. "You girls. Pan American Games. That is something."

"It's the trials," I corrected him, not wanting anyone to think I didn't know the difference between trials and games.

"I wish the games were going to be somewhere besides Chicago. Why couldn't they be in Brazil or Argentina?" Lynn *knew* she'd make the team. She'd already proved that she was the second best backstroker in the world. All I could expect was to fly from Portland to East Lansing. Lynn leaned over and bumped my arm. She promised that we'd be roommates and that we'd sit together on the plane. She even offered me the window seat.

Lynn and Nancy shopped downtown and found red blazers for us to wear with white skirts, our Club travel uniform. Mom sewed the MAC insignia, a Winged M, on the pocket and then bought me a red purse with a long strap, a pocketbook like Helen Burke's. At the airport we posed for pictures, and then Lynn insisted we all buy flight insurance from an airport kiosk so the plane wouldn't crash.

Mom pulled me aside before we walked down to the concourse and delivered her final instructions. "Carolyn, I want you to behave yourself. I've talked to Mr. Burke—"

I interrupted her. "Bob. He told me to call him Bob."

"And he promised to look after you and your money. I'm going to tell you something that they taught me in my sorority."

This sounded really serious. Mom talked about being a Theta as if it were a religion. She had a little sermon she needed to deliver, one I would hear in various forms over the years that went something like this:

"'Remember who you are and what you represent.' The Multnomah Club is paying your way. They expect you to swim fast, yes, but you are representing every member of the Club at this meet. It's an honor, Carolyn. So don't make any trouble. And when you get there, I want you to send a thank-you letter to Mr. Perry." She straightened the collar of my blouse while she looked at me.

"Okay." Usually I'd feel like pulling away, but I looked hard at Mom. She meant it. For the first time since her illnesses, when I'd gone to scout camp, she was letting me go off by myself.

"Remember who you are and what you represent," she repeated as she pulled me into a hug. "I know you will."

Mom's words made me think past the excitement of a plane ride and the chance to be on my own. We weren't a swirling gang of age-group swimmers about to converge on some local pool. We four girls wearing our matching white skirts and red blazers were like Cody's Kids, those MAC swimming stars from the 1940s, or Maureen Murphy the Olympian. We represented the Club, which had paid for our plane tickets, room, and board. Mom was worried that in her absence, I'd be influenced to take a dare or run wild. But I wouldn't. I'd do my best for the Club and the team. I couldn't let them down, and I wouldn't disappoint Mom either.

Our plane left late in the evening. At the counter Lynn picked our seats right next to the galley. We'd get served first and might even get seconds, she said. When we got on, she gave me the window like she'd promised, but the seats didn't recline. Not one bit. At first it didn't matter. I watched the four propellers start up, and then the ground rushed by and slowly receded as we lifted off. Below, the Columbia River snaked along and headlights flooded roadways. It looked like Richard's train-set world, the trees tiny and the fields dusky-brown squares. Pretty soon we flew into the clouds and then above them; after that there wasn't much to see. The stewardess brought us dinner on a tray with silverware and cloth napkins like in a restaurant. Lynn fell asleep sitting upright as soon as she finished dessert. I stared out the window through the condensation trapped between the panes. Everything vibrated and buzzed. Off in the distance, I spotted the first forks of lightning.

"Lynn. Lynnie." I nudged her. "There's a storm." I'd never seen lightning so close before. What if we got hit? The plane lurched and dropped, righted itself and dipped again. Lynn nodded, mumbled something, and curled away. I watched through the night. The storm went on and on— sometimes close and sometimes lighting the bulging clouds and ground far, far away. When we landed in Chicago that morning, my eyes felt swollen and sandy. I wished Lynn had been awake and seen the storm too. For the first time, I felt the regret that comes when you experience something intense alone and want to have shared it.

The trials ran from Friday until Tuesday with Sunday off. Coach only entered me in the butterfly, even though I swam faster than either Noel or Nancy in the freestyle. Butterfly was scheduled for Saturday, Lynn's backstroke not until Monday. We lay around in the dorm room most of the time when we weren't warming up, eating, or watching a race. Lynn shaved her long legs, painted her nails pink, touched up her hair with peroxide. She offered to give me a haircut, but I declined, content to read a comic book on my bed.

Michigan State had a brand new outdoor fifty-five-yard pool, the same length as Jantzen. The women's locker room held a modern sauna, something foreign to us, different from the Aero Club's tiny, tiled hot room with old canvas sling chairs or the MAC's men-only steam room. On Thursday after warm-ups and a light practice, we sat in the wood-paneled sauna with a swimmer from Philadelphia and three others from Los Angeles: Carolyn House, Molly Botkin, and Patty Kempner. Carolyn House told all about how she'd been blind since her premature birth, and Molly told us about their plane dropping a thousand feet over the Rockies and all the dinner trays flying up to the ceiling. I told them that we had flown through a storm, too, but that nothing happened. I felt kind of disappointed our storm hadn't been as dramatic as the LA kids'. Probably if Lynn had awakened to see it, she would have made it into a better story.

Coach got pretty mad when he heard we'd spent about an hour in the sauna. He said that it would sap our energy and that we were in Michigan to compete not relax. "What's the matter with you girls? Don't be so stupid." His dark mood reminded me of Richard. For some reason it felt like we were fighting with Coach even though no one said anything back. My event was two days away, and Lynn's was four. It didn't seem stupid to be in a warm place telling stories. The next day, Chris won the 110-yard freestyle in a new national record. Molly Botkin came in second, and Joan Spillane third. The sauna hadn't hurt Molly much.

Saturday morning I qualified for the finals in the 110-yard butterfly—sixth out of eight. Nancy Ramey set a world record in the prelims, but Becky Collins beat her in the finals. Molly Botkin finished third, qualifying her for the USA team in two different strokes. I moved up one place to fifth with my best time ever, two spots away from making the team. *Next year, Olympics*, I told myself. It actually seemed possible.

My perspective changed after that trip to Michigan. Being on a college campus with young women from across the country provided a view of my competition in ways magazine articles and time lists couldn't. It was completely different from saying, "I want to go to the Olympics," or pledging with Lynn, "Let's make the team together." I had met the girls who stood between me and the Olympic team, sat beside them in a sauna, observed them in the cafeteria. Between nationals and the Pan Am Trials, famous swimmers had become real people, and those girls whose times were barely better than mine became vulnerable because I had seen them, seen their bodies, their strokes and turns, had heard their stories, dreams, and fears.

In a way I felt like I had gained an edge, a way to beat them. Molly goofed off, Shirley Stobs was short, and Joan Spillane trained alone. On national teams, four girls qualified for the freestyle relay. I could be one of the four if I kept working hard and improving. In butterfly I needed to pass three competitors to be one of the top two. Now I knew who they were. It never crossed my mind that they might be observing and evaluating me too.

There's nothing friendly about racing when the point is to beat people. Swimming for fun or for medals, for pictures in the paper or a personal best would not get you on the team. At the Pan Am Trials, you came in first, second, third, or you were nothing. Only place counted. The goal became clear: next year I would have to finish first or second to make the Olympic team.

Lynn took me to my first-ever Catholic Mass on Sunday. Inside, the church was dark and smoky, and the priest spoke in Latin and never even looked at the people. Lynn prayed on her knees as I sat on the bench and watched. One time she stood up and caught me with her elbow, and I started to laugh. "You brat, " she whispered. When her shoe kicked the kneeler and made a loud clunk, my shoulders shook, but I kept my eyes down, held my breath, and swallowed the giggles. Afterward on our way out, she called me "brat" again and said she'd prayed for me and that she'd make the team. Her prayers worked because the next day, she finished second in the 110-yard backstroke. Lynn made the team with Chris and all the American and world record holders.

Coach and Nancy stayed on in Chicago, Lynn went off to train with the US team, and Noel and I flew back to Portland, where our parents met us at the airport. In the car Mom chattered away about how she'd missed me and what had happened at church and what Georgie had said. Then she turned around. "We have a surprise for you."

"What?" I wondered if they'd gotten me a dog or a new radio.

There was no dog when we got home. She led me to my room. The Goldilocks and Three Bears wallpaper behind my bed had been covered with a pink, floral-patterned paper; the other walls, once papered in cheery red polka dots, had become pink. An early American maple twin bed set had replaced my old bed, plus a new bed stand, bureau, and fancy lace-shaded lamp. I hated everything about it.

"Isn't it beautiful? You're a young lady now, and here's your new—"

"I'm not a young lady. I'm going to the Olympics with Lynn."

Mom's smile fell away, and she said I'd get used to it, that it had just surprised me.

Another girl, some mythical daughter she didn't have, would have thanked her, but I didn't want this change. I wanted the old wallpaper and the comforting pictures of the Three Bears. Maybe her friends' daughters wanted pretty clothes or redecorated rooms, but I didn't. She would never know me, I thought, angry that she tried to make me conform to her hopes and resentful of her pressure to change or hide who

I was. In Lansing, I'd set my own priorities: practicing focus, improving my time, racing the best. There I could be who I really was—a swimmer. With Lynn, not my parents, as guide, I'd navigated the world of national competition and become more confident. Back home, nothing had changed except my bedroom decor.

The bedroom was almost as bad as the Junior Olympics the next week. I hated the dinky pool at Wilson High—not even long course—and all the pokey kids from all over the state. Driving home from the finals, I tried to tell Mom that it wasn't fun racing kids that you beat by a mile, but she answered that everyone was doing their best. Of course they were doing their best, but that wasn't it. I'd learned that doing your best meant more than trying hard or improving your time. It had everything to do with evidence: finishing first, setting a record, making a national team. Anything less was not good enough.

I wished I were with Lynn and the kids from California. I wished I were still in Michigan, eating in the cafeteria, talking to the girls from Vesper Boat Club and learning chess or laughing in the sauna with Molly Botkin instead of back home. It had been so different at nationals and the trials. There we all had dreams that stretched beyond the ocean. The races mattered. But Mom didn't know what I meant any more than I could understand why she'd painted my room pink. We were in different places now.

After Labor Day, high school classes started. The MAC team took September off, so I swam with the high school team some afternoons. Every day I scoured the paper for news from the Pan Am Games. Chris won all her events, but Lynn didn't win a single medal. She sent one long letter telling all about training with George Haines, the team coach, and she sent a little USA patch that I sewed inside my MAC sweat suit. In late September, when practices started up again at the Club, Lynn still hadn't returned.

Late one Saturday afternoon, the phone rang and I knew it was Lynn. "I'm not coming back to Portland. I'm going to Santa Clara. And guess where I'll live? With Chris, your idol!" She sounded so excited. "Now you gotta make the Olympics, Woody. Blood sister. We're all going to Rome. Veni, vidi, vici. Right?" She talked so fast, I couldn't even answer. I couldn't think.

"But what about Coach? Does he know?"

"My dad told him. Listen, Woody. You gotta work hard. I'll see you at the Far Westerns and nationals. And then..." She rattled on, her voice dissolving along the line, the long wire stretching from my house out into the darkness and across all that land we'd flown over, a barely discernible voice far, far away in the dark.

"I've got to go now, Lynn." I could feel hot tears starting. "I gotta go."

Curled on my side in bed, I wept, grief unfamiliar. If my mom hadn't recovered from her cancer, if she had never returned from the hospital, I'd have known grief, but this was my first loss and I didn't think I could bear it.

After a long time Dad came into the room. "Enough. Enough tears now." He never talked sharply, but he meant *stop*.

"She's not coming back. It's not fair."

He sat on the bed and told me I'd have to train on my own. I'd have to train hard and make the team because Lynn and Chris would be on it. Then he patted my shoulder and left me alone.

I had counted on Lynn's return: training another year, making the team, and being on the relay together. I had believed in it, but now everything had spun away and disappeared without explanation. I felt abandoned and utterly alone, as if someone I loved had died. All those tears may seem silly now, teenage hyperdrama. And yet, then I could no more have explained the depth of my loss than I could have recited the capitals of South America again.

I lay in the dark thinking about what I had lost—a spirited training partner who'd been on the Pan Am team, a blood sister. But I still had the dream. Lynn didn't have to be in Portland for me to work hard. She didn't swim my laps or race my races. I could rise up to the next level, hers and Chris's. I belonged with them. I just needed to prove it—every day at practice and in every race.

LOST AND FOUND

2012

AN EARLY ARRIVAL AND A meander through town leads me to the convent albergue, but somewhere between a park bench, the bakery, and the convent courtyard, my pencil case goes missing. I rifle through my backpack, empty everything from the front pack, plow through my pockets. Gone. And with it two pens, a pencil, glasses cloth, tweezers, and an eraser. I know every item because when you pack to carry only sixteen pounds for forty days, you notice what you've got. I can let my glasses film up and the chin hair grow, but I need a pen. Journal and pen are my most reliable companions.

The loss occupies me for hours. I backtrack my route through the tiny town, check under benches and around the fountain. I ask inside shops in a combination of charades and lousy Spanish: *"Perdo un caso de lapiz? Rojo? Ve?"* Everyone nods, looks around as if they might find something, then shrugs in sympathy with my loss. *"Lo siento."*

It's only a pencil case, I assure myself.

But it's from that trip to Guatemala, I lament. *It's handmade.*

It's nothing. You can buy a pen anywhere. Let it go.

The sadness feels disproportionate and familiar, a sunken collapse after the initial energy of search.

I've had plenty of practice losing things over the years: keys, glasses, sweatshirts, socks. We all have. Things come and go. Even when something's been gone forever, it may reappear like an old wood-handled weeder that emerges among the daisies in the spring. Or an earring gone who knows where that comes back one day to its drawer. Once I found a yellow nailbrush in the compost pile two years after it disappeared. Some things, you keep hoping will return. Others, you know never will. My thoughts push toward Rose, but instead I remember another day on the Camino.

I'd been hiking four or five hours when I passed two Swiss girls sitting off the trail sharing lunch. I'd watched them in the village that morning stocking up for the day, a loaf of bread, a hunk of cheese, tomatoes and grapes, while I bought my yogurt and apple. They waved as I approached, but I pressed on without stopping, without asking if I might join them. A lost opportunity.

I blink away tears, my memory bumping into emotion. The title of a book, *The Loneliness of the Long-Distance Runner*, comes into my mind, a time when I saw it on the library shelf and broke into tears without knowing why. Now my left foot aches and pain sears through the big toe joint; the ball of my right foot feels ablaze. The loneliness of a long-distance hiker.

Why do I choose to be alone? I wonder. *Why do I push on when I'm hungry, tired, and in pain? Do I need to know?* I try to laugh. *Is anything wrong with my choices?*

My father, dead now over forty years, comes into my thoughts. His presence fills my mind as it did halfway up the Kilimanjaro summit when I didn't think I could take another step. A silent, happy presence suggested, *You can do it, sis. Come on. You can do it.* Not insistent, not excited, just matter of fact and sure, confident that I could carry on.

I think of him in those last days in his gut-swollen pain, still convinced he'd beat that cancer. I was twenty-four. We never talked of death or love or fear. My last night with him, we smoked cigarettes together in the hospital as I described the riots at Portland State the evening before.

"What the hell do they think they're doing?" he asked, and I wasn't sure if he meant the protesting students or the police who beat them bloody.

Now I wonder if he meant his doctors who had filled him full of chemicals, an early chemo experiment.

On a walk that stretches forty days, old regrets will find you. I'd lost an opportunity then. I could have told him that I forgave him for missing my last race as a competitive swimmer in the 1962 Chicago nationals when he went to the dog track instead of the pool. Or for gambling away all my college money. I could have told him how proud I was that he'd joined AA and finally quit gambling. Or how sad I felt that he would never know his grandchildren. I could have told him a lot of things that mattered. On the path now, in my pain and loneliness, I want him to know that I loved him for all his kindness, his gentle ways, his joy and childlike belief, always, that I could do it, whatever it was.

In León a few days later, I find a stationery store that sells pens and pencil cases before meeting up with Monica and Gordon, my Canadian friends. We stay late talking after dinner, my first conversation in English for days, and take a long goodbye. I will not see them again because they are hurrying forward to the finish while I am spending two nights in the city. On the walk back to the hotel, I think of the many pilgrims who have woven into the fabric of my walk: the British talker I hurried to avoid, the old Quebecois, a Romanian man who shared his lentils and eggs late one night, the New Hampshire mother and two daughters who walked all the way from Le Puy, the Swiss teacher who started from her front door in Geneva to see how far she could go on her own feet. We come together and separate like swimmers from different clubs coming to meets. You never know who you'll find at the end of a day or who will show up weeks down the trail. I'll miss Gordon and Monica.

Back in the hotel, I discover my neck gaiter is gone, the second loss in three days. I race back to the restaurant, but it has closed. The same rush of emotion as before, the sudden catch of loss, the push-pull of disappointment, anger, sadness, and blame, floods in.

Not again, I begin. *I might as well be thinking about Rose. Enough.*

Where is a stone to pick up and carry?

Practice release, I advise.

Didn't my father teach me this years before when he helped me study for the South America test? Go to sleep, he said, and you'll remember in the morning. When Lynn left and it felt like I'd lost the world, he said, "Enough." He meant, let go, move forward. Wasn't that the secret of a good stroke too? A swimmer's arm enters the water and makes a catch, then pulls, pushes, and finally releases it in recovery. Without letting go of the stroke, the swimmer can't move forward. *I need more work on the release*, I think. After all, I have another day in León to check the restaurant or find a replacement and some heavier gloves. Reports predict snow ahead in the mountains.

FRESHMAN

1959–1960

BEAVERTON HIGH SCHOOL HAD MORE to offer than grade school did—different teachers every period, interesting and entertaining kids from other schools, and a swim team loaded with talent and a friendly coach, Rod Harman, who made workouts fun for everyone. The first weeks swirled with new students, pep assemblies, and homework. We had long lists of vocabulary words to learn for Mrs. Ward's biology quizzes, book notes for novels in Mrs. Zeller's English 1C. Spanish wasn't as hard as I'd feared, and it was actually kind of fun practicing ridiculous role-plays. Algebra made absolutely no sense, so I joked my way through each day by making fun of the geeky teacher. The young and beautiful PE teacher, Mrs. Malcolm, came from back east and wore shirtwaist dresses with unrolled bobby socks over her nylons, a look I recognized from the Philadelphia girls at the trials. Nobody in Portland wore socks anymore, but I started wearing them with some of my pleated skirts.

Our first novel in English was *Great Expectations*. I loved the title. In the afternoons waiting for swim practice, I'd spread out my notebook and the novel. At first I had no idea what was going on with Pip and Mrs. Joe and Joe Gargery, but I could feel the cold, damp air rising off the dark water and see the ferocious guy who came after Pip. Reading that book transported me the way *The Secret Garden* had years before. In class, we all hated Estella and couldn't stop talking about Miss Havisham. Sheila Herman, who wasn't as threatening as she had been in seventh grade, shared a locker with me. After class we'd walk the long halls and replay scenes from the novel or list details described in Miss Havisham's room.

I wanted to impress my English teacher, but I wanted to dazzle Mrs. Malcolm. In the late fall, we had a swimming unit in PE. Kids who didn't know how to swim got lessons. The rest of us swam laps or learned new strokes or life-saving techniques. It seemed a waste of time to walk over to the pool, dress down, swim for thirty minutes, and then get ready for the next class, especially when I was going to be training after school for another two hours. Mrs. Malcolm, when she demonstrated the breaststroke for the beginners, had a scissor kick, and for the final she told us to swim crawl breathing every stroke. I was not going to breathe every stroke. It was wrong technique. Mrs. Malcolm obviously didn't know much about swimming. She walked along the deck with her clipboard, then whistled to get our attention. Again she insisted that we turn our heads to breathe every stroke so she could verify that we were breathing.

That seemed ridiculous, and I would not do it. Instead, I held my breath for the whole lap. When the nine-week grades arrived, I had an A in every subject except PE: C!

I couldn't believe it. She gave me a C because of swimming. How could she do that? Dad thought it was funny, but Mom made an appointment.

When she came home, she said that it was just a nine-week grade, but I needed to show more respect for my teachers. She reminded me that my father had once been a teacher.

"She doesn't know anything about swimming," I argued.

"But she's the teacher. Follow her instructions. No more Cs."

Mrs. Malcolm turned out to be a much better square-dance teacher than swim instructor. We learned how to do-si-do, allemande left, and promenade in the gym with the boys' class. At the end of the semester I had straight As despite giggling through Spanish role-plays and fending off entertaining asides from the boy seated in front of me in world history.

Mr. Schultz, the orchestra teacher, also taught world history, and he trained us to take notes while he lectured. Over the summer he traveled abroad and brought back slides from Greece and Rome and Egypt, which he used to supplement his lessons. One late morning I studied the photos of Rome: the Colosseum, the famous fountains, the Vatican. Wes whispered that I would be going there that summer.

"*If* I make the team," I corrected him. It was bad luck to make assumptions. I glanced at my arm resting across the desk. My biceps flexed even when relaxed, and my arms looked twice as big as Wes's. I wore a size 16 dress now, even though my waist and hips were size 10. *I'm bigger than every freshman boy*, I thought, looking around the room.

Mr. Schultz ended his lecture on the Minoan society, a matriarchal civilization, with slides of bare-breasted women, snakes draped around their necks. My cheeks burned, my stomach growled; Wes backed his desk into mine. We nervously waited for the lunch bell.

I liked Mr. Schultz, his sense of humor, his handsome tweed jackets, his short-cropped hair and precise manner of speaking. Before Christmas he had read us Alfred Hitchcock's "Specialty of the House." He smiled at us like a cat when he said it was a Christmas present and added, "Be careful what you eat."

During lunch one day, I said that I thought Mr. Schultz was like a college professor, but Gretchen raised her eyebrows and, using the same insinuating tone my mother had when she called Henry Walsh "arty," said, "He's not married."

I felt a twinge and a blush as if somehow exposed. In that moment I wanted to disappear. Was she suggesting that I was like him? In 1960 I had no words to describe who I might be. Perhaps I'd heard *homosexual* or *queer* by freshman year, but those were references to men like Liberace—sissies, fruits, fairies. They had nothing to do with me. But Gretchen's comment had touched a nerve no one could know was raw. Whatever made me blush that day, whatever I feared might be recognized, was something so shameful, it had to be denied and hidden. I was careful to wear the right clothes, affect nonchalance, and keep a distance at school to hide me from myself as well as others. How tightly I closed in, how much energy spent in denial and disguise.

To be on guard all the time was wearing, and the pool provided protection. There, strength, drive, and effort were rewarded—muscles, guts, and single-mindedness. Work chased away any contemplation of desire. If a suggestion of shame ever emerged, I would return to my safe self-understanding: I was someone pursuing an elite goal that differentiated me from my classmates and excused my difference.

When the Winter Olympics began in Squaw Valley, California, my parents and I watched with Grandma Green on the black-and-white set she'd bought in 1953 for the coronation of Queen Elizabeth. We bunched up on the couch for the Opening Ceremony as the athletes marched into the stadium in their national uniforms and followed a teammate carrying their country's flag, but we'd have to wait a week for *Life* to publish pictures showing all the flag and uniform colors. As all the teams stood at attention behind their flags, thousands of white pigeons flew up from beside the stadium toward the mountains. Skiers swept down a slope toward the stadium, the lead one carrying the Olympic torch, which he handed off to a skater who crossed the ice, climbed some stairs, and lit a giant cauldron that would burn for the rest of the Olympics. On television we could see all the flags waving behind the cauldron, the Olympic flag above them all. I wondered if they'd have pigeons in Rome, too, because they symbolized peace, an Olympic ideal.

Immediately I identified with the ski racers and imagined competing when I quit swimming and learned how to ski. It looked so easy and fun. Skiing, skating, and every other sport were forbidden by Coach, even though some kids snuck up to Mount Hood regularly. For now, I joined the rest of America rooting for our girl racers in the downhill, Penny Pitou and Betsy Snite. The United States hadn't had an alpine champion since Gretchen Fraser in 1948, but this year we had a chance.

On Saturday morning in the women's downhill, something terrible happened: Betsy Snite, my favorite racer, fell on her second run.

Weight training in the MAC pool balcony, 1960

They replayed it more than once: she sped down the hill, caught a tip, then tumbled head over ski, snow spraying around her. Officials rushed onto the course. I couldn't believe she fell and that we had to watch it over and over again. Every time it almost made me cry. How could a champion or someone predicted to win be eliminated just like that? It didn't happen in swimming, although sometimes a diver hit the board. I'd never seen winter sports and had no idea of the risks skaters and skiers and jumpers faced. It was like getting knocked out in boxing, which I did watch on TV Friday nights.

At school on Monday everybody talked about it, especially Sheila Herman, my locker partner. I can almost recall our exchange that day.

"She was going so fast. About fifty miles an hour I bet, and then *bang*. Head over skis."

"Yeah. And her ski went flying straight up and probably hit some spectator on the head." I imagined the ski zooming by.

"What if it hit a television camera?" Susan continued.

"What if it hit Walter Cronkite?" We took off on a tangent of what-ifs and how we'd feel. What if we were the best and were heading straight downhill and then—*pow*—upended? We were still laughing when the class bell rang. Gretchen, always quick to counter injustice, turned around to shush us. Betsy Snite had the fastest first run and she deserved to win, she told us, and it's not really funny.

Gretchen was right, of course. But it was too agonizing to contemplate all Snite's work and her dreams smashed in a split second on the slopes. I didn't want to think about it. It was easier to laugh it off. In the end Penny Pitou, the other American, finished second in the finals. On television she apologized, "I'm sorry it wasn't gold."

At least you're on the team, I thought. *What's wrong with a silver medal? It's better than falling down.*

Training and meets took more and more time that winter, forcing me to squeeze in homework down at the Club or after practice. I still wanted to be a scholar, but straight As seemed less important than Olympic Development, Far Western Championships, or indoor nationals. When Mrs. Malcolm announced that we'd be doing track and field the last six weeks of PE, Coach Schlueter absolutely forbade it. He and my parents met with the principal, and on the day track started, I reported to study hall with the juniors and seniors, carrying a copy of *Crime and Punishment*, a book from the college prep list.

Even though I'd begun high school with new clothes and a fresh attitude, it hadn't taken long before it felt as if I were watching freshman year from the far end of the cafeteria or the upper corner of the bleachers. Classes could be interesting, but my focus was aimed in a different direction than my classmates'. I wanted to be more than just a freshman at Beaverton.

The people who understood that, my tribe, serious swimmers, lived somewhere else—Santa Clara, Philadelphia, Los Angeles. All of us worked toward a spot on the Olympic team, not a date to the Friday-night dance. Nobody at school knew what that meant. Every afternoon I made my getaway to the Club and into the pool to work my guts out the way Jim had taught us.

19

Shame and Pride

2012

Fewer and fewer of us hike along the Camino in November as daylight grows shorter and weather colder. I wait a couple of hours for others to arrive in the village elementary school-turned-albergue, but by dusk no one has come and I lock the door. They must have stopped somewhere before this town or hiked past while I was in the shower. It is an empty, lonely feeling to be the only occupant in a three-room school. Here I'd hoped that Silvia, new on the trail since León, a Valencian and a Basque separatist sympathizer who loves to explain politics and speaks excellent English, would share dinner, or the old Quebecois who is still determined to make Santiago. When it gets dark, I start dinner. The school office, converted to a small kitchen, offers a two-burner stove where I heat water for lentils and packaged soup. In my pack I find crackers, cheese, and an apple. Enough for now. There are no stores, cafes, or even lights on in the tiny village.

The day before, Silvia had described another albergue where she'd stayed that was hosted by a married gay couple. They were celebrating the supreme court's ruling that upheld Spain's 2005 legalization of same-sex marriage. She said they'd served sparkling wine and cake for dessert, and everyone sang and bashed "the corrupt *ratón*, Rajoy," Spain's prime minister who had tried to overturn the law. It seemed unbelievable that a Catholic country, one with its history of fascism and oppression and patriarchy, was more progressive than America, more progressive than the Multnomah Club had been in 2004.

In my first year of retirement without a daily job to go to, without assignments to prep or papers to grade, I began to spend more time at the Club taking yoga classes and working out. Because Rose would retire in another year or two, it seemed a shame that we couldn't use the Club together. We'd registered as domestic partners in Portland years before, and her health insurance now covered me. But the MAC required a proof of marriage, an official marriage license, in order to qualify for a family membership, impossible for us with the current laws in Oregon. But not in British Columbia, where same-sex unions had begun to be legally recognized. We flew to Vancouver, BC, in December 2003 and were married in a simple ceremony. We sent in our application the Monday we returned.

Several months passed before we heard from the Club. I remember walking toward the house from the mailbox, looking through the mail, and seeing the envelope with the Club's red lettering. I tore it open. Inside, a letter from the Club manager informed me that he was sorry but the board of directors had asked him to write to explain that they would not consider Rose's membership application at that time. They were not prepared to admit same-sex couples as a family.

I felt a wave of nausea, one that comes from a blow to the gut. Blood rushed to my cheeks as if I were fourteen and had been shamed at school, or nine and had been called out for going shirtless, as if I were still all alone on the dock incapable of meeting the standards for a white cap. Small. Insignificant. Humiliated. I had loved the Club, worked hard for it, represented it in my childhood, been part of it for most of my life. I had imagined it almost as one might a beloved person, but in that instant I saw that it did not care about me at all. It did not seem to be "committed to treating everyone with fairness and respect" as its new diversity policy proclaimed.

And then I felt angry. Rose and I both did. We would right this wrong, fight the battle for basic rights offered to every other member. We found powerful allies within the Club and among our friends. We even married a second time in Portland when Multnomah County granted marriage licenses in 2004 and sent in the second license to prove our legitimacy. It took a year and half, but the Club changed its policies. We had stirred the pot.

I might have shared this story with Silvia if she were here. I have seen her anger in action. A few towns back, she accused a local mayor—a fascist, she called him—of skimming money from the albergue and not paying the villagers who tended to it. He had tried to appease her by offering her a drink, which she slammed down on the table before she walked out. The next day I heard much about Spanish corruption, especially in Galicia, the birthplace of Franco, former dictator of Spain. If she were here, we might have talked about current American factions that want to deny rights to gay people.

My first job after graduate school was teaching special education at a new high school in far western Hillsboro out among the dairies and tree farms and hill folk of North Plains.

It was the year Mount Saint Helens erupted and Rose moved in with me—1980. I wasn't closeted among the faculty and staff, but I didn't fly the rainbow flag. I talked about Rose when others talked of spouses and brought her to department potlucks. When an uninhibited student blurted out one morning, "Are you a dyke?" I laughed and redirected the question without embarrassment or blush, but I wasn't going to announce my sexual orientation anywhere in rural Hillsboro.

In Portland Public Schools, the district where Rose worked, domestic partners were recognized and covered by insurance. There, gay teachers formed a support group, the Cascade Union of Educators (CUE), which met monthly in a teacher's home, usually a gay man's. What a relief to be among others like me, to feel "free to be...me," as Marlo Thomas sang on Michael's record.

Glencoe High School was only about twenty miles west of my house, a very long day's walk on the Camino, but a world away from Portland.

At the long, empty table in the albergue, I slurp my Knorr soup and think about the CUE potlucks. The men had tried to outdo each other with exotic salads and elaborate main dishes. These were not church casseroles or string beans mixed with a can of mushroom soup and potato chips crunched on top. One time someone brought his own torch to caramelize the sugar on a crème brûlée, a dessert unknown to me then.

We'd talk about issues in our schools, about students we recognized as gay or probably gay and if or how we might help them. We talked about harassment and the frequently used slur *faggot* shouted at students and teachers. Increasingly we talked about HIV and AIDS. Some among the group had friends, lovers, partners who were affected. Some in our group died. By 1985 Portland had a gay newspaper, *Just Out,* the city council had passed an ordinance prohibiting discrimination against gays and lesbians, and the Portland Gay Men's Chorus had sung at the secretary of state's inauguration.

We had to be out of the closet, everyone agreed. We had to be the models, to show our students, our faculties, and parents that we were normal people whom they'd known and respected for years. To be invisible and silent would allow myths and lies about gay people to perpetuate, we reasoned. That was fine for Portland teachers, whose district protected them from discrimination, I thought, but out in Washington County, out where a judge had decided I was not fit to parent, and where gay nondiscrimination laws would not pass, I felt vulnerable.

"You don't need to march in the Gay Pride Parade," advocates argued, "but you can be out to your friends, your family. Claim the words they use against us. 'Yes, I'm gay. Yes, I'm a dyke. Queer! Yes.'"

Rose and I had lived together for six years. We had kept no secrets from our neighbors, our parents and siblings, our friends. *But have I ever told Michael explicitly?* I wondered.

He was ten years old and beginning to run with me on weekends. He was training for a two-mile race, the Crimson Classic, out at my high school. We started out jogging on Hewett Boulevard, a narrow, little-used road that ran along the rim of the West Hills.

"I want to talk about something," I started. We plodded along for a few paces. "I just wanted to say..." On we trotted. "Well, Michael, Rose and I are gay."

"I know." We ran on at the same pace.

"Well, if you have any questions or anything, I want you to tell me, okay?" We ran. "Well? Do you? Have any questions?"

"No."

The next summer he and I marched in the New York City Gay Pride Parade among thousands of participants in khakis and costumes: fairies on stilts and drag queens, Dykes on Bikes, queer cops, firefighters, teachers, doctors. Every group imaginable had a banner and a group marching behind it waving *Lesbian Gay Vote 86* pink triangle posters or rainbow flags. From the south side of Central Park down Fifth Avenue, the street was lined with cheering, happy people—everywhere except outside St. Patrick's Cathedral, where shouting protestors waved angry signs: *Protect Our Children, Christians Say Shame on You, Down with Cuomo's Evil Empire, Sodomy Will Be Punished.*

We stayed with my first lover, now a law clerk for a federal judge, and slept on the floor of her minuscule apartment on the corner of Gay and Christopher Streets in Greenwich Village. We rode the Staten Island Ferry, stood atop the World Trade Center, and watched the Yankees beat Detroit in a night game. We saw *Little Shop of Horrors, La Cage aux Folles,* and *Cats.* I raced in the Fifth Annual Gay Pride Run through Central Park and won the women's division. We even took the train to New Haven to visit a friend teaching at Yale before Rose joined us later in the week. After visiting the mummies in the Metropolitan Museum of Art, after walking the Brooklyn Bridge, after swimming at Coney Island, on the Fourth of July we all sat together on a pier in Hoboken, New Jersey, and watched the Liberty Weekend fireworks over New York Harbor, a centennial celebration for the Statue of Liberty. What a week we had shared together. Within ten years, Michael would be a Yale graduate, and I'd be an English teacher at his high school alma mater and the advisor for the Gay-Straight Alliance.

It's late in the albergue. I wash the dishes, lay out my clothes, and crawl into my sleeping bag. When the lights are off, I can see the starry night sky, the Milky Way as wide and bright as the memory of fireworks.

MYSTERY-MAN COACH

1959–1960

COACH SCHLUETER SEEMED TOO REMOTE and too secretive for me to ever know him. He never talked about Lynn not returning. In November the *Oregonian* interviewed him about our team, questioning why she had left. He shrugged it off: "It's a mystery to me." It was a mystery to me, too, but I thought there had to be a reason, something that Lynn wasn't telling. And I was pretty sure that Bob Burke had told Coach why. How could it really be a mystery? But that was Coach—Mr. Mystery. They ran a headline: "Olympic Swimming Prospects Due (Maybe) From Winged M" and named Nancy Kanaby as a candidate in the 100 freestyle, Noel Gabie in the 100 backstroke, and me in the 100 butterfly. I didn't want to think about the *maybe*, but I knew it was true. I wondered why Coach hadn't said I was a candidate in the freestyle too. My times were always faster than Nancy's. The question that had bugged me in the summer came back. Why hadn't he entered me in both freestyle and butterfly at the Pan Am Trials?

An athlete needs to believe in a coach, that he or she has your best interests in mind even when you're overworked or made to stretch beyond what you think you can do. Tye had been a lovable teacher first, a coach second. Gruff Jim had yelled and stormed during practice and then teased and hugged when we finished. He taught us all about toughness, and we knew how to push through a workout or to finish a race hard. These men, like Rod Harman, who coached at Beaverton, were basically optimists who believed you would do what you sometimes thought you couldn't. I loved these coaches because they believed in us. They inspired us. Unlike those other coaches, Mr. Schlueter seemed pessimistic, as if he expected the worst to happen and needed to protect against it.

Coach liked to set up opportunities for us to break records at infrequently raced distances. It created good publicity, he told us. After Christmas he arranged an invitational meet he called Olympic Development, but since nobody built fifty-meter or fifty-five-yard indoor pools in Oregon, we had to make our little twenty-five-yard pool "stretch." In practice we had been swimming repeat 125s or 150s interspersed with faster repeat 75s. Now we would test ourselves with a five-event contest, an invitational time trial, racing Olympic distances. We would swim the short-course one hundred yards, four lengths, and then turn to finish at a rope dropped ten yards past the end, creating a 110-yard race. For the women's 110 butterfly, he invited Nancy Ramey, the world record holder from Seattle.

On the weekend before the meet, Coach concentrated on starts. From the sidelines he demonstrated what he wanted: squat position, arms back by our sides, ready to pull forward when the gun sounded. Keep low, he told us, and he crouched then sprang forward on the deck. When we hit the water, he wanted us to feel the glide. I climbed up on the starting block. A boy held a long bamboo pole across lane one. It looked too high and too far away to dive over. Coach gave me more instructions: to start my dolphin kick as soon as I entered the water, to take three strokes before my first breath.

"Take your marks...hut," Coach commanded, and I launched off the block, arcing high over the pole, relieved that my ankles or shins hadn't hit it. But the arc was too high, and he grumbled when I surfaced and made me get out and do it again. I swam back and tried again. By the third start, I had the feel for it: stretching out long in the air, skimming over the pole. My hands pierced the choppy water, and then I knifed into the glide and kick, no body torque like in a freestyle start, but fluid, legs and hips dolphin kicking me up to the surface and into a powerful forward fly, almost halfway down the pool from the dive alone.

Later in the week, Coach brought a starter gun to work on our reflexes. Grouchy and serious, he ordered us never to straighten up at the sound of the gun, to be ready, our weight slightly forward on the balls of our feet. We'd never done this kind of technical training before a meet, but races come down to tenths of seconds, he told us. A fast start. An efficient turn. A push to the finish. We needed to find the tenths and shave them off. Every night that week, he paced the deck unsmiling, his pants soaked from our racing dives.

On Friday he called some of us into his office one at a time. It smelled of cigarettes and chlorine, his desk piled with papers. Nancy K. wasn't racing because she'd been sick, but she sat in on the meetings, slouched in a corner chair. This time Coach didn't have a splits card—he simply said that I could beat Nancy Ramey and he'd tell me how. I was to go out hard right off the start, take her out fast on the first fifty, then just ease up on the third lap. He asked if I knew what he meant, to hold a pace and relax. I nodded and looked over at Nancy, who wore a funny grin, like she already knew what he was going to tell me. *Why is she in on the secret plan?* I wondered. Coach said the most important time would be about ten yards before the last turn. He wanted me to put my head down—no breath—and to crank it up. He said she wouldn't be expecting that. If I could accelerate into and out of that last turn, I'd break her.

"You can do it. You're ready," he said.

I am ready, I thought as I looked over at Nancy K., Coach's shadow, always down at the Club in his office instead of at college where supposedly she took classes. I felt jealous and a little resentful that she got such special privileges. Sometimes I wondered if she might have been part of the reason Lynn left Portland for Santa Clara.

Saturday night when I made that fourth turn and saw Nancy Ramey behind me, every bit of fatigue faded away, and I lifted up and over the water to the finish. We each swam back to the wall in our lanes. She looked straight ahead at the tiles, panting, and then she turned to me and reached her hand over the lane. "Good race," she said. MAC kids leaned down and hit me on the head, and my dad said something impossible to hear. He held out his stopwatch and pointed at it, laughing.

Teammates swamped me when I got out of the pool—Donnie, Patsy, Noel. Mom tried to get my attention from lane six where she was timing. I gathered my sweats and listened to Patsy and others retell the whole race. Down at the shallow-end bleachers, Nancy Ramey's coach pulled her into a hug and patted her back. I began to make excuses for her. Maybe she didn't have time to train because she was in college. Maybe she had a cold. These could be reasons I won. "Don't get cocky," Mom often reminded me. But another voice inside whooped it up: *I beat the Olympic silver medalist and world record holder.*

I looked around for Coach, but he was nowhere to be found. Nancy K., when she came to congratulate me, explained that he had been there for the start but that he'd left because he couldn't stand to watch important races. They made him too nervous.

"You mean he doesn't know I beat her?"

"He'll find out," she assured me, because one of the parents was out looking for him and would tell him all about the race.

What a letdown. I'd gone through with his plan, and he hadn't even watched.

When we got home, Mom told me that Marthadent Schollander told her that Coach had gone to the Bull Pen, a tavern across from the stadium. He was drunk when they found him.

"That's so weird," I said.

"Sometimes a guy gets wound up," Dad said.

"But he missed my race." I felt mad and disappointed. If Jim were still my coach, he'd have jumped in the pool, he'd be so excited. I imagined Jim in his khakis and blue sweatshirt leaping off the balcony. Nancy Ramey's coach had consoled her when she lost. But where was my coach? The thought occurred to me that maybe Coach didn't like me because I missed Lynn and talked about her, and he disapproved. Or

AAU officials clocking a close finish, 1960

maybe I didn't like him because I suspected that somehow he and Nancy K. had made Lynn want to leave.

When I tried to explain it, Mom told me not to think about it, but Dad said it didn't matter.

"Work hard, sis, and you'll win when it counts." Dad was my optimist.

On Sunday I called Lynn long distance to tell her the news. The next week Chris von Saltza sent me a letter:

Dear Carolyn,

Congratulations again and again on the wonderful swimming. We are so proud of you. As soon as Lynn hung up the phone she

Swimming butterfly

gave our coach, George, a ring and he was amazed. He thinks that is just fabulous. Keep up the good work and we will see you set an American record at Portland.

Lynnie and I are working real hard too. We have our first meet at the end of this month. We hope to do as well as you. Again, nice going. We will all make that "O" team yet.

See ya soon. Love, Chris

I kept the letter next to my bed and read it practically every night. "We will all make that 'O' team." The *Oregonian* headline had added "(Maybe)," but if Chris believed I'd make the team and set American records, I (almost) felt sure I would.

By the time Lynn returned to Portland in March for the Far West Invitational, I hadn't set any new records. On Friday night she warmed

Bob Burke, Lynn, and me after the Far West Invitational, 1960

up with her new Santa Clara teammates and barely looked at any of us. I didn't think about how she might feel coming back to Portland. I just thought she seemed very serious and all grown-up. Saturday morning before the preliminaries, she left Chris and her teammates, and we finally talked in the big locker room. She asked me why I wasn't swimming the 100-yard freestyle. I didn't know for sure, but I thought it might be because Coach wanted to save me for the relay. She squinched her eyes but didn't say anything. I added that he hardly ever let me race against Nancy. She shook her head, so I changed the subject and asked what I'd been wondering since September. Why had she left the MAC and gone to California?

She paused as if she wasn't sure what to say, and then she told me that her dad decided George Haines would be a better coach for her. At the Pan Ams when she roomed with Chris, they talked about George and Santa Clara, and after the games the von Saltzas offered her the chance to live at their home. She loved George's coaching, and she wanted to room with someone her own age.

"What's it like?" I asked. I meant what was it like living with the von Saltzas, but she went on about training. She said that the first month there, she thought she'd die, they worked so hard. She laughed and repeated, "*Die!*" They trained twice as much as we did at the MAC. Twice a day all winter long. Outdoors. She said it was hard but fun because George made it fun, not like Coach Schlueter.

I didn't want to think about Coach or about how much fun Lynn was having in California training harder than we were. It made me feel left behind, as if I needed to pedal faster to keep up. In need of encouragement, I asked if she'd get Chris to write more than her signature in the old *Sports Illustrated*, the one with her on the cover. I was too timid to ask her myself, and it felt a little like begging, but I thought Lynn owed me something.

On Sunday after the meet, we drove Lynn to the airport so Mom and Dad could chat with her. Before she left she pulled my arm and turned me toward her. She told me to trust Schlueter because he'd had a freestyler in every Olympics since 1948. She said that continuing that streak meant more to him than anything. "You're the one who will do it. You can do both butterfly and—" I started to interrupt, but she kept on. She told me to watch out for myself, to train hard, and to race both strokes. To be on the medley relay with her and Chris, I had to make the team in butterfly. But I had a better chance of making the team if I raced the freestyle too.

"Remember, you're the fastest," she said, "not Nancy." She pulled the *Sports Illustrated* out of her shoulder bag and handed it to me, turned to my parents and gave them each a hug, then me, and off she ran to catch her teammates.

National Indoor champions, 400-yard freestyle relay, 1960: Noel Gabie, me, Joan Matich, Nancy Kanaby

"See you in Bartlesville," I called down the concourse. In the car I looked for Chris's inscription. She'd written: *Carolyn, To a real great gal as well as swimmer. May you always have the very best of luck and I hope to see you winning at the Nationals shortly. As always, Chris.* Nothing about the "O" team this time. I wondered if she saw me as a threat.

We missed a week of school for the indoor nationals in Bartlesville, Oklahoma. It was too far and too expensive for my parents, but Mr. Johannesen, the Club's assistant manager, came along to room with Coach—or to find him, I joked to Noel. In this meet, Coach entered me in the 100-yard freestyle, and on Thursday I finished fourth behind Chris, Joan Spillane, and Shirley Stobs. Molly Botkin, who had qualified for the Pan Ams in two strokes, didn't even make the finals. Everybody knew that Chris would be first, but those other two, Joan and Shirley, were now the ones I had to beat in August. The freestyle relay, the event most important to Coach, raced on Friday, the same day as butterfly, but Coach, the doubter, didn't believe I could swim two races on the same day. He held me out of it, and I watched Nancy Ramey win with a record and someone new come in second, Carolyn Schuler.

Before the freestyle relay finals, we arrived at the pool early to warm up. Santa Clara swimmers made a lot of noise from their lanes, splashing each other and laughing. We kept ourselves serious, loosening up in a slow four hundred. Coach called us together at one end to practice starts. He reminded us to keep the swimmer in our sights and to follow them with our arms as they approached. For the hundredth time, he warned us to beware of false starting but to be quick off the block. While he talked, I watched Santa Clara warming up. I'd be up against Chris again at the anchor. Her blonde head bobbed two lanes over. *If I have a lead, I'll beat you*, I said to myself. *If I have a lead, you'll never catch me.*

"Woody. Are you listening to me?" Coach barked.

That night spectators packed the bleachers and the balcony, which stretched the full length of the pool. It looked like the Beaverton gym at a pep assembly. Noel Gabie led off the relay and broke a minute for the first time, but we were in fourth place when the next girl dived in. She swam a personal best and pulled us into third. Usually Coach put the weakest swimmer third, but this time Nancy K. swam it, and she closed the gap on the first fifty yards.

Was she going out too fast? I shook out my arms, shoulders, each leg, breathing long and deep. She started to pull ahead on the second fifty. I never once looked over at Chris. My focus stayed on Nancy K., watching as she faltered and then accelerated to the wall. Bam! I took off in a full sprint, hit the first turn and could see Chris a little behind me as I shoved off. In and out of the second turn, Chris still lagged behind, but coming into the third she seemed even, a blur of green-and-white bubbles and water. Pushing off that third turn, my legs strong springs, I felt like I had in Portland against Nancy Ramey. *It's only twenty-five.*

It's only twenty-five, I chanted, calling up power, calling up whatever defies pain, that lesson Jim had pounded into us with all those no-breath sprints. Up surged the power, and I held Chris off.

The next day the Bartlesville paper wrote: "Little Carolyn Wood battled the great Chris von Saltza to a stand still in a thrilling anchor lap." Another paper called it a "tremendous stretch duel." They printed my split as 0:55.6, half a second faster than Chris's new record. We were national champions who had smashed the American record. The *Oregonian* ran a banner headline on Sunday's front page. "The girls went berserk they're so happy," they quoted Coach. He said it was the most exciting race he had ever seen. Mom saved the clipping.

"He wasn't there again. Why does he make this stuff up?" I asked when I got home and read it.

Mom said she thought he probably wanted to be there and that Mr. Johannesen must have told him all about it. When he saw our splits, he could imagine he'd seen it, she said. Mom was so good at explaining other people's thoughts and behaviors. She seemed to hear more than they said sometimes. I was beginning to pick up on a kind of code grown-ups used when they talked about certain things. But right now all I had were questions.

"And why doesn't he let me swim both the butterfly and the freestyle in important meets? Lynn thinks I should be doing more. All of them swim four and five events. It's like he doesn't trust me. And why doesn't he ever tell me how I'm doing? He talks before the races but he never says anything after because he's not even there." I could feel myself getting all worked up, but I couldn't stop the words. "He tells Nancy—"

Mom walked over and started to put her hands on my shoulders, but I shrugged her away. "He's just not very expressive," she said quietly. "But I know he thinks you are going to do really well this summer. Marthadent told me he thinks you—"

"But why does he tell Mrs. Schollander and not me?" Mom stood out of reach.

"Whatever you do, Carolyn, we'll be so proud of you." That wasn't very consoling. It sounded like code. It sounded like, "If you don't make the team, we'll still love you." I got up from the table and tramped upstairs.

Coach gave another interview with even more details about the race he didn't watch. "People knew we could move, but it made them notice when Woody pulled away. She had a short lead on von Saltza, then Chris caught her with about eight yards to go, but Carolyn just out fought her.... She's a tiger, real tiger."

It was the best compliment Coach had ever given me. I sounded dangerous, and I wanted to believe that he meant it even if he hadn't told me directly.

WAITING

Spring–Summer 1960

DAY AFTER DAY IN APRIL as it stormed and rained in Portland, Jantzen Beach remained closed. Coach wanted us to practice there, but the park never opened. Lynn wrote that Santa Clara was already training twice a day at a long course in a reservoir. Everyone worried that we were falling behind. By mid-May Coach had found a long-course pool in California where he could train those of us who would be going to the Olympic Trials in Detroit. Families scrambled to find housing with friends or cheap motels. My dad talked to Mr. Erickson, the principal, requesting an early release from school. Mom arranged for us to stay with an old friend in Menlo Park, and we headed to California where the sun shone every day. We would swim in a brand-new pool set far out in the countryside on the construction site of Foothill, a new community college.

Mornings felt cool under the wide oaks but always with the hint of heat to come. "Itsy Bitsy Teenie Weenie Yellow Polkadot Bikini" and "Alley Oop" filled the car on the drive to the morning swim. Golden-brown hills scattered with oaks and bulldozers rolled away from the pool, which sparkled turquoise, like an ad in a magazine. California, where all the great swimmers trained now, felt so different, so bright and warm, so vivid.

We trained hard there, harder than we ever had in Portland. But two days before an Olympic Development meet in early June, Coach eased up on us a little and cut back our distances—a taper, he called it, an experiment to see where we were. Most of the entrants came from Northern California, and Carolyn Schuler, the butterflyer who'd placed second in Bartlesville, was the one to beat.

On the blocks late that afternoon, the sun hot on my back, I felt a pulling in and a holding energy, like when you hold your breath for too long and you're ready to gasp. Explosive. Even the water didn't cool the heat. I beat Schuler by a half stroke. Like Nancy Ramey had done in January, I reached over the lane and shook her hand while I thought, *I'll beat you in Detroit too.*

Another week passed before our final California test, an age-group meet at Santa Clara, which replaced the old Livermore AquaRodeo. It was loaded with top swimmers from the West Coast, including an exuberant contingent from the Club. A little bit of home arrived cheering. Donnie and I showed what a few weeks of solid training can do: we each set two national age-group records in butterfly and freestyle. In six weeks we'd be in Detroit.

Lynn, too old to swim age group, came to watch us race before we headed home. She advised me to watch out for Donna de Varona, that she'd schmooze me up and talk a lot before the races telling me all about her illnesses or muscle pulls. Lynn said it was all a distraction.

"She told me she had a broken toe," I said.

"I'm just warning you. Keep your concentration. Keep to yourself. Do what's best for you." She was talking about more than de Varona. She meant all the distractions that can pull anyone away from focusing on a goal: a competitor's psych-out, tension at home, silliness among teammates, a coach's pessimism, self-doubt.

Mom and I left for home after the Santa Clara meet. I stretched out on the mattress we'd set in the back of our new Ford station wagon. I dozed, read, daydreamed, and replayed Squaw Valley and the national teams marching in together, imagining myself in Rome. Every time we passed a hay truck on the highway, I'd say the good luck chant, "Load of hay. Load of hay. Make a wish and turn away," then close my eyes to wish: *I'll make the Olympic team with Lynn.* Going through tunnels and over bridges, I held my breath, repeating the wish. I must have made a thousand wishes that year.

The trials were finally approaching, and the wishes would come true or not. A few things pointed toward good luck: I'd beaten Nancy Ramey and Carolyn Schuler. My freestyle times were faster than Chris's had been at my age. Long course suited my stroke better than short course. But the notion that everybody thought I would make the team seemed risky, as if tempting bad luck.

Our yearbook had come out a few days before we left for California, and I pulled it now from the stack of *Mad* magazines and books piled in the corner. Almost everyone who'd signed it wrote the same things: *Best of luck in the Olympics. You deserve the Olympics. Best of luck in swimming and get 'em at the Olympics.* And, *Good luck in swimming this summer. I'm sure you'll take first in the Olympics.* Reading those inscriptions made me feel sick. They didn't understand about qualifying. They wrote as if I were already on the team. What would I say at school in September when they asked, "Why didn't you go Rome?" They'd think I'd lied.

But I never said I was going, I argued to myself. I hadn't talked about it at school, especially after the race with Nancy Ramey. But when Coach said all those things in the paper after indoor nationals, the kids at school read them. Even kids I didn't know came up and talked to me like we were friends. But they didn't get it about Detroit, about the trials. It was important not to be flattered or overconfident, and I honed techniques to keep people away—an offhand response, a distant look, absorption in a book.

The hot California air streamed in the windows and across my bare arms and legs. Mom hummed along to the radio, but the wind blew away the music. I thumbed through the yearbook and found a note that made me laugh: *To Carolyn the Clod I have in two classes. If I didn't have you in algebra I think I'd die of boredom and quietness. Well, anyhow, good luck, you fish—Ruth.* After that came the entry Lynn had written at the Santa Clara meet. *You are the greatest girl I've ever met. You are my little sister even though we have different names. Really go this summer and we'll be roommates in Rome. You can do it. Lots of luck to my best friend and blood sister—Lynnie.*

She said it: we'd be roommates and teammates. She and my dad felt sure. The dream and the once-distant goal hurtled toward me. Time seemed to simultaneously speed up and slow down as my emotions shifted between hope and fear. All I had to do now was train and wait.

Sometimes that summer, waiting felt almost unbearable. It reminded me of those times before a piano recital in the waiting room with everyone dreading their performance. The little kids would be running around, uncertain what to do with their excitement. Others would be reading comics, pretending not to care. The older you got, the more you'd replay the score in your head, in your fingers. I was a terrible pianist, with haphazard practice and little feel for the music, but at recitals something magical happened. I'd try to remember the piece, play it through in my mind, but parts of it would somehow vanish. I'd start again and again until finally the whole thing would disappear. Yet, when Mrs. Enright called my name, when she introduced me and my number, I'd sit on the bench, shut out all the faces looking up at me, place my hands on the keys, and the music would flow without thought. Afterward I never knew if I'd played the right piece or made mistakes or left out sections. I'd stand up, bow, and scurry back to the waiting room, light and happy, relieved to be finished. That's what it was like that summer. I knew what I had to do, and I wanted to get it over with, to find out whether I'd get through the piece without forgetting, without messing up.

Outside the waiting room and beyond the swimming pools, life went on as always. At home Grandma Green puttered around her room and her garden. Dad went back and forth to work at the store. Richard, a senior at Oregon State, worked two summer jobs again and spent his free hours down in Salem with his girlfriend. If I hadn't been focused on getting to Rome, I might have heard that Russia shot down a U-2 spy plane and captured Gary Powers or that Adolf Eichmann was found and arrested in Argentina. I could have followed Richard Nixon and John Kennedy as they crisscrossed the country campaigning for president. Perhaps the news that the United States had launched Echo 1, a precursor to communication satellites that would provide the first live broadcasts of Olympic events from Tokyo in 1964, would have meant something. But all this, current news and the future, lay outside my narrow focus in the summer of 1960.

By the time Mom and I got home in late June, we'd been away for almost five weeks. A mimeographed letter from Betty Baldwin, the Olympic women's swim team chaperone, had arrived while we were gone. PROSPECTIVE OLYMPIC SWIM TEAM MEMBERS, she started and listed twelve things we needed to do before the trials in Detroit. This was the second letter from her. The first had come a month after indoor nationals and suggested that everyone who'd made finals should get a passport and a smallpox vaccination.

Before we'd left for California, an official United States Government envelope arrived—in it was a green cloth passport with my picture and ten blank pages. Hope rose so fast that day in May, I thought my skin might split. Nobody in my family had a passport. Richard, home from school, grabbed it away and thumbed through it. Mom reached out to keep the peace and commented that it seemed so official. Then she said that my picture looked cute.

"No, it doesn't. I look stupid." I always contradicted her when she talked about how I looked, but I liked the way my blonde highlights looked in the picture. Later that night Richard's friend, Mike Kline, who played varsity football at Oregon State, came over. He called me a jock, and I thought we shared athletes' camaraderie. I'd shown him the passport, almost bragging, as if it proved I was on the road to Rome.

Now in this new letter, Betty Baldwin wrote, *You cannot re-enter the United States without a smallpox vaccination. GET IT NOW; it will be too late on August 1st.*

I skimmed through the two pages of notes, which listed everything from when the team would leave Detroit to where they'd stay in New York to when they'd leave for Rome. She ended the letter, *I wish our team could be made up of 50 girls, but since there can only be 20 at the most, I will have to say...*

My chest felt hot inside, and I went back to the beginning and started to read it out loud to Mom. I got through less than half of the instructions, stopped, and folded the papers.

Mom prodded me to keep reading. She reached out for the letter, but I stood up from the table, ran to the bathroom, and locked the door. "What?" Mom called after me. "What is it?"

But it wasn't anything. I didn't know what it was. I just couldn't stand it. I sat on the toilet and opened the letter again, reading:

> *Come to Detroit prepared to go into training.*
> *The next few weeks are going to be busy...but all your swimming could be in vain.*
> Don't be a disappointed swimmer.

I started to cry and then flushed the toilet, stood up, and looked in the mirror. "Don't be disappointed," I said. "Veni, vidi, vici."

Mom knocked on the door. I pulled it open, handed her the letter, and hurried down the hall and outside. "I'm going next door." I slammed the screen behind me.

My techniques to ease the anguish of uncertainty were limited. Books like *Exodus* and *On the Beach* led me to faraway times and places. TV shows like *Gunsmoke* and *Have Gun—Will Travel* rekindled Western fantasies. But after reading that letter, I needed to run wild.

A deep trench gouged across our front lawn from White Pine Lane, through the next-door neighbor's driveway and yard, all the way past the Wolfes'. Fresh dirt from the three-foot ditch mounded in a kind of barrier alongside it. The county was changing us from septic tanks to sewer that summer. I knocked on the neighbor's door and pushed in at the same time.

"Steve?" I yelled down the basement stairs. "Wanna go for a ride?" He was only nine, but he'd been my playmate since he'd moved in five years before. His older sister liked Nancy Drew and dolls, and even though she was closer in age, we never played together. "Let's ride to Rexall," I hollered down to him. He clomped up. His fresh buzz cut made him look a little bald.

We rode our bikes over the boards that crossed the trench and started off toward Raleigh Hills, a long ride on a summer's afternoon, and soon Steve slowed down. Bribes helped when he lagged behind, so I offered to buy him a Popsicle. After he'd caught up, he asked when I'd gotten back from California.

"Last night. Late. And no practice today." I was glad to have the day off, happy now to be riding bikes with Steve. I didn't want to think about Betty Baldwin's letter and being a DISAPPOINTED SWIMMER.

Shadows stretched over the trenches when we got home. In the backyard Susie and her friends lay propped on blankets reading. "Let's see how far we can follow the trench," I said. We jumped down into the pit where the dirt walls came up to my waist and almost to the top of Steve's shoulders. "Let's pretend it's World War II and these are connected fox holes. We're on a mission to get a message to another platoon." These military words came from reading *Battle Cry* that winter. Steve was pretty much willing to pretend anything I suggested. When Mary and he and I played, he'd be an Indian, an outlaw, a captive, a cop, anyone we wanted to fill out the story.

We crouched down and began running. "Keep your head down," I whispered when a car passed. If felt cool and quiet hunched in the damp earth where colors shifted brown, orange, black in undulating layers. Little holes pierced through where worms had tunneled. "Let's go to the end and see if the dirt changes."

Another car drove by, and we ducked. I felt that little rush you get when playing hide and seek, a kind of scared excited flutter. I bent to pick up a dirt clod that had tumbled from the side pile. "It's a grenade," I said, smiling at Steve. I stood, reached way back, and slung the clod out across the street. He grabbed another clod, put it up to his mouth as if pulling the pin, straightened, and hurled it into the Woodwards' yard.

A car rounded the corner, and I picked another grenade and lobbed it. It splattered right behind the car. Steve advised me to lead the target like a pass in football. When a white Impala cruised by, I popped it perfectly. Thwack. "Bull's-eye," Steve yelled a moment before we heard the brakes squeal, the gears shift, and the car reverse back to the driveway.

"Run! *Run!*" We scuttled up and out of the trench, ducking behind Steve's garage, past his sister and her friends. The driver, a big guy, parked and threw open his door, but we were gone across the grass, over the fence, through our fir grove, across the street, and into Mr. Miller's woods. Back in the mossy grotto where we'd once played Indian scouts, we collapsed and caught our breath.

"Geez, Carolyn. You really hit him." We laughed. In the fantasy, we'd demolished the tank. After a while Steve wondered if the guy might still be waiting for us. "What if he tells my mom?"

I started thinking about the man talking to Bev and about her telling him who I was. Maybe we'd really damaged his car. Maybe it would be in the paper. "I can't get caught before the Olympics, Steve. I can't get in trouble. They might not let me be on the team. Will you say you did it? Please?"

We circled through the woods, coming out at the Hunters' house where we could see Steve's driveway. The Impala was gone. "The coast is clear," Steve said, but still we backtracked through the woods, just in case. Steve climbed over the fence and into his yard, where his sister still sat. She looked up at us. "You're in big troub—" she started.

"I didn't do it," I said. "If you tell on me, I'll kill you." This sounded like one of my brother's angry threats, but I felt desperate, sure that if caught I'd be thrown off a team I hadn't even made yet, and angry at myself for doing something so stupid. Threatening Susie fooled me into feeling, for a moment, that at least I had control over something, while Betty Baldwin's capital-letter warning—DON'T BE A DISAPPOINTED SWIMMER—echoed in my head.

A few days later, Mom dropped me off at the Club for the afternoon carpool. Downstairs beyond the swinging doors, Coach looked up from his office desk, raised his arm, and motioned to me. He stood up, walked out on the deck, and pointed to the little space in front of the elevator. This was weird. Coach never talked to me alone. My scalp felt prickly. He faced me, his hands in his back pockets, and started talking about our race results in California, specifically my time in butterfly and a teammate's in breaststroke.

I nodded. *What did he want?*

"We've got a medley relay now." He paused. I wondered if I was supposed to say something. "What do you think, Woody? We have a good chance of winning both the freestyle and the medley relays at nationals. Do you think we should go for it?"

I looked at Coach, his brown face a wrinkled frown. *Why is he asking me?* We'd never even talked about nationals. They were in Indianapolis. We'd have to fly there. We'd lose a week of training.

"I thought we were peaking for the trials," I said. I felt kind of panicky, like he was changing things. *Is he testing me?* Long ago Richard offered to read to me and would suddenly stop and quiz me on what he'd read, and my mind would go blank and he'd yell or hit me. Coach might yell at me for saying the wrong thing now.

He reached for the pocket with his cigarettes and then dropped his hand. He explained that we would only race the relay and we could use it to peak. He sounded like he was trying to convince me.

I looked down at the old gray linoleum. He'd told the paper we'd lost all that practice time. He'd said he wasn't optimistic. Maybe he'd given up on any of us making the team. But I *was* going to make it. I had to. I didn't want to go away again after we'd been gone so long to California. He already thought we couldn't swim more than one race a meet. And he'd made such a big deal about training and peaking for specific races. I must have been holding my breath, because he looked blurry. I felt certain that if we went to nationals, I'd be saying goodbye to making the team with Lynn.

"This could mean a national championship for your teammates," he said from far away.

I looked past him toward the tile steps leading into the ladies' locker room and thought: *But they don't have a chance for the team. I won't live in a motel for weeks and weeks. Lynn said, "Do what's best for you." That's to stay home and get ready.*

"I can't go to nationals," I said. "It doesn't make sense. The trials. That's what's important."

He reached out toward my shoulder, but he didn't touch me. Then he turned away scowling, nothing more said.

When I'd told Tye no to a summer swim meet five years before, or had my mother tell him, I'd only wanted to play. This time it was a thoughtful decision, made harder because Coach wanted me to choose between the team and myself. He made me feel like my choice was selfish, and I was torn between feeling ashamed of it and proud that I'd stood up to him. I didn't tell anyone about our conversation, not even my parents. At practice that afternoon, he announced who'd be going up to Tacoma for the last Olympic Development meet July 9. He made no mention of nationals.

We tapered off for the meet as we had done before in California, and everyone had personal bests. I beat Nancy Ramey again and barely missed the world record. If only that had been the trials, it would be over. Instead, we returned home, and Coach increased our yardage, working us into a stupor. I'd felt light and speedy in blue-gold California, strong and sure in Tacoma, but piling on distance buried me in fatigue. Only two weeks remained before we left for Detroit, but two weeks can stretch forever when you're exhausted and waiting.

Training was as repetitive as the lines on the bottom of the pool. We started with the same warm-up day after day: 400 IM pull, 400 IM kick, 400 IM swim. Sometimes we'd do repeat hundreds or fifties. Sometimes we'd do over-distance or under. We couldn't talk in this underwater world, and all I heard was my own audible breath and whatever flowed through my head. I might pick someone to beat on each repeat. I might find a song whose rhythm my arms caught and kept lap after lap. If I was swimming fast, it might be Sinatra's "High Hopes." But for slow laps, it was always the Andrews Sisters singing "Sentimental Journey" over and over. I might want Coach to notice me and say something so I'd go harder. Or maybe he'd tell me to go slower and take it easy for a while. Maybe I'd hum, letting the bubbles trickle past my cheeks.

One cold, breezy morning, Patsy's scream woke us all from dozing on our kickboards. "A *rat*! There's a *rat* in my lane." She sprinted straight to the side and scrambled onto the deck. Coach strode down the sideline looking into the pool where Patsy pointed. The rest of us circled well away from the large black animal floating on its back next to the gutter. Coach had us clear lane one while we watched him drag the bug net through the water, lift the rat out, and walk back down the pool to the pump house.

They don't swim with rats in California. Or with rain. Or wind. Or jets. I swam along listing all our hardships with each stroke: no rats, no rain, no wind, no jets. If I swam slowly enough, I could feel the powerful water jet at the end of the pool shove my legs slightly to the right. *It's like swimming in a river*, I thought. *Like a river, like a river.* The words repeated over and over.

Thoughts never finished when swimming. Words floated through and sometimes stuck, pounding in rhythm to my stroke and spiraling away. Today it was rat, rain, wind, jet. Jet. *If I swim hard into the jet, it'll be like Jim's harness*, floated through. I liked the idea. If I was side by side with someone on a repeat and came up to the wall with the jet, I'd have to swim harder to stay even; in a regular pool, I'd actually power ahead. And then I'd get a boost out of the turn. Yeah. *Good idea. Good idea. Good idea.* I pressed hard into the wall, bucking the current.

Coming from Oregon that wet summer, swimming at Jantzen Beach, withstanding the cold east wind, water currents, chlorine, and rats made me feel as tough as a pioneer. Every day held a hardship to overcome, all leading toward the ultimate test.

Coach ground us down those last weeks, and physical exhaustion became another way to hold thoughts of the future at bay. By noon when I'd wake from my after-practice, after-breakfast nap, my room would be hot, light pulsing against the white shades, the images on the ceiling shifting into familiar patterns like the bottom of the pool, the same cracks in the same places. I'd push back the blankets and turn to my side, but still the heat would press down, flattening me, my arms and legs heavy, as if filled with warm Jell-O. Somewhere far down the back hall, the vacuum hummed. Outside voices rose and fell from across the street. I'd roll onto my back, arms stretched wide to the ceiling. *Only two more weeks.* Light wavered like heat waves rising off pavement. My eyes still stung from the morning's chlorine. *I should get up. I should get ready.* I felt paralyzed—by the heat, by muscle fatigue, by time's seeming suspension before events would finally reveal the future, either the one I wanted or the one I dreaded.

I could barely handle my energy and exhaustion, excitement and dread. I must have felt that first combination of hope and fear as a child as I waited for my mother to return from the hospital. Certainly I would come to know it again—waiting for grades to arrive in college or through those long, joyful, uncertain months of pregnancy; and later, waiting for a judge's decision on custody or a partner's on divorce. That July was my first conscious experience of waiting, and its terrible weight wore me out.

On the Sunday before we left for Detroit, instead of listening while Reverend Brown preached, my mind was busy packing. *I'll need suits and sweats and shorts and shirts and muumuus. But I'll also need clothes for Rome,* if *I make the team. Or will we have to wear a uniform all the time?* Betty Baldwin had asked our sizes for uniforms, but what would they be like? Dr. Brown's sermon droned on. *Will everything fit in my suitcase? It's big, but not that big.* A fragment from his sermon reached my brain: "...students will return to schools in September..." I shifted in the pew, thoughts of my suitcase gone. "Return to school in September" stirred a different unease.

Down in Fellowship Hall, all our family's church friends crowded around and wished me luck for the trials. Betty Baller wrapped me in a big hug. "We know you can do it, Carolyn. We'll be praying every day." Eldon pounded me on the back and kept repeating, "Go, champ!" Martha Johnson reminded me of the Twenty-Third Psalm, and Jeanette Sulmonetti linked arms with my mom, laughing. I'd known these people all my life. Picnics and potlucks. Christmas bazaars and rummage sales. Sunday school. New Year's parties. Weddings and funerals.

Mom and I walked through the Park Blocks to our car. "I will not go back to Beaverton High if I don't make the team," I announced. The words came out before I knew I'd thought them.

"Of course you will," Mom said.

"No, I won't. I can't. They all think I'm already on the team, and if I don't make it they'll..." I looked around; my voice sounded too loud.

Mom started with her sympathetic voice, but nothing she could say would help. The church people didn't care if I made the team or not. They'd love me anyway. But at school...

Mom interrupted my thoughts. She wanted to share a secret, she said, a surprise she and Daddy had for me in case I didn't make the team. Before I could object, she continued, "We know you will make it, but if you don't, we have plans to go on to Washington, DC, and New York after the meet. Daddy's always wanted to see the Statue of Liberty. We have tickets for all of us."

I stopped walking and looked at her, tears hot on my cheeks, and then hurried on trying to get away. She didn't think I'd make the team. She and my dad were betting against me.

"We don't want you to be disappointed, honey. We don't want you to be sad. Just in case." Here was my mother's technique to protect herself and others from disappointment. She imagined the worst and prepared for it, but it sounded like she'd given up on me, if she had ever believed. The stupid kids at school thought I was on the team, the church people didn't really care, and my parents wanted to go sightseeing with me.

Ahead, pigeons scuttled off the sidewalk onto the grass. I stepped toward them to make them run then stomped my feet, and they flew up and away from me.

My mom and I didn't talk about their travel plans again, but I carried my grudge like a wet towel all the way to Detroit.

WALKING ALONE

2012

AFTER THIRTY DAYS OF WALKING, this simple act becomes a meditation and time loses its grip. I stop looking at my watch and pedometer, eat when hungry, stop only when the distance to the next inn has been covered. A week passes almost without notice, though detail along the trail remains vivid. It feels as if I am wading through a viscous liquid, pushing gently but constantly forward, a thick wave emanating out and away, not caring what I might encounter but knowing that I can greet it with humor if not grace.

Weeks ago, the pilgrim family of mother and daughters from New Hampshire told me that when they made mistakes and hiked past a trail marker, they'd say they were getting stronger, and when they followed the trail all day long, they'd congratulate themselves for getting smarter. In the morning I start out from Triacastela, intending to take a short but scenic route to the next town. The trail should climb over a mountain, but after an hour I am still beside the river. When I overtake a German couple and ask if we are on the road the Samos, the long way, they confirm it. I will be walking five miles farther than planned, but I'll be getting stronger. The greater gift from this error, however, is coming upon a sixth-century monastery, one of the oldest in the Western world, the largest in all Spain, now an almost-empty, sprawling, stone compound that fills the remote and narrow valley. It houses only thirteen monks and three sisters. How do they feel about a world that has changed so drastically in their lifetimes? How do they cope?

When Rose and I traveled across Spain in 1987, we rode the narrow-gauge railroad along the northern coast from San Sebastián to Santiago, hopped off in tiny towns to explore prehistoric caves and walk along the beaches, stayed in no-star hotels and boarding houses. One day strolling the streets of Santander, we passed a quaint hotel that we wished we could afford. We'll come back someday and stay there, we said. And we did return, in 1998 for Rose's fiftieth birthday, and walked the streets again searching until we finally found it: condemned and partially collapsed. It was a lesson taught and retaught throughout a life: Things change. People too. Every cliché holds a little truth: Tomorrow is now. Seize the day. Don't count your chickens. Improve the nick of time.

The summer before I retired, I began to imagine a future without the ticktock of schedules and the rectangle of a classroom. In a summer workshop, I wrote myself a letter, a proposal for an experiment, a challenge.

You want to begin the year with a new look. You want to break away from the old routines: the Grape-Nuts and bananas, the seven-minute drives, the rice cakes, string cheese, prunes. The bells. The break, duty, prep, peacocks, and princesses. Every Friday football, every Saturday papers, every Sunday the New York Times.

The bells remind you of clocks ticking away what's left of your life, a diminishing flow, like a summer stream. No longer full with rain and snowmelt, but just a stream, a rocky creek. Every forty-seven minutes a reminder: start, stop, start, stop, pass. Minutes like water over rocks, seeping into sand, pooling up and spilling into small, diminishing trickles. The bells that call to order and dismiss, the bells that push forward the day, over and over again in a pulsing rush toward afternoon and night.

I wonder what would happen if the days were not pushed? What would happen if the time flowed in its natural sequence? The sky edging from darkness to gray, rising like a tide of light, pushing the flotsam of cloud upward. And then the sun's rim, liquid gold, the slant of light through twigs and leaf. What would happen if you watched time's river rise and flow, lifting you on its back and carrying you on its crest, until, lying back, you rested on the receding light, languishing in the slow pools of afternoon, the tips of the firs trembling and lifting, the ropes of birch leaves swaying in the light like sea kelp. To the west, the evening glow would linger, holding on to color. What if you could watch until the last drops spilled from the edge and then you came to know the night?

Oh, but what would be served by such a life?

Observation. Contemplation. Deliberation. What if your life came unplugged, disconnected, out of sync with the rest of the world? What if you rode this planet on one full circle round its star paying attention to light and plants and water? Seeing the way rain gathers in puddles or dew beads on grass, noticing the day violets open under the firs or ants appear in the bathroom?

You could, you know. Shut off the bells. You could cut loose, unplug, begin. You could improve the nick of time.

I thought about how slowly time passed the summer I waited for the Olympic Trials, how endless each day until the qualifying race, wondering and worrying about the outcome. Yet my last year teaching had ripped by with few doubts about what lay ahead in retirement, and a naive belief that I could control or predict my future. I'd been confined to a pool or a classroom, limited by laps and periods for over fifty years. I longed for freedom and wanted to follow paths out and away and later inward. I wanted to explore the world outside books, to visit locations that had been the settings in novels I'd taught: Kilimanjaro, Vietnam, India, Kingcome Inlet. I wanted to backpack off-season, when trails were mosquito- and crowd-free. There was so much to explore.

But my dreams were not Rose's. She retired from one job and took another, teaching art in a college. Her artwork had shifted from drawing on film and direct animation to spectacular digital installations presented in historic buildings, projects that demanded hours of computer work, grant writing, fundraising, research, and coordination. She did it all, driven toward new goals in her teaching and art making. We'd begun to swim in separate lanes, explore different trails.

On typical days in the spring and early summer, I worked the garden, waiting for her to take a break. I'd start out weeding grass roots that wound through the daisies and among the lavender, take clippers to water spouts on the viburnum, spread a load of compost. Through her studio window, I would see her hunched toward the monitor, her hand gripping the mouse, as she manipulated the images that would become her next piece. While she mastered advanced digital projections, I pruned lilacs and dreamed of trekking to the Annapurna Sanctuary. Summers filled up with school institutes and course planning; deadlines and academic schedules still ruled our lives. Disappointment and anger lurked beneath my resignation.

Why didn't you...? I could let my mind begin to gallop away with blame and accusation. I could set loose a litany of questions that initiate now-familiar stories that will keep my mind agitated. I could ignore my feelings and spin a tale instead. But in thirty days of practice, I've begun to recognize that when I hear *you* or *she* in my thoughts, I am moving away from the present and into a fantasy.

I stop on the trail, bend down yet again, and lift a stone. *Here I am. What feeling started this story? Anger? Sadness?* Maybe I actually am getting smarter. My breath comes steady; my legs feel strong. *This is it, here.* In a distant field, three white chickens move in fits and jerks across the green as if pulled along by a string. Twice a garnet-breasted bird whistles a multinote tune from the stone fence. Far ahead a hunter and his dog cross the road and enter the field.

Detroit: Just Another Step

July–August 1960

Nothing stirred in the motel parking lot. Even at seven o'clock under the tall oaks and elms, Detroit's air felt thick and wet and seemed to sway. Walking that morning felt like wading chest deep through a warm green pool, alone, like Rima in the *Green Mansions* jungle. I found the small diner we'd been to before for breakfast.

"Two soft-boiled eggs, whole wheat toast, no butter, and hot tea."

"On your own today?" The guy wiped at the counter.

"I'm up early," I answered, opening my book.

It was good being alone in the morning on race day with a book that took me away, in a cafe where nobody knew me or why I was there. Maybe someone would know my name someday. Maybe tonight after the finals. The endless waiting was almost over.

Competing had been an ongoing performance, not only the race but all the stages leading up to it: the training, the tapering, the previews at development meets. We'd been on display to teammates and parents, coaches and competitors, reporters and fans. All that summer we'd been in rehearsal for this show. Since arriving in Detroit, we'd given a few sneak previews during workouts in short time trials. Joan, Nancy, and I had swum 100-meter freestyle preliminaries and semifinals, but tonight only I was left to perform for our team.

That weight felt as heavy as the air outside. In the cafe, though, no expectations. No one cared.

I tried to read, but my thoughts jumped ahead to the finals and back to everything that had happened so far. We'd be under the lights again tonight. Yesterday we'd swum prelims in the afternoon and returned long after dark for the semifinals, the last event of the night—almost midnight. It felt otherworldly to be up so late swimming under lights surrounded by darkness. My qualifying time put me in the lane right next to Chris for the finals. All I had to do was stay up with her—and beat everybody else.

It's possible, I thought, stirring honey round and round the cup. On Monday Coach had timed my fifty meter in a record split. He actually laughed when he told me the other coaches had checked and rechecked their watches. Driving back to the motel after the semifinals, he'd given me advice. He wanted me to take Chris out fast like I had Nancy Ramey back in January. "Push her on that first fifty. Make her work at the start, and then ride her in," he said. I liked having a plan.

But first, before the freestyle finals, came the 100-meter butterfly heats that afternoon. Coach said it would be a good warm-up. He wanted me to swim for place, not for time. "All you need to do is make the finals. Wednesday night: that's the big one. That's the one you want."

I did want it. I'd been waiting for today more than two years. You get an idea about something you want, and you wait years for the chance. Life fills up the time with ordinary things—school, meals, homework, telephone calls and TV shows, books, play, practice. But when the thing you want gets a date—say, August 3, Olympic Trials 100-meter freestyle final—time becomes stretchy, changeable, surging forward and then slowing to an ooze.

After breakfast, the day crawled toward noon, and finally we left for the butterfly heats. When we returned Joan was awake and ready with her razor and shaving cream. None of us had ever "shaved down" before, but we'd heard that Santa Clara was doing it for finals, even the boys—to reduce drag. I'd been shaving my legs for two years but only up to my knees, exactly where Chris stopped her razor at midkneecap. I wasn't sure how to begin a full-body shave.

"What should I do?"

"Start with your legs like always, I guess, and keep going all the way to the top," Joan advised.

I spread the lather up my shin and thigh, but the razor, soon filled with long blonde hairs and soap, pulled and yanked. It hurt. Joan suggested I clean the head and use more lather. When I finished, my legs felt bare and skinny.

"Now your arms. 'Fuzzy Wuzzy was a bear.'" Joan teased in a singsong voice, pinching at my long forearm hair. She helped lather my arms and stood behind me to draw the razor up from my wrist to my shoulder. When she finished, I felt stark naked. There was nothing to do but wait some more.

I'd hardly seen Mom and Dad since they arrived four days after we did. Coach didn't want us talking to anyone, not even our parents, but Mom had brought me a pile of letters from friends back home wishing me well. She'd waited until Coach was out having a beer, and she didn't stay to talk. She and Dad waved and cheered from the stands at preliminaries and semifinals along with Marthadent and the other MAC parents. It seemed weird being kept away from everyone, like we were in a movie and they a distant audience. At some point that evening, Mom and Dad both stopped by the room to wish me luck before they drove on to the pool to watch the events scheduled before my final.

"You can do it, sis. We know you can," Dad said. He took my shoulders and turned me around, massaging my muscles. "Nice and loose," he said.

Mom stood a bit behind him smiling. "I know you'll do your best, honey. We'll be watching."

She always said that. It sounded so stupid, but what else could she say? Everybody's parents and teammates were probably saying the same things: do your best, you can do it, just go hard, win. Tonight, though, I wanted to show her how good my best could be. It had to be good enough to escape the sightseeing trip she'd planned for us. When she'd let that slip, she might as well have said, "Betcha can't do it." If she didn't think I could make the team, if she was betting against me, I would prove her wrong.

After they left I lay on the bed waiting for Coach and replayed yesterday's race. I'd felt fast swimming under the bright lights strung above each lane, buoyed by the light that reflected off the bottom, everyone in the stands and poolside invisible. Tonight we'd be swimming under those lights again.

Someone tapped on the door.

Joan asked me if I was ready and got up to open it. Coach stood outside and asked me to come out for a minute, then nodded Joan back to her seat and closed the door. He handed me a cup and placed a small oval tablet in my hand. I looked up with a question.

"It's niacin and vitamin B. It'll dilate your blood vessels to get you more oxygen."

No coach I'd ever had gave us choices. They told us what to do, and we did it. Without questioning Coach now, I swallowed the vitamin he gave me, gathered my gear, and off we went. I had a race plan, more oxygen, and a body smooth as a porpoise. The wait was almost over, my mind already at the pool.

An evening thunderstorm rolled in while we drove the winding drive to Rouge Park, the clouds so black and heavy, they practically crushed the car. By the time we got to Brennan Pool, the first splats hit the windshield, and ozone rose from asphalt and dust. We were running toward the pool when lightning ripped the sky and rain pounded in a deluge, the way it rarely does in Portland.

Spectators, swimmers, and officials fled from the stands as swimmers emptied the warm-up pool. "Tonight's finals will be delayed," a voice blared from the loudspeakers. "All coaches report to the pool office."

We huddled under an overhang watching the chaos. My parents and Marthadent Schollander scurried toward the parking lot, programs held over their heads, their clothes soaked through. Mom started to tell me to stay warm and dry and to ask how I felt, but Coach ordered me back to the car. Off he ran to the coaches' meeting, my parents to their car, and Mr. Johannesen and I to ours. We drove round and round the park in the hammering rain until finally it let up.

The officials reopened the warm-up pool after an hour-and-a-half delay. The men's 100-meter freestyle final, the first final event of the trials, would begin in an hour. That meant the women's wouldn't start until very late, almost midnight. It felt kind of thrilling to have the schedule so upset. Anything could happen tonight, it seemed.

Lights hung over the Olympic pool, casting shadows on the warm-up pool. I pulled off my MAC sweats and stuffed them in my duffel. Next came my old lucky Caplan sweats. The temperature had dropped with the rain. For the first time in over a week, it felt cool, almost cold. I curled my toes over the edge and looked out across the dark water, my freshly shaved arms tingling. I tensed and dove. My arms cut through the water without resistance, like hot blades. I felt as sizzling as the dry ice Dad brought home sometimes and dropped in water to make it crackle and smoke.

All the night's finalists, twenty-four men and eight women, stretched out for a few laps and then bunched up at the shallow end. The California girls complained it was so cold, they had goose bumps. Joan Spillane, the Texan, drawled, "Why don't they start this thang befo' we all turn blue?" Donna de Varona began to tell us about some ailment.

Lynn's advice came back: "Keep your focus. Don't listen to your competitors before a race." I dived under the water, sinking and dolphin kicking along the bottom, before I pushed off and launched into a quick sprint. I felt loose and ready, excited and absolutely silent inside, the way you feel playing hide-and-seek when you're in a perfect hiding place and the seeker walks right past you and you know you'll beat her back to base.

After a few more laps and a couple of short sprints, five- or ten-stroke bursts, I pulled out of the pool, picked up my duffel, and started to the locker room. Coach Schlueter stepped out of the shadows. "Don't worry, Woody. You're completely ready," he said. "Now go get warm." He patted my back and headed another direction. He would soon be off to wherever he was going to wait for news.

After a hot shower softened my muscles, I got out, dried off, and changed into my lucky black suit and my old red-and-white cotton sweats before pulling on the MAC sweats. I lay back on a bench behind the lockers, a long towel around my neck, one end draped over my face. I could hear the other girls talking back and forth, but I did not want to join in. Chris would be alone somewhere, too, as she had been in Livermore before setting a record. I thought about Coach's words, "Don't worry...you're ready," and started to hum an old Kingston Trio song and then to sing, louder and louder, crowding out the girls' voices, filling up the locker room: "It takes a worried man to sing a worried song...I'm worried now, but I won't be worried long." I wasn't worried: Not about the late start. Not about the cold night. "Ready or not, here I come," I said into the towel.

After the men's 200-meter breaststroke started, an official came into the locker room to announce: "Ladies. Time to report to the clerk of the course." Outside, the crowd cheered but from far away. She led us to chairs where we waited for the men to finish.

Time jumped, and suddenly we finalists stood on the starting platform. Lights strung over each lane pierced the water, highlighting the wide black line on the bottom. Around us everything disappeared except the lights, the lanes, and the timers huddled behind each of us. Detroit's air had an edge to it, all the thick roundness gone. We stood above our lanes on the long wooden starting platform, shivering now in our thin nylon suits.

The starter commanded, "Take your marks." We slowly bent forward together. *This is it this is it this is it*, I thought. But Donna de Varona rolled through her start, jumped the gun, and brought all of us with her. The water bit hard. I popped up and shook off the cold, turned around and sprinted back to the wall. We waited for everyone to climb out and get set again. The stars from California, Texas, Florida all moaned. "Damn that wind," Shirley Stobs muttered.

She thinks this is a wind? I thought. *Ha!* It was probably still seventy degrees, cool compared to the humid eighties and nineties, but hardly cold. I thought about our mornings at Jantzen Beach, the east wind blasting down the Gorge, the filthy, turbulent, cold Jantzen pool where I'd spent two summers training. This was nothing. *I'm not cold at all,* I thought as I looked across the field of competitors. *I'll beat every one of you.*

The first fifty felt like Monday's time trial. The lights lifted and propelled me. I went into the turn right with Chris; coming out, my vision seemed to extend in all directions through the water. She pulled ahead around seventy-five meters, but something kicked in for me. I felt buoyed again, on top of the water, effortless and fast, closing the gap, not even needing to breathe, just speeding toward the wall, hitting it, and rolling onto my right side. Chris's arm still seemed in motion, but nobody else was near the wall. We looked up at the timers huddled around their watches.

Chris reached over the lane line and pulled me close. "I think we're on. Nice race, Woody." Voices blurred along the poolside. I lay back on the water, my face burning, not daring to celebrate, hoping. We had to wait for the official times, the turn judges' reports, and the final judges' decisions. I swam back to the wall, shaking out tension and fatigue. Bob Burke's voice boomed from the deck, "You're on the team, you brat! You're on!"

Lynn ran over and crushed me in a hug as I climbed out of the pool. "You almost beat Chris. You're going to Rome, blood sister." Still, we didn't know for sure.

Finally the announcer made it official: "Chris von Saltza and Carolyn Wood are the first two members of the 1960 Women's US Olympic team."

Everything got fast and confused after that. George Haines, Santa Clara's coach and now the Olympic coach, handed us official team certificates, and reporters asked questions. Somehow my parents got on the deck, found me, and wrapped me in hugs. Mr. Johannesen, Marthadent, Donnie, and the rest of the team crowded around. Everyone except Coach. People handed me programs and asked for my autograph. It was crazy all around, but inside I felt calm, as if I had known all along what this moment would be like. A kind of nonchalance replaced all the anxiety and wondering that had been my companions. I stepped into a familiar pose—cool, sure, inscrutable. It was the way I'd played Tarzan when I was nine and Mickey Mantle when switch-hitting in backyard baseball. It was the way great athletes behaved.

Even so, what I wanted most was to tell someone back home that I'd made it. From a pay phone by the pool, I called Patsy Walsh collect. Her dad answered and refused to accept the charges, but added to try again in ten minutes. When I finally got through, she screamed, "I prayed and prayed for you."

"Tell everybody" was about all I had to say.

"You'll get to see Pope John," she said as I was hanging up.

The next morning bouquets of roses and about twenty telegrams arrived. Dad's sister's came first, *The tree is proud of its twig*, and then one from Tye, *Take the butterfly*. They came from swim team friends, church friends, my parents' friends, neighbors, aunts and uncles, and two from Mr. Perry, who surely had forgotten his threats to suspend my MAC membership: *Knew you'd come through like the champ you are*, and, *Just announced our new champion on Club House speakers. You should have heard the cheers.*

No storms interrupted Thursday night's 100-meter butterfly final, and Coach gave me no vitamins. I'd qualified sixth, so I swam on the outside in lane two. As it had the night before, the light seemed to lift and propel me, my stroke effortless. I could see through the water across the whole pool. When I hit the wall, I knew I was first. After everyone had finished, Nancy Ramey struggled in—last. *How could the world record holder be last?* I wondered.

It didn't really matter if you were on a previous Olympic team or set records in the preliminaries. All that mattered was what place you finished one time: in the finals of the trials. It didn't seem fair. Jeff Farrell, the best sprint freestyler in the world, wasn't on the team. He'd had his appendix out four days before the trials started. All bandaged, he swam the prelims, semis, and finals only to finish third. Maybe he would make it on the relay, but that meant another three races.

We're on the team! Chris von Saltza, George Haines, and me after the 100-meter freestyle finals.

I watched Nancy Ramey bob up and down in the water. She was crying. All she had wanted was a second chance at the Olympics, a chance to win gold. Now it was over for her.

That will not happen to me, I thought. No young nobody would beat me off the team. In 1964 I'd be in college and no longer swimming. This was my time. Now.

Water plashed against the wall, mixing with the gasps and pants of swimmers as they recovered their breath and waited for the results. The announcer finally came on: "Carolyn Wood, first; Carolyn Schuler, second." And that ended the trials for me. I believed that I'd be on the medley relay with Lynn, *if* she qualified. The women's 100-meter backstroke would be the first event the next night.

With all my races over, my parents could finally talk to me. In the morning, Dad sat and read telegrams out loud, chattered about the races, detailed which parents were going on to Rome, and repeated what he'd heard about different swimmers and coaches.

"Tonight's Lynn's turn," he said. We were careful not to be too sure because even though Lynn had qualified first in the backstroke prelim, you couldn't count on anything until the race ended. We didn't want to jinx her.

How quickly excitement disappeared and the mundane returned. I'd have liked to savor the victory, wallow in it, but right away the next step rose up: packing.

"Do you think you'll need two dresses or three?" Mom asked, refolding the red-striped Lanz that hung, unworn, in the closet.

"They're giving us uniforms. Why would I take dresses?"

"Well, you might have receptions or dances."

"Dances? This is the Olympics, Mom."

She didn't look up from her work. "I'll pack two, the red one and the blue one." She placed them in the Samsonite bag.

I watched her busy herself with my clothes. She packed as if I were heading off to college, which was all she could imagine, I thought, because she had no idea. I didn't really have any idea either. Emotions washed over me, and I didn't want to think about clothes, I wanted to get back to the euphoria I'd felt the night before. But the adrenaline and serotonin had drained away, replaced by irritability.

Mom filled a little travel kit with Nutri-Bio, toothpaste, shampoo, and a mini-clothesline with pins. She told me to get Lynn to help me with laundry and asked if they'd have washing machines over there. She hadn't been listening to Dad and me.

"I don't know. How would I know?" I exploded. "Besides, Lynn isn't on the team yet." My voice sounded harsh, but really I felt like there was so much I didn't know. Like where would we sleep, and where would we eat? What would the food be like anyway? And how would we understand anything when they talked? Italy seemed really far away.

I didn't know a thing about it. How long would we be gone? What about school? My calm center began to slip away.

Mom ignored my outburst and gave me an I'm-sorry look. "Oh, I wish you were going with us."

"Mom. I'm going to Rome."

"If we'd known you were going to make the team, we'd have made other plans. Your father wants to be there so bad, but..." Dad slipped outside to have a cigarette.

As I watched her carefully packing my clothes, I might have wondered what she thought of her little Olympian. I might have asked if she was sorry for doubting my chances. I might have told her how much I needed her and Dad to be there to cheer for me. Instead, I still carried that wet towel of resentment, made heavier now with the unknown yet to come.

"Maybe you could buy the Rameys' tickets," I suggested offhandedly.

"We already have all our other reservations." Her voice trailed off.

She didn't really want to go that far away because it scared her, I thought, but Daddy could go. I'd forgotten that neither of them had a passport; the expense did not cross my mind, nor the idea that they might actually enjoy a vacation by themselves, somewhere they'd never been and had always wanted to visit.

It was all sinking in. I'd made the Olympic team. We were headed to Rome, and we'd be there more than a month. When I raced, no one from home would see. If Lynn didn't make it, I'd be on my own.

PART III

GO

1960–1963

On the Team

August 1960

AFTER THE EXCITEMENT OF MAKING the team wore off, exhaustion and uncertainty set in. I'd hardly finished packing and saying goodbye before we were whisked away on Saturday afternoon—all fourteen swimmers, including Lynn, of course, and three divers—for New York and the Renaissance Country Club out on Long Island, our training site until we left for Rome. It had a fifty-meter pool—with a set of bleachers from Ebbets Field, home of the Brooklyn Dodgers, a fact that someone mentioned every day—and an upstairs ballroom outfitted with camp cots. It reminded me of the Portland Golf Club, dark and cool inside. Some of the members, Helen Burke and her friends, served all our meals in the club's dining room. Members' kids hung around and watched us eat and swim, asked for autographs, or pointed out the bleachers. A donor bought us white sweatshirts with *USA* on the front, but otherwise we wore only our swimsuits or the clothes we'd brought from home to Detroit.

George Haines's "easy" workouts lasted longer and felt harder than any of ours in Portland, and we trained twice a day. The week of late nights, expectation, and excitement at the trials left me limp and worn out. I could barely stagger to my cot after lunch before falling facedown, arms hanging over the edge, knuckles on the floor. Too tired to sleep sometimes, my mind would skitter across everything that had happened or was going to happen. I might think about our workout and how far ahead Chris always seemed, or how close Molly Botkin came in behind me. *What will the pool be like in Italy? Where will we sleep? Why doesn't Lynn hang out and kid around like before?* Doubts kept me awake. *Will I ever feel fast enough to race again? Do I belong on the team? I might not even be on the medley relay for the finals.* George would determine who would swim each relay based on our performance at the trials and in training and time trials afterward. He could choose among the six of us who had qualified in the 100-meter freestyle for the freestyle relay. Some would swim the preliminaries; the fastest would go on to the finals. For the medley relay, he told us, whoever won each event at the Games would swim the relay finals. Nothing was for sure.

On Sunday a huge scandal about pep pills erupted in the newspapers. Sylvia Ruuska's father accused swimmers from Santa Clara, Multnomah Club, and Los Angeles Athletic Club of using them at the trials. Bob Burke told us that the headline had streamed across Times Square in Manhattan. Sylvia was on the team, so none of us wanted to say her father was a crackpot, but Bob and Helen Burke said just that when I saw them one afternoon after practice. Lynn said it all had to do with Donna de Varona leaving Mr. Ruuska's team and swimming with Santa Clara. She knew something else, too, a rumor about the 1956 trials when Coach Schlueter had had a really good backstroker. Right before the finals, he'd given her a pep pill, but the finals were delayed by a thunderstorm. Just like this year. So much time went by that the pill wore off, and she ended up last. She was a total basket case, Lynn said.

I listened and nodded. Coach had been secretive about the vitamin he'd given me before the 100-meter freestyle. The finals had been delayed, as in 1956, but the pill hadn't wrecked me. It must have been a vitamin like he said. Still, I would not tell Lynn or Bob or anyone. I wondered if I would have told my parents if I'd been home. Mom would have had an explanation, or Dad might have talked to Coach Schlueter. In New York there was no one to talk to, really, not about this.

US Women's Olympic Swimming and Diving Team, 1960, at Renaissance Country Club. Back: Ann Warner, Chris von Saltza, Sylvia Ruuska, Lynn Burke, Joan Spillane, Nina Harmer, Molly Botkin. Middle: Betty Baldwin (chaperone), Donna de Varona, Carolyn House, Carolyn Schuler, Shirley Stobs, Paula Jean Pope (diver), Carolyn Wood, Patsy Willard (diver), Patty Kempner, Juno Irwin (diver), Susan Doerr. Front: Unknown, Sammy Lee (diving coach), George Haines (swim coach), unknown.

George Haines told a reporter that it looked like "jealousy and sour grapes." The *Oregonian* quoted Coach Schlueter: "All we gave our kids was the same old vitamin B tablets they've been taking all season." That wasn't exactly true—unless he was talking about Mom's Nutri-Bio. Someone else suggested that Ruuska had confused honey syrup and vitamin C for a pep pill. Still, you can lose faith in yourself pretty quickly if you suspect someone has cheated for you. It's like winning because someone lets you.

At the Schollanders', I'd once watched Jim Campbell crush every opponent in ping-pong. Donnie had begged Jim to let him win one game, but Jim told him to never *let* somebody beat you. "You don't do anyone a favor by letting them win," he'd said. If Coach really had given me a pep pill instead of a vitamin, he hadn't done me a favor. Still, I had won the butterfly without any vitamins or pills. That thought consoled me, and by midweek the distraction had all died down.

Nothing felt normal those days out on Long Island—seventeen girls sleeping on cots in a ballroom, George Haines as coach, people always milling around, dining-room food. One afternoon somebody brought us a special dessert from *the city*, and everyone got all excited. It sounded terrible: cheese...cake. When I tried it, it tasted sour and felt grainy. The kids from New York, Pennsylvania, and Florida could have their cheesecake. At home in August, we'd be eating peach cobbler, home-made. My thoughts drifted back to Portland, and I wondered if Stevie knew I'd made the team. I missed the familiarity of home. The empty hours between workouts in that strange, isolated place left me way too much time to stew. It was a relief when Bob brought Lynn's little brother, Bobby, to the pool one morning.

"Lynn says you might want some firecrackers. I got 'em in Chinatown last weekend." His dark eyes twinkled like his mom's when he handed me a brown paper bag with a double string of about one hundred lady fingers inside, bright red with yellow-twined wicks. He warned me not to get caught because fireworks were illegal in New York.

"I'm taking these to Rome, and when we win the relay, I'll set them off!" I said, energized as I imagined the future.

Long Island resembled Detroit with its broad-leafed trees and sultry air. New York City was a whole different world. Maybe I slept on the bus ride from Roslyn to Manhattan, because I don't really remember seeing the city come into focus, but when I stepped off the bus onto the sidewalk and looked up and up to the tops of buildings so unimaginably far away, I got dizzy. This was a city like the ones Mr. Rosebraugh had made us draw when he taught perspective in eighth grade, only instead of four- and five-story buildings, these rose so high, their tops almost touched across the sky above the street. I had to reach out and steady myself as I looked up, my mouth open, like the country mouse in Uncle Ernie's Cheeser stories. Lynn had known this world when she'd come to Oregon. I had no idea anyplace could be so big, dirty, noisy, tall, and exciting.

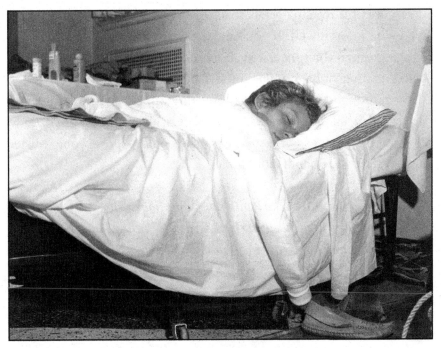

Asleep on my lumpy cot in New York between practices

We stayed two nights in the Vanderbilt Hotel on Park Avenue. All the teams heading for Rome stayed there to be processed. On our first afternoon, a *Life* magazine photographer followed Lynn and Chris, our team's big, blonde stars, and took pictures of them trying on uniforms. I'd had a little brush with fame when Jim McKay, a television man who'd be covering the Games, came to the Renaissance Club. He sat on a catamaran in the pool with Donna de Varona while Lynn and I swam up and were interviewed in the water. A cameraman knelt on the deck filming us for a TV show.

"Do you think you can beat the Aussies? Do you think you'll do well? How does it feel to be the youngest competitor?" he'd asked.

Lynn, more experienced with interviewers and far more confident than I, answered most of his questions. The whole setup struck me as stupid. What was he doing out in the pool? How were we supposed to answer questions while treading water? At least the magazine reporters took more time to actually talk to us. Even with them, though, I did not like being interviewed. If you talked about winning, it sounded like bragging, and if you speculated about the future, you were inviting bad luck. I'd rather sit back and let others answer the questions.

Even though Mom was still in Washington, DC, with Dad, I wrote a letter home telling her everything we'd been given. She'd want to know all about our clothes and presents so she could tell everyone. I listed them as they were handed out:

navy-blue blazer and skirt with navy-blue pointy shoes
red jacket and white pleated sharkskin skirt with red high heels
a red beret and a white straw hat with red, white, and blue ribbon
a red belt with an Olympic rings buckle

The navy outfit with the white hat was for the Opening Ceremony. It looked horrible, I told her. The skirt hung way below my knees, and the jacket fit like a big box. When Betty Baldwin's summer letter had asked about my sizes, I'd written that I wore a size 16 top. This could have been a size 20.

For casual wear, Van Heusen gave us two shirts: a long-sleeved, olive-green, button-down, printed with torches surrounded by laurel leaves; and a short-sleeved, powder-blue polo similar to the ones Coach wore, only with a tiny Olympic torch instead of an alligator on the breast pocket. Swimmers each got two new bathing suits, a Jantzen and an Ocean Pool, one red, one blue. Of all the gifts and clothes, though, the best by far was the uniform every athlete would wear to the races: a royal-blue Champion sweat suit with *USA* on the front. It reminded me of the special Aero Club set that Tye had loaned me to wear in Livermore, only this one really fit.

Grasshopper provided a zip-top suitcase and an Olympic duffel bag. A zippered carrying case with a USA insignia contained an electric Lady Remington razor, Breck shampoo, cosmetics, toothbrush and paste, and a comb and brush. I added a batch of little enamel USA pins to the case. They were for trading with athletes from other countries to foster friendship, the officials told us. We raced around the hotel suite trying on clothes and laughing. It felt like Christmas or a birthday party.

On Friday, a Renaissance Club member arranged for us to tour the Garment District. Lynn pulled me through the factories and advised me what to take even though everything looked strange and frilly. *I wouldn't be caught dead in this stuff*, I thought, but on Lynn's advice I ended up with a negligee, a garter belt, a strapless bra, and a merry widow. She said the merry widow would be useful for prom, but that seemed doubtful. I could hardly hook the hooks. She explained that was the whole point and why I needed it—to make me look like I had a waist. We laughed like crazy kids again, like the old days.

Our team perks were meager compared to now, when Olympians are often professionals, supported in training at development camps or sponsored by companies—sports apparel, shoe, soft drink, insurance, car. In 1960 we were all amateurs. To accept any gift valued more than ten dollars would risk expulsion from the Amateur Athletic Union. Olympians were allowed their uniforms, which were gifted to the USOC and then provided to us. The swim team's underwear tour must have been granted special approval after someone made a donation to the Olympic Committee.

When we got back to the hotel, a photographer took four of us—Lynn, Nina Harmer, Donna de Varona, and me—to the roof for a photo shoot with the Empire State Building in the background. The *New York Times* ran it the next day on the front page of the sports section, along with a send-off article. We stood in our USA sweats looking off in the distance, happy and confident. I felt part of the team now, ready for Rome.

FINDING PACE

2012

LOW RAIN CLOUDS HAMMOCK BETWEEN stone buildings and over cobbled streets. Night comes early now. There's no heat in the bar, and I've got my wool hat pulled over my ears, my hands cupping a mug of hot chocolate. Several days of climbing up and over the mountains to the highest point on the Camino and down through remote terrain start tomorrow. This will be the last stage of the journey.

I arrived in town today in time for Sunday *comida* in the *restaurante* filled with families in this working-class section of town. A feast, really: *vino* and paella, *pollo asado, patatas fritas,* flan. Patrons arrived in clusters and pairs and filled the dining room with energy. Beside me two couples shared a table with five raucous kids all dressed up for church. At another a grandmother and her teenage grandson quietly conversed. Four young men in their twenties swaggered in and sat together laughing over their paella, while nearby a family of five sat formally in near silence. Older couples, more families, and bustling waiters filled the dining room all afternoon.

It was like watching a film, I think now at the bar with my hot chocolate and beer. I replay the scene and add it to my journal before heading out to my room in a cheap pension on a hill above the market. All day I've been alone, walking, arriving, finding shelter and food, trusting that all will be well whatever arises.

A hand taps me on the shoulder. "Hello there." An Irish pilgrim smiles and nods toward her friends. "We're headed out for dinner. Want to join us?"

"No, thanks," I answer without thought or excuse. Later in my dreary room, with an old man lodging on one side and a traveling salesman on the other, I listen to the floorboards creak with their every move and a television soundtrack bleed through the walls. A single bare light-bulb casts strange shadows on the stained white walls. I wonder at my choices. Why do I push further and further away from the camaraderie of the Camino? Would I be happier if I became part of it all instead of apart? Questions and criticisms pile up beside the bed. Can I let go of judgment? Can I make peace with the notion that I am a person apart, one who most enjoys watching others, listening, observing, questioning but not diving into the group?

Now is the time for observation, I console myself. This walk is long enough to explore being alone and to find my pace. *And I have found my pace*, I think with a laugh. When I try to keep up in order to talk, I feel pain. If I slow down for someone, I feel antsy and then resentful and my knees hurt. It's like running road races—to finish well, you must know in your muscles your pace and ignore the fleeting impulses to pass someone or slow down, to get ahead or to quit.

When Michael was taken to live with his father, my world filled with fog and I struggled to find my way through the long gray days between our visits. Driving to pick him up at his father's house, I'd see runners climbing Terwilliger Boulevard, a heavily wooded parkway above the city, some plodding along and others fleet-footed as deer. I started running on the days he was gone, round and round a nearby track, first a mile and then two miles and then out on the road, dragging myself up and down Terwilliger for almost a year before I began to feel slightly deer-like.

An Oregon track coach, Bill Bowerman, started the jogging craze, and by the late 1970s, road races in Portland filled the calendar from New Year's Eve to Christmas. Once I'd managed to run two miles without walking, I wanted to go farther and faster. I tried a two-mile fun run first and then a five-mile race. All the preparation and planning, the nervousness before the start among the jostling runners, the gun and that release into movement and the body taking over, finding a sustainable pace and holding it, all felt wonderfully familiar. Training and racing reorganized my life, helped me regain a sense of self-worth. By the time I met Rose, I'd run in several big races, including the first Cascade Run Off, a fifteen-kilometer run through Portland, up Terwilliger Hill, and back along the Willamette River.

The first time Rose and I ran together, she took me to a short circular track where she jogged a few times a week. She'd never run on roads, through neighborhoods, or on trails, but that soon changed. Throughout the 1980s I trained for races, but on Saturday evenings we'd run the four-mile loop around Fairmount together after we drove Michael to his father's. On Sundays we'd wind our way along the Wildwood Trail in Forest Park for an hour or more, at a pace slow enough to talk. We were young, fit, and happy to be together.

A long, solitary walk provides a time to observe and experience the undulations of geography, the shifts of light and weather, the fluctuations of one's mind. This retreat into myself is nothing new. The solitude of neighborhood woods and vacant lots enticed me in childhood. The quiet plash of the pool and the muted footfalls along running trails provided escape and comfort from social expectations and high-spirited classrooms. Oscillation between encounter and withdrawal is as natural and necessary as the ebb and flow of the sea.

In the morning I'm half an hour along the trail before light finally leaks through the clouds. There's ice on the puddles, frost on the heather, but in the mountain villages, window boxes still overflow with geraniums and carnations. The trail climbs steadily up to the apex of the Camino, Cruz de Ferro, while the capricious weather entertains with rain, snow, and sunshine. For a time I follow two vertical rainbows, brilliant against the dark storm clouds ahead, which threaten but then move away to the north where the mountains are snow covered down to three thousand feet.

It's an exhilarating trek that ends in an old Celtic-style chapel, a fire in the center, benches tiered on four sides, bunks in an upstairs loft, showers below. Pilgrims arrive one by one or together: a young French girl, a Czech couple, a Japanese youth, an older French threesome. I'm happy to greet Silvia, the Valencian, when she arrives an hour or so later, her pace much slower than mine. After she sets up her bunk, we walk back into town together, she to find a *farmacia* and a store, me ready to share her company. We'll have a glass of wine and tell stories of the day's climb.

No Roman Holiday

August 1960

My parents' East Coast trip ended in New York in time for them to see the team leave for Rome. Dad gave me a big hug and whispered, "I know you'll come home with a medal. I wish I could be there to see." Mom sort of cried when she said goodbye. "Do your best, honey. And be good. Don't go horsing around. Remember who..." I joined her in the now-familiar refrain, "who you are and what you represent." She reminded me it was a lot more than the Club now. It was all of Portland. And the country. I didn't want to be too proud, but I felt it: proud to be on the team, to wear a uniform, and to possess a passport the president had signed.

I looked at my happy parents standing together. I was going off to Rome, to Europe, places they would never go, leaving behind everything familiar, everyone who knew me—except Lynn. I felt scared and excited at the same time, like right before a race.

We were flying with the men's water polo team, on an overnight flight in a big, chartered propeller plane. My parents would probably watch the plane for as long as they could see it climbing and flying away. Bob and Helen Burke would drive them back to Long Island, and together they'd speculate about how long we'd be flying and what time it would be when we finally landed in Rome. Bob would promise them he'd look after me when he got there. In later years, Mom wondered why she and Dad hadn't gone too. "How could we have missed something so important?" she'd ask. Back then there was no question. They couldn't afford it. They couldn't even imagine it.

As soon as we took off, the water polo guys started unhooking seats to make open areas so they could play cards or stretch out to sleep. After an hour or so, the card players got really loud. Lynn leaned over the aisle and told me they had brought booze on board; they were drunk.

I couldn't believe it. "They shouldn't be drinking if they want to win. What if they get sent home?"

Lynn looked back toward the noisy men. "It's a rowdy sport."

I'd never heard of water polo. Sometime after midnight I fell asleep.

We stopped to refuel in Shannon, Ireland, where rain pounded into the darkness. In Rome, hours later, the sun blazed. White-uniformed officials led us to a waiting bus, a big, clean, modern bus with windows from the seat bottom to the middle of the ceiling, nothing like the stinky blue one with its tiny, streaky windows that ran up and down Canyon Road. Beside the highway here and there stood classical white columns. Ancient viaducts threaded across the hills. Under their arches women and kids sat in doorways of lean-to shacks. The modern and the old lived next to each other in Rome. The ancient part looked like a seventh-grade diorama on Greece, and for a moment I confused Greece and Rome and the Olympics and coliseums. Where was I again? I leaned my forehead on the glass while the bus crawled through Rome. Outside, old women in black scarves, men wearing wool jackets, and ladies dressed up in high heels all crowded the sidewalks while motorbikes and tiny cars zipped along the road.

It took over an hour to get to the Olympic Village, clusters of elevated apartments and shops built alongside the Tiber River. The women's complex, modern three-story yellow-brick apartments atop concrete pillars and arranged at right angles around a grassy courtyard, sat behind a fence within the Village. The United States

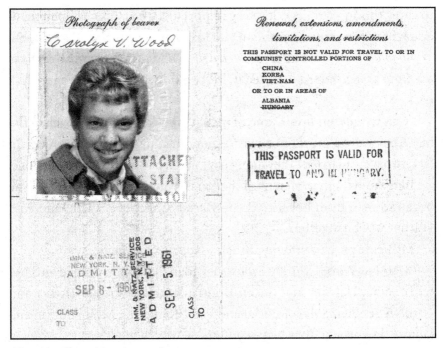

Photograph of bearer
Carolyn V. Wood

Renewal, extensions, amendments, limitations, and restrictions

THIS PASSPORT IS NOT VALID FOR TRAVEL TO OR IN
COMMUNIST CONTROLLED PORTIONS OF

CHINA
KOREA
VIET-NAM

OR TO OR IN AREAS OF

ALBANIA
HUNGARY

THIS PASSPORT IS VALID FOR
TRAVEL TO AND IN HUNGARY.

IMM. & NATZ. SERVICE
NEW YORK, N.Y. IC 205
ADMITTED
SEP 5 1961

IMM. & NATZ. SERVICE
NEW YORK, N.Y.
ADMITTED
SEP 8 - 1961

CLASS
TO

CLASS
TO

Olympic village identity card

and some other English-speaking teams were housed in one building, swimmers on the first floor, with track and field, gymnasts, and others rooming above us.

Before we got off the bus, Betty Baldwin handed each of us a participant badge, a beautiful bronze medallion encircled with laurel leaves and cast with Rome's insignia, the she-wolf suckling Romulus and Remus above the five Olympic rings and an inscription: *Roma MCMLX*. The badge sat atop a light-blue enamel panel with the word *ATHLETA* in bronze relief. The back was also engraved, *Giochi della XVII Olimpiade* and an image of an arch. "You must wear this at all times." Her high, piercing voice was emphatic. "You will not be admitted to the Village or to the women's quarters without this badge." George, our coach, turned around and raised and lowered his eyebrows as if to agree and make fun of her at the same time. Next she handed out a little green book, *Carta D'Identità*, an Olympic passport with our own photo inside. "Now. You also need to carry this in your gear. It's very important. It's an official document. You will not be issued another if you lose it."

So what then? I wondered. *Do we sleep on the street or have to make a lean-to somewhere?* I doubted it. Betty Baldwin made me want to talk back.

"Can we get out now?" one of the divers asked from the back of the bus. They were almost fifteen years older than most of us swimmers. In fact, two were married. They didn't have much patience with a chaperone.

Betty told them to wait until she gave us our room assignments. She began to read from her list: "Lynn Burke, Chris von Saltza, and Ann Warner will be together."

My heart pushed into my throat. *I thought...I thought...*

"Carolyn Wood, Shirley Stobs, and Joan Spillane will have another triple. Nina Harmer and Susan Doerr together. Carolyn House and Carolyn Schuler. Sylvia Ruuska and Patty Kempner. Molly Botkin and Donna de Varona. That leaves you three divers together, Paula Jean, Juno, and Patsy. All right then."

I kept my head down; my cheeks burned. I thought I'd be with Lynn. That was what I'd worked for. I ordered myself not to cry and hurried off the bus. Shirley put her arm around my shoulder. "Come on, roomie. Let's see this triple and fight over beds."

Shirley Stobs looked like her name, short and muscular, stubby, with dark, curly hair and a sharp sense of humor that reminded me of Lynn. She didn't hold it against me that I'd beaten her in the freestyle. She was happy to be on the team, she said, traveling to Europe before she started college. While she hoped she'd be on the freestyle relay, she wanted to have a few dates too. I didn't think she sounded very serious about winning or even training, but I relaxed around her because she was kind and made me laugh. My other roommate, Joan from Texas, was much quieter and, while pleasant, acted too old for fun. When we were alone in the room, we had nothing to talk about ever.

I chose the bed in the corner where the sun didn't come in so harshly. I unpacked my things and put them in the little bureau next to my bed,

Postcard home from the Olympic Village

then lay down. Across the room Shirley and Joan chattered; outside in the hall, Ann and Lynn laughed. I pulled the cover over my head. I didn't want to talk to anyone. This wasn't what I had dreamed about and worked for at all.

We took our meals in a massive cafeteria about a ten-minute walk from the women's quarters. Cases of warm Coca-Cola leaned against the wall near the door. Inside, cooks wore white uniforms and chef hats and stood behind long tables to dish out food. They had all kinds of cold cereal in big metal bowls, and the milk was always warm. Poached eggs filled a huge metal tray, a weird kind of bacon lay piled in another, and heaps of steaks in a third. At the end of the line, they stacked up cold toast. Nothing ever changed at breakfast.

Betty told us what time to be at the bus each morning because we didn't have a regular workout routine. All the national teams had to share the few training pools around Rome, so training times changed daily. We wouldn't practice in the Olympic pool until Friday, one of only two times before the first event.

Joan and Shirley liked to sleep late, but as usual I got up early, put on my suit and sweats, and headed over for breakfast alone. Outside the fence surrounding the Village, a group of Italian boys hung around and chanted "OoooSa. OoooooSa," when they saw USA on my sweats. A boy waved a *Sports Illustrated*, the one that had come out right after the trials with Mike Troy on the cover. Inside were pictures of Carin Cone and Becky Collins. *SI* had guessed they'd make the team—instead, Lynn and I had.

"OoooSa," they called, and I walked over to the gate.

"*Quale sport?*" the one with the magazine asked.

"Swimming. *Nuoto,*" I answered, feeling pretty smart that I knew some Italian already.

"*Quale?*" He mimed a few strokes of crawl. I mimed back butterfly, and he grinned and opened the magazine to Becky's photo. "*Si scrive. Autografo.*" He pointed to Becky's photo.

Lynn and me heading to practice before the Games begin, Rome

"That's not me," I said, shaking my head and pointing to her and then to me.

He made butterfly strokes and pointed, insisting. "*Autografo!*"

"It's not me." I gave up, shrugged, and signed it anyway. He didn't really care who I was. He'd seen what he wanted to see: a USA swimmer whose autograph he could get in his magazine.

Inside the cafeteria I took my eggs and toast and sat at a side table. I watched an enormous guy load up his tray and lumber past me with steaks stacked on a plate and two bottles of milk on his tray. He sat down and stabbed a steak right in the middle, and then he jammed the whole thing into his mouth, his cheeks bulging. He picked up the milk bottle, threw back his head, and drank the whole liter in one swig. I couldn't turn away even though it looked disgusting. Ann Warner sat down beside me. "That's Dave Somebody," she whispered. "Shot put. What a gross-out." We watched him stab two more steaks and glug a second liter of milk. He did not look like a very good representative of the USA.

We got to the practice pool just as the Australian team finished a cooldown. Chris pointed out a short-haired giant standing at the shallow end—Dawn Fraser. Even in the water, she looked taller than Chris, with a big Roman nose and sharp blue eyes. Beside her I recognized Ilsa Konrads from her pictures in the papers. She and her brother were famous distance swimmers. Dawn, Chris's main competition, held world records in the 100- and 200-meter freestyle and had been a gold medalist in Melbourne. As we filed onto the deck, she watched us. Suddenly, she turned and dunked an unsuspecting guy standing next to her.

Lynn bumped into me while I still stared at Fraser. "She's notorious," Lynn said.

"What's that mean?"

"She gets in trouble a lot. *A lot.* But she is so fast."

I watched Fraser horsing around and thought she must be showing off for Chris, trying to psych her out.

Olympic swimming pool, Rome

When Shirley and I went into the dressing room to use the toilet, we couldn't find it anywhere. An old woman in a pale purple wrapper swabbed the tile floor. We asked her, "Where's the toilet?" She stopped mopping and looked at us.

"The toilet?" Shirley repeated and squatted down pretending to sit.

The tiny lady laughed and pointed to a stall down the way. I opened the door and saw a hole in the tile floor.

"She sent us to the shower," I called to Shirley and came out to find the attendant. "Toilet?" I repeated, shaking my head and pointing to the cubicle. "Toilet?" This time I pretended to sit.

She started talking fast in Italian, took my arm, walked me into the same stall, and pointed at the hole. Then she squatted down and smiled up at me.

This was the toilet? I couldn't believe it. A hole in the ground? When she left, I pulled my suit down to my ankles and tried to aim at the hole. How could I pee into that and not get my suit wet? And no toilet paper.

213

"How do they do this?" I asked from my squat.

Shirley laughed and laughed from the other stall.

"Do not leave anything in this dressing room," Betty Baldwin announced from the front of the bus. "*I mean not anything.* People want what you have." She repeated herself, "Do not leave..."

The bus stopped beside a wide park, and we walked through it to the new stadium in the Foro Italico, our first chance to swim in the Olympic pool. My stomach got a little queasy, so I sped up, trying to get to the front of our group. The dressing room was ultramodern with lockers and benches, a wall of frosted glass, and a wide-open doorway that led to the pool. Like Jantzen Beach, it had a footbath. Lynn splashed through the bath and called back to everyone to hurry. The pool was fantastic, she yelled.

I jammed my sweats into my duffel, stashed it under the bench, and ran to catch up with her. Stadium seats for twelve thousand people towered on each side of the pool. From the dressing room, we walked the full length to the shallow end, where concrete starting blocks stood behind each of the eight lanes. A wide deck at the end separated the swimming pool from the diving pool. Our divers waved to us as they waited in line to practice on the three-meter springboard.

That day we shared the pool with two other national teams. George had us take off from the blocks a few times, and after that we settled into the usual warm-up followed by a workout based on what we'd be racing. The pool felt cold at first, and during the repeats, I noticed a choppiness, as if it weren't completely filled. From the water I looked up and around. *I'm in Rome,* I thought. *In Rome in the Olympic pool.* The stands looked huge and rose so high, I couldn't imagine them filled with spectators. Bob Burke would be in Rome soon, but I wished my parents were coming too. I wanted them to see everything. It was all too fantastic to describe.

After practice, back in the dressing room, women in light-pink housecoats and scarves tidied up benches and swept the floors. Two stood guard by the toilets, real toilets here at the Olympic pool. On the floor under the bench, my bag lay open. My stomach churned. "Oh no. My sweats!"

"Look around," Shirley said. "They probably dropped out."

"You weren't supposed to leave anything in the dressing room." Carolyn House sounded like Betty Baldwin.

We searched everywhere. I even tried to ask the indifferent, house-coat-ladies to help, but the sweats were gone.

Betty's voice rose even higher than usual when I told her. "You left your...?"

"I'm sorry. I was in a hurry." It sounded weak.

She went with me one more time to look in the locker room, but when we couldn't find them, she said that I would not be getting another set. She had specifically warned us.

"I have to have sweats. I'm on a relay." Now my voice escalated. She had to get me another uniform. She *had to*. Everybody wore the uniform for awards. Besides, it was the only thing I wore every day. I looked around at all the locker-room attendants. It was their job to watch out, wasn't it?

Betty followed my gaze. She said that the women had probably been waiting for a chance to take something and that one of them had snatched a prized USA uniform. I felt miserable. Lynn loaned me her cotton sweatshirt for the return to the Village, and I sat in the back of the bus as far away from Betty Baldwin as I could get.

We worked out hard on Saturday and Sunday and had 80 percent time trials on Monday. On Tuesday Betty Baldwin informed me that she had put out an emergency request to the other chaperones and one had answered. A gymnast had been injured and couldn't compete, so she was giving me her uniform. It was not my size, but Betty said it was the best she could do for me.

I thanked her. Mom had written recently and reminded me to be my "sweet self." It was very hard to be sweet to Betty Baldwin. She was soft, doughy, and so bossy. Somebody said that her husband made lots of money and that's why she was chaperone, not because she knew anything about swimming or kids. When I tried on the sweats, the bottoms fit fine, but I could barely tug the top over my head and get my arms into the sleeves, which hit just above my wrists.

"Better than nothing," Betty said as she watched me struggle with the sweatshirt. I wanted to hit her.

Dad only wrote me three letters during the month I was gone, but they meant the most to me. At home Mom sometimes made fun of him. She'd laugh about how he had asked someone if her earrings were "looms" when he meant heirlooms, or how he mispronounced "co-lo-nel" in front of company. She made fun of his spelling and said he couldn't write, that's why he was a PE major. He was not my first choice to proofread school essays. His letters to me in Rome were short and to the point:

My Darling Daughter

Keep working hard and do your level best. I know you will win. All your races follow instructions and give till it hurts. The rewards will be the greatest in your young career. What you have already won will be peanuts in comparison to a Gold Medal in the Olympics one or more.

I am sending a note for Coach Haines. Will you give it to him.

Good health and lots of success

Love, Dad

This was the first letter I'd ever gotten from my dad. I read it twice and thought about what he said about rewards. It seemed like when you got something big, something you really wanted for a long time, that it was hard to be satisfied. As soon as you got the reward, you thought of something else better. It wasn't enough to make the Olympic team. Now I had to win a "Gold Medal...or more."

The next time he wrote, he called me sis: *A week from today is your first race and a week Tuesday is the fly. I can hardly wait. Enough about races. I know you are plenty keyed up. Try to keep calm and be relaxed—but with determination.* This sounded like Dad, advising me to take it easy at the same time he was bursting with excitement. He went on, *Richard is working out. You brag about his muscles when you get home. Say hello to all the girls and good luck every day. We all say our prayers daily—you do the same. Love, Dad.*

I love you too, I thought and wished he were here in Rome to give me a rubdown before the prelims, following with his roughhouse tousle that always made me feel like I was tough and he was proud of me.

Mom wrote me every day, sometimes twice a day. The aerograms arrived at Villaggio Olimpico about two o'clock each afternoon. "Geez, you get a lot of mail." Shirley laughed. Some were from classmates and neighbors, and some from complete strangers. Mostly they came from Mom. She reported on who had called and who she'd seen and what was in the paper. Like at home, you didn't have to listen to understand her messages.

After the chatty part, she'd start the guilt trip: Why hadn't I written to Mrs. Leovich? Marthadent hadn't heard from me yet. Coach was feeling hurt I hadn't written. She'd slip in that she wondered where my letters home could be. She hadn't heard a thing since New York.

I had written home once. There really wasn't much time, and I didn't have anything to say: I slept, I got up, I ate, I swam, we rode around in a bus; back at the Village, I slept or talked to Shirley or listened in on conversations. I didn't want to write letters.

Mom's other main topic was shopping. She and Dad had given me one hundred dollars in traveler's checks to spend in Rome. At first she wrote to spend it on anything I wanted, *Something that will be treasured or something unique in clothes that you really want badly—that isn't out of reason.* She always added a limit. I told her I'd been invited to stay at the Burkes' in Flushing after we came home, and she wrote, *I hope you see Rockefeller Center and the United Nations and some cathedrals but* not *Coney Island. That would be* bad *just before your trip home with school and make-up work ahead of you.*

When the next stack of mail arrived, I lay on my bed reading

Mom's aerograms, two written on Sunday. She had a new idea she'd read about in a magazine, *Something that might be nice for you to start collecting—to put on a gold charm bracelet—a charm from Rome and also from New York. It's a lasting memento and always a good conversation piece. Will you be going to Paris?*

A bracelet? I didn't wear bracelets. Conversation pieces? Why would I be going to Paris? I understood now why Richard got so mad at her. She just parroted something she'd read about, probably in *Seventeen* magazine. Mom was like the Italian boys who only saw what they wanted to see. She kept at something until she got what she wanted. She'd present me with a gold bracelet when I got home, and I'd better have a gold charm from Rome to put on it. *And not,* she wrote, *some piece of junk or trinket that will seem silly to you later.*

She always ended her letter with a prayer to stay well and strong or to get in TIP TOP shape or to do my very best. When she hadn't heard from me in a week, she started her worries. *I have a vision of you working so hard you are too exhausted to write.* I reread her lines, *Bet you are tired of all my scribblings. I don't have the technique of Mr. Burke.* She must have felt she couldn't compete with Bob Burke who could get anybody to talk and laugh and who soon would be in Rome. If she couldn't be there, too, she longed to hear about it all, to know what I was eating and how I was sleeping and what it looked like in Rome.

I sat on my lumpy bed, mattress stuffed with gunnysacks, in the corner of our sweltering room, and I sort of wished she was there to get mad at. I missed her asking if I was tired so I could answer: "*No!* I'm not tired. I'm *hot!*" I couldn't do that with my roommates nearby. I had to be quiet. Actually I'd been quiet for about a month, ever since we'd left Portland. I missed goofing off with the kids on the team and yelling at Steve next door and slamming the screen at home.

I missed Mom's worrying too. If she were here now, she'd be worried that my first race was the day after the Opening Ceremony. I imagined her telling me that I'd get too hot walking from the Olympic Village to the stadium and then standing out there in the sun all afternoon. "You

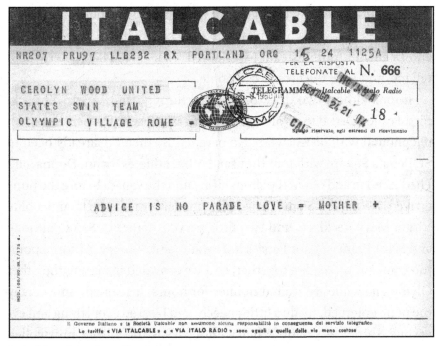

Italcable advice from Portland

better remember why you're at the Olympics, dear. If you get overtired, you'll get sick," she might warn me. "You won't do your best if you're all worn out." My thoughts bumped into each other, the desires and cautions, and I tried to sort them.

All the athletes from every country were invited to Vatican City on the day before the Opening Ceremony for an audience with Pope John XXIII. Attendance was voluntary, George told us, but I would definitely be there. Mom had added a PS in three of her letters: *Don't forget Patsy's holy water. You owe her for that collect call.* It was the next day, the Opening Ceremony, that worried me.

When Joan Spillane left the room, I asked Shirley if she thought I should march in the Opening Ceremony parade. I didn't want to sound uncertain in front of Joan, but with Shirley I didn't care. Shirley said she thought the parade would be a very long walk and our parade shoes, the pointy ones, would be murder.

"Why don't you ask George what he thinks?" she said.

But I felt shy. George didn't feel like my coach; he belonged to Chris and Lynn and Ann. Instead, I wondered what Coach Schlueter would tell me, and I got the idea to call home.

It took almost two days to get a call through and an answer back. First I called Dad at the store to ask him to ask Coach. The next day Mom telephoned with his answer: "No parade." By then I'd already been to St. Peter's Square with four thousand other athletes. Lynn, Donna, and I had raced in and out of the shops all around the square before the pope arrived. I bought a Saint Christopher medal for good luck, and a blue Virgin Mary necklace, and two little carved statues of Saint Anthony and Saint Francis. I got Patsy's holy water and a rosary. At some point the US team was called together, and we crowded in among the other Olympians while we waited in lines for hours, it seemed, until finally the pope emerged, made a little speech, and blessed everything and everyone. Shirley was right. When we got back to the Village, my swollen toes wailed and my feet screamed.

CITIUS, ALTIUS, FORTIUS

1960

WHEN THE UNITED STATES TEAM marched into Stadio Olimpico and the crowd around us jumped up to cheer, I felt sorry to be in the stands with Bob Burke. The USA uniforms looked sharp on the athletes as they marched in tight formation, four abreast, behind our flag bearer, Rafer Johnson.

"Why's my race tomorrow?" I moaned, wanting to be down on the field with our team. I knew the answer. I needed to do well in the preliminaries to qualify for the semis, but I felt like I had years before when Mom made me come home early from the slumber party—like a baby.

Bob reached around my shoulders, hugged me, and assured me I was smart not to waste energy walking around all day. "Priorities," he said, and together we tried to spot Lynn down on the field. She didn't have any races for a week.

After all eighty-three countries marched in, an Italian athlete took the Olympic Oath for the rest of us. Up on the stadium's huge scoreboard, the Olympic Creed flashed across in almost every language: *The important thing in the Olympic Games is not winning but taking part. The essential thing in life is not conquering but fighting well.* Mom had sent me that quote in her last letter. It was the ideal, but we swimmers believed that we were there to win our races. Bob nudged me and said, "Winning's good, too, right, brat?"

Most of the athletes standing out there representing their countries would not be competing for medals. Most wouldn't even make finals. In Rome, over 5,300 participants (600 female) vied for 450 medals. The majority of competitors came for the higher principles of the Olympics: to do their best, to compete in peace, to forge friendships. But Coach expected me to win a medal. So did my parents and everyone else back home. My mission was completely different from those others'. I wasn't supposed to go *citius, altius, fortius*—"faster, higher, stronger"—but fastest.

All the flag bearers stepped forward and formed a semicircle while an Italian hoisted up the Olympic flag with its five colored rings. Right when the Italian president declared Le Giochi della XVII Olimpiade open, cannons roared five times, and hundreds of white doves flew up from the field and out into the late-afternoon sky. In the midst of all this, a single runner entered the stadium with the Olympic torch, circled the track once, and climbed to the top rim of the stands. He turned and stood silhouetted against the sky, raised his arm, and the big cauldron beside him burst into flame while all the bells in Rome began to chime.

"Geez," I kept saying. "Geez." I tried not to cry.

On the way back to the Village, Bob told me to pack a bag for one or two nights. He said that George was moving Chris and me to a hotel so that we could have a good night's rest. We'd be in the same hotel where all the parents were staying, the von Saltzas, the Botkins, Bob.

"You mean leave the team?"

Bob said that the parents had all discussed it and raised enough money so the night before a race, swimmers could have air conditioning, a good bed, and quiet.

"Chris'll be there too?" I sounded as worried as my mother might have if she'd heard this. "We won't get disqualified?"

Bob laughed and promised. "It's legit, brat. George's idea. This heat is killing us all."

So I had a room to myself at the Hotel Caesar Augustus that night, and if I qualified for semifinals, I'd be there the next one too.

US Women's Swimming and Diving Team in Rome. Back: Betty Baldwin, Molly Botkin, Lynn Burke, Nina Harmer, Joan Spillane, Chris von Saltza, Patsy Willard, Sylvia Ruuska, George Haines, Ann Warner, and Carolyn Wood. Front: Patty Kempner, Carolyn Schuler, Susan Doerr, Juno Irwin, Donna de Varona, Carolyn House, Shirley Stobs, Paula Jean Pope, and Sammy Lee.

When Chris and I got to the pool for the preliminaries of the first race in the Olympics, our teammates had finished their workout and were heading back to the Village for lunch. They wished us luck; everyone expected us to make the semis without their cheers. After we warmed up in an outside lane, George instructed us to "stay loose, swim easy"—all we had to do was win our heats. I could do that.

White-uniformed officials herded us onto seats set behind the blocks. There must have been more than fifty of us waiting to swim the hundred meters. Because more than half were really slow swimmers from countries that didn't have developed training programs or pools, each heat took forever while the last girl struggled to finish. The Olympic Creed, the bit about not winning but taking part, applied to almost everybody swimming the 100-meter freestyle. My time qualified me fifth for the semifinals. Two races later, Chris set a new Olympic record. She hadn't followed George's instruction to swim easy.

At the hotel for a second night, Chris stayed with her parents, and I was alone in my room with nothing to do. I explored the hotel for a while and found some steps up to the roof. From there I looked out across the ancient city. Hazy hills rose in the distance, clusters of dusty trees squeezed among the squatty, red-roofed buildings. It was too hot to be outside. On the roof it felt as hot as Detroit, heavy and thick, too much to bear.

Back in my room I reread Coach's letter. *You are a well-poised champion now and your training and natural confidence will serve you under pressure. I do hope that you will remember to 'control your power' and use it on Fraser, or anyone who may be near you at the right time. You can win that 100 free at the Games.* I'd controlled my power in the prelims, all right, and it hadn't felt very good. Questions and thoughts rolled around in my head until Bob finally arrived to take me to dinner.

He carried the conversation while we ate. The girls had sent greetings, especially Shirley, who told him she missed my mess in the corner. I liked that. He shared stories about the team but nothing about Lynn until I asked.

"Lynn sends a big hello and a sock in the arm." He reached across the table and pretended to hit me. I liked it when he teased me. It felt more like home.

The next day when we got to the pool, the team talked about a Danish cyclist who had died. Donna de Varona said he had died of heat stroke, but Molly Botkin, who knew more than anyone about what went on behind the scenes, said she heard he took uppers, that all the cyclists took pills. She told us that the officials were changing the starting times of certain events, like the marathon, because of the heat. In the dressing room, the girls complained that it was *so* hot, *too* hot in Rome. Chatter rippled past me. I needed to concentrate, but I liked listening to English again and hearing the netter-natter of swim kids together.

"Don't forget your sweats," Shirley teased before she left me to psych up for the semis.

My time qualified me for the finals, but it was even slower than in the prelims. I'd been in the same heat as Dawn Fraser, who smashed the Olympic record Chris had set on Friday. I wasn't even close. With no races on Sunday and the final not until Monday night, Chris and I returned to the Village for some fresh clothes and to pick up mail. The dorm room didn't feel that hot, and I really wanted to stay with the rest of the team, not alone in Hotel Caesar Augustus.

I took a bunch of new letters from home with me to the hotel and read Donnie's first:

Dear Funny One,

I sure would like to be there with you, but maybe my time will come in 1964. I hope we both can be there one way or another. Be sure and tell me all about it. Good luck in all your races, and the way you are going you just might win the butterfly.

Don

I wished that he were in Rome to talk to. By the time he got a letter to tell him all about it, all my races would be over.

I shuffled through Mom's letters, checked their postmarks, and read them in order. *I hope you weren't disappointed about the parade, but I'll bet you did want to be in it,* she wrote. *I pray you will win the butterfly so you can be on that relay because I know how* much *that will mean to you—you can do it—and everyone says you can and this time I believe them.* She was almost admitting she hadn't believed in me before. And she knew and understood my reason for wanting to make the team. I read on. *Some say get 3 or 4. They just don't understand, do they, what a tough order gold medals are. But I do and I'm proud of you no matter what you do—you've done plenty already to satisfy me.*

That's when I started to cry, my palms pressed over my eyes and forehead, fingers through my hair. I sat crying on the bed until I couldn't sit anymore. I got up and climbed back to the roof, but all my thoughts made me cry: *My freestyle times are too slow. I want to go back to the Village and see Lynn and listen to my roommates. My time is too slow. I'm too slow. I'm out of shape. I'm too slow.*

I shambled back down the stairs to my room and tried the door. Locked. I'd left without my key. Late-afternoon sun filtered in through a high window over the silent stairs, the halls empty. I sat on the steps and wept deep, wracking waves. I couldn't think anymore, and I couldn't stop. Tears took time away. It may have been an hour or fifteen minutes or all day before someone touched my shoulder and spoke softly in a foreign language. I didn't look, my face wet with tears and snot. He kept talking and patting my shoulder and back. I quieted, hiccuped, gasped for breath. He murmured some more, put his hand under my arm, coaxed me up, and gently led me to a room where he sat me down on the bed. I peered up at him through swollen eyes. He pointed at my sweats. "OoooSa," he said and motioned me to lie down. I curled on my side, still crying a little. The door closed. Some time later he returned with Bob Burke.

After the tears I felt empty, lost, and hopeless. "I got locked out of my room," I told Bob.

"What else, Woody?"

"I swam terrible."

"It's only the semis. You're holding out for the finals. And you have butterfly prelims Monday too. You're saving, the way George wants you to." He talked softly, not kidding around at all.

I wondered if George really wanted me to swim better. If I did what Coach said in his letter, I'd beat Chris. George wouldn't want that, I bet. But I didn't say that to Bob. When we got into my room, he sat down with me and asked if I felt homesick. I started to well up again. "I wish..."

"Your mom and dad could be here to see you race?" he asked.

"I guess." But that was only part of it. "I just wish Lynn and I were roommates like we planned and that we were on the relay for sure." George had told us at a practice that whoever won the butterfly final in

Rome, Carolyn Schuler or me, would swim in the medley relay final. Our place at the trials, me ahead of her, didn't count. Only the final in Rome.

Bob consoled me. He said that Lynn felt nervous, too, because everybody expected her to win. It was a lot of pressure to carry around inside, and she had to wait more than a week to compete while everybody else had races.

"Yes, but..." I didn't finish. I didn't even know what I wanted to say. The Olympics weren't anything like I thought they'd be. I couldn't have imagined what it would be like to be somewhere far away where nobody spoke English and everything that was usually cold would be warm, like water and milk and Coke. I didn't think we'd be eating in giant cafeterias and that American food would all taste like pizza, or that dorm rooms would be hot and stuffy, the beds as lumpy as our backyard. I guess I thought it would be a series of happy events, like when we played as little kids: let's be in college now; let's go to a dance; let's pretend our bikes are horses; let's play store, you buy cookies and then we'll take them home. In my dreams, Lynn and Chris and I would be roommates. We'd march in the opening parade. Then we'd be on a relay and win. After that, we'd play a prank on somebody and not get caught. It would all happen like fast cuts in a movie. But the Olympics weren't anything like that. It went on day after day after day. And right now I was stuck far away in a hotel waiting to swim the butterfly prelims and the freestyle finals, and I did not feel very good.

Bob told me to put on my suit and he'd give me a rubdown to get rid of the knots in my legs and lumps in my back. "This'll get you ready for tomorrow."

When he rubbed my back, the tender spots between my shoulders screamed, but I stayed quiet until something popped into my mind. "Chris told me they aren't keeping the pool filled enough. She said to watch out for the wave."

"That's right," Bob said. "We're sending a protest." He rubbed in the wintergreen oil and pushed his thumbs into my shoulder blades, and I kept talking.

"There aren't any gutters at the ends, so a big wave builds up, and when you turn, you have to swim past it or you might choke. She said it happened to her."

Bob said he thought it happened when the field was spread out like it was in the preliminaries.

"If I hit the wave and choked with twenty-five meters to go, I could hold my breath and power in," I told Bob after a few minutes. "I know I could do that because of Jim Campbell's no-breath twenty-fives. But if I choked with more than twenty-five—"

"You're not going to hit a wave," Bob assured me. They would fill up the pool for finals, he said. And I could miss the wave by taking a few strokes no breath off the turn.

I don't know what put those thoughts in my head. Maybe I needed to invent worries so someone would reassure me. Maybe I was trying to pull up those inner voices that could spur me on: Jim shouting, "Guts. Guts, ladies and gentlemen. Show me you've got guts." Or Tye saying, "Get steamed up and go, go, go."

I felt better after talking to Bob, like when my dad gave me rubdowns on swim-meet weekends and believed I'd do my best. Mom's last letter said it was raining at home. I wished it would rain in Rome.

The butterfly prelims, scheduled for noon on Monday, would serve as a perfect warm-up for the freestyle final, George told me, which was exactly what Coach had said in Detroit. Butterfly and freestyle on the same day, a good warm-up.

"Just qualify," George reminded me.

The Detroit trials seemed far away now, back where everything was still hope. I'd traveled past hope into lonely, murky waters. I couldn't shake the doubts about my preparation. I wished Coach had entered me in double events all summer so I'd be used to it, that his workouts had been harder so George's wouldn't leave me feeling so tired. And I wished he hadn't given me a vitamin that people suspected was a pep pill. Even rereading his letter didn't make me believe I could beat anybody.

Dutch swimmer Atie Voorbij and me after the butterfly preliminaries

I finished first in my butterfly heat and qualified third overall, a couple of seconds slower than in Detroit. *Good enough*, I thought. Carolyn Schuler, however, did what Chris had done in the freestyle prelim—set an Olympic record. She wanted to be on the medley relay.

Officials kept the finalists for the 100-meter freestyle, the first women's final in the Games, isolated in the dressing room after warm-ups. Nobody was allowed near us. Garbled Italian drifted in from the stadium loudspeakers.

"Let us out," I muttered. "We're trapped in here."

Dawn Fraser looked at me and laughed. Outside on the deck, we could see about twenty young women lined up, all of them wearing white dresses. An older official in the dressing room started putting us into a line.

"I want to be behind Chris," I said. But the official didn't speak English or she wasn't listening. She shuffled me into line for lane two.

"Doo-ay," she insisted.

Chris and Dawn lined up behind me somewhere. The young women marched on either side of us along the deck to our lanes, where we were seated behind our blocks while they introduced us one by one. Too nervous to sit, I stood and jumped up and down and swung my arms back and forth. I wished Donna de Varona was in the race so she'd false start like she had in Detroit, but no one in the final did.

The race went by so fast, I couldn't even remember what happened. Before the gun, the pool looked beautiful and still, its lights in the walls and on the bottom creating the illusion of an aquamarine rectangle about to lift off into the black night. The stands may have been full, but I didn't notice. Dawn Fraser beat Chris by more than a second. I finished fourth.

The opening Olympic race was over. I had taken part and fought well like the creed exhorted. But tomorrow would be different. Tomorrow would be my night. I'd know all about being held in the dressing room and marching in and how to get psyched. I'd be ready. Now, it was back to the Caesar Augustus.

Fortius.

Citius.

RACES

2012

TWO DAYS BEFORE THE US presidential election, a storm blows across the Camino, drenching everyone walking. Twice I stop to empty my boots and wring out my socks. But the next day breaks cold and clear, with hunters and hounds out in the fields stalking rabbits. A single-lane road weaves through the cut and tilled fields up toward forested ridges and back down to a smattering of ochre-colored brick buildings with red-tile roofs. Blue sky stretches over the autumnal landscape. On a path that veers off the road, I find a small rock printed with black felt-tip pen: *God and Santiago please Vote for Obama.* I add it to a pile of stones beside the trail with my best wishes.

The omnipresent blare of news and analysis, the dismal speculations and terrifying threats from party operatives, the nonstop barrage of advertising have all but disappeared for me in Spain. Not that there aren't televisions in every cafe, bodega, or taverna, wall mounted and chattering away. But here fútbol, Basque separatist arrests, and Hurricane Sandy take priority.

Four years ago, Rose and I were in Utrecht, Holland, for the presidential election. She'd mounted a show in the city hall there, and we'd watched television late into the night as results came in until finally they declared Obama winner. The next morning, every newspaper ran full-page headlines and people on the streets beamed, everyone hopeful for the future. I'd felt proud to be an American, just as I'd felt in Rome watching Rafer Johnson carry the flag in the Opening Ceremony. Here on the Camino, you could almost forget that the vote was coming.

Wednesday morning after the election, I wake early, so excited to hear the news that I dress and leave before anyone else has stirred. In the darkness I twice lose the way and have to retrace my steps. Even with daylight, the trail markers are hard to locate, and soon I'm off the direct route, instead wandering through vineyards and hillside neighborhoods all the while eyeing my destination, which lies tauntingly distant. The approach to town is excruciatingly long, and I feel the old insistence that I am missing out on something up ahead. Who has won? Finally on the town outskirts, I duck into an open cafe and see the news. What a relief! But that familiar feeling—anxiety and urgency to know an outcome that will not change whether or not I want it to—leaves me feeling unsettled and edgy the rest of the day.

Over a pilgrim dinner and a glass of wine offered by the host to celebrate Obama's victory, I consider the day. We've grown accustomed to living with that anxiety of missing out, tuning in to television, podcasts, radio, and computer, checking Facebook, email, Instagram, all the while missing the moments we are experiencing—the catch in our breath, the bee in the hellebores, the stone on the trail with a prayer printed in felt-tip pen. I haven't brought a camera on the Camino because I want to encounter it all without a screen between me and the experience. Later, what will remain are those moments, the burning images that made a connection, that carried meaning.

A few years ago, I took a trip to India while Rose was working, and my group sailed on the Ganges in Varanasi at sunset. Butter lamps floated out from shore, priests and worshippers chanted on the banks, and sitar music drifted from another craft, but my friends who'd started out taking photos became obsessed with showing each other their images and videos. "Watch this," someone said. "Look what I got." They huddled over their tiny screens, each insisting they had the best pictures while our boat passed smoking ghats and temples and evening bathers, the night rising around us, the lamp flames flickering and vanishing among the river currents. For a long time, I had worked to disregard pointless competitions.

On the Camino I rarely feel the urge to compete. A good part of my childhood was spent practicing to win—that was the point of racing, whether to beat my brother in finishing dinner or to place first in the butterfly. When Mo Murphy gave a speech after she returned from the Melbourne Games, she concluded with an inspirational rhyme attributed to Saint Jerome, "Good, better, best. Never let it rest. 'Til your good is better and your better is best." What I heard then was: "Don't quit until you are best," a terrible misunderstanding that took years to untangle. Now on the Camino, I am in practice—not to be best or first but to be awake. There is no need to hurry. It is not a race but a walk, a wander, a meander, an opportunity to slow down. It is the opposite of competing in Rome.

In June when I thought about finding the gutsy girl I'd been, the defiant child at the lake first came to mind. But I couldn't separate her from the swimmer, the competitor. The tough little girl I sought at the beginning of my walk is part of a well-crafted story that entertains and sustains me. She doesn't exist in my past like some character in a book, but within me. She's walked along the trails just as she's raced down the pool and will accompany me into the future. We have much to offer each other. *Finish hard to the wall*, she reminds me. *Look. Stay awake*, I reply.

RACE DAYS

August–September 1960

When we got to the pool the night of the butterfly final, Shirley snuck into the dressing room with piles of letters. I opened a couple of Mom's and skimmed through. *Everyone's reading the sports page—even Grandma's friends.* That made me laugh. I opened one of the blue-and-white Italcables, Italy's version of Western Union. It was from the Multnomah Club's manager: GOOD GIRL TOMORROW YOU WILL WIN A MEDAL VERNE PERRY.

I set the pile aside. I didn't want to be reading about yesterday or predictions for tonight. I lay back on the bench, my eyes closed, then sat up again and thumbed through the aerograms and letters. One plain white postcard addressed in pencil stood out. I turned it over. A line curved across the card with two stick figures, one on skis holding its poles out, the other flat on its back, one ski loose. Under the line was boldly printed: DON'T FORGET BETSY SNITE*!!!* At the bottom in cursive: *What an artist, huh. Oh well, you get the idea. Sheila*

I looked at the card for a long time. Sheila? I couldn't think who that was, until I remembered my locker-mate from school—Sheila Herman. *What does she mean?* I wondered. *Does she mean don't fall down? Don't blow it?* I remembered us laughing and making fun of all the publicity Betsy Snite's fall got. *Does she think…?* I didn't let myself finish the thought and buried the card in the stack of mail. It should have made me mad.

As Shirley left, Lynn came in to wish me luck. She said that she'd be sitting right at the finish screaming her head off. She was all confidence for me. "You're going to be first with a world record. I know it. And Friday—gold on the relay." She added a reminder to swim through the wave and scooted out to get her seat.

I couldn't see Carolyn Schuler because she'd gone around the back side of the lockers. The Dutch girls sat together laughing. They didn't worry me. Nobody's time was even close to Schuler's and mine. I spread my towel on the floor next to the frosted glass wall. Pool lights filtered in through the stands, creating angled shadows. *Get psyched*, I thought. *Get psyched.* I hummed "Worried Man" in my head and stomped my feet up and down. From outside came distorted announcements in Italian, cheers, silence, and the gun: the start of the men's 200-meter breaststroke.

My stomach fluttered. Fifteen minutes left. Cheers and clapping, a few whistles seeped through the dressing-room doors. The crowd noises rose and fell with each turn, and then a roar on the final lap. I lay on my back listening and not listening, floating in that prerace emptiness. The wave of noise ebbed. I kept my eyes closed until the announcer started up again. *He must be announcing the next race*, I thought, *ours*. I hit my fist against the glass wall—once—twice. It shook with a flat rattle right next to my ear. The woman in white from the night before walked by, pulling the swimmer for lane one by her arm, dictating in Italian and sign language for the rest of us to line up behind her.

Everything seemed in slow motion compared to the night before. Sandwiched between our Italian-girl guides, we stepped through the cold footbath and walked into the darkness between the bright-blue pool and the steeply rising stands. As soon as I got to my lane, I pulled off my sweats and plunged into the light, took three or four quick butterfly strokes, and rolled into an easy crawl. I swam almost to the end, flopped onto my back for a few strokes, and flipped over again into a quick sprint. My heart sped up. In the next lane, I could see streams

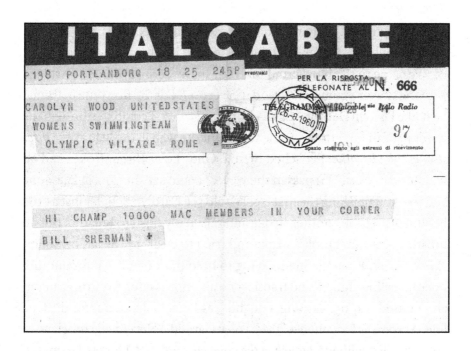

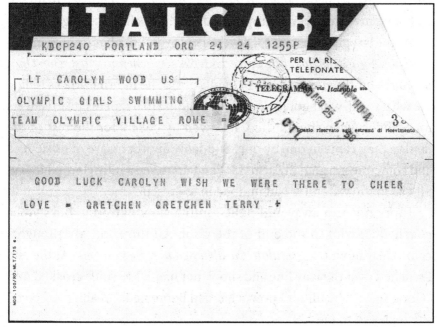

Italcables from Portland

of bubbles from Carolyn Schuler's nose as she raced past me. Tonight everything looked clear, each bubble edged in silver.

We came to the blocks and took our marks, crowd sounds dissolved with the starter's commands, and we were off. For the first time in Rome, I felt like I had in Detroit—light, effortless, strong. I could see through the water in both directions. At the turn, I hit the wall in the lead. *Take three strokes then breathe*, I coached myself. One. Two. Three strokes and up for a breath. Clear! I'd passed the wave. I could see the girls in lanes one and two still finishing the first lap. I could see Carolyn Schuler just a little behind me. I took another stroke and raised my head to breathe. But no breath. All water. I took a stroke and tried to clear my throat, my lungs. *Relax. Relax*, I commanded, trying to hold back panic. Up for another breath, feeling choked and frantic—no air, more water. My arms caught, and I raised way up, gasping, coughing as I reached out, out for the lane line. As soon as I touched it, Tye's voice warned, "Never hang on a lane or you'll be disqualified." *I touched the lane. Disqualified*, I howled to myself and hung my arms over the ropes, coughing, spitting, starting to cry.

As the last girl swam past, I covered my eyes, breath returning in ragged sobs. *Finish the race*, one voice said. *No, let them finish first. Don't butt in. You're off the medley relay.* I couldn't stop the internal voices telling me what to do, what not to do, what was going to happen. I heard cheers for Schuler when she finished, followed by cheers for the rest of the field as they came in one by one. Suddenly another wave of noise rose and someone grasped my arm. I looked up to see a fully clothed Italian official in the water. He had jumped in to "rescue" me.

I tore my arm away and pulled into a slow butterfly. Jim's voice coached, "Swim to the end of the pool. All the way." My thoughts came clear now: *Congratulate Carolyn Schuler. Be gracious.* At the end I reached over the lane line and shook her hand. My voice croaked out, "Good race." She didn't know what had happened. "Yeah, good race," she repeated to me.

Timers and officials leaned over my lane and tried to help me out. I pushed myself up onto the deck right as Betty Baldwin came running.

She grabbed my shoulders and wrapped a towel around me, asking questions I didn't want to hear. "What happened? Are you all right?"

"Where's Lynn?" I asked her calmly.

She held on to me, babbling.

"I want to see Lynn. Let me go."

She patted my back and pulled me toward her as I strained to get away. A lady wearing a nurse uniform rushed up and grasped my arm; I dragged them both along behind me, trying to escape. I wanted to be alone. I wanted to find Lynn or Bob. When finally Lynn appeared, I yanked free of the nurse, elbowed Betty Baldwin, and ran into her hug. We walked behind the diving pool, sat down, and cried, and after a while I started to laugh, and then she did too. She didn't even ask what happened.

We sat on the steps up to the cafe behind the pools. She would swim the medley relay preliminaries the next day, and I would too. "Even if it's not the finals, we'll be on one relay together," she said. So my wish would come true, sort of. At the opposite end of the pool, the small band began to play "The Star-Spangled Banner," but they played only half of it, no longer than it took to raise the flag. Carolyn Schuler had her gold medal, and now she'd probably get another on the medley relay instead of me.

George sent me back to the Village that night. "You better cable your parents," he told me. "They'll be worried." Inside the compound I found the Italcable stand and wired home: *AM FAIRING WELL GOT SOME WATER GET THEM NEXT TIME DON'T WORRY LOVE CAROLYN.*

Someone shook me awake in the morning for a long-distance call.

"Oh, honey, are you all right? They showed it on the TV. You must be devastated," my mom's voice wavered over the line.

"I'm okay now."

She went on and on.

"I'm okay, Mom. I just choked." I wasn't going to go into every detail on the phone in the middle of the team apartment. Besides, she'd already written that it had cost four dollars a second when I'd called about the parade. "Today's the medley relay prelims, and I'm swimming," I told her.

"Are you too disappointed?" she asked again.

"No, Mom. It was only a couple of gold medals, that's all." I sounded like Richard with his sarcastic voice, but I wished she sounded mad at what happened and not so sorry. I wanted encouragement for the next race, not pity for the past. I told her to tell Dad hi for me. "I'm okay, Mom, really," I finished.

After the medley relay prelims were over—and because the freestyle relay, the last event for swimming, was Saturday night—I had two nights in the Village before our whole relay would go to the Caesar Augustus. Donna de Varona and Ann Warner showed me where I could get a haircut. We visited the girls track team on the floor above us and sat trading stories while they straightened their hair. Mostly I listened. I sent postcards home to Richard and Auntie Mildred with official Olympic stamps on them. I liked being with the team again.

Both nights we went to the pool to cheer. Ann Warner finished sixth in the breaststroke on Wednesday. Thursday night, Lynn, Patty Kempner, Carolyn Schuler, and Chris won the medley relay, the first time it had been part of the Olympic program. I sat with Ann Warner and Donna de Varona and everybody else on the team. When Lynn set a world record on her backstroke leg, we jumped up and down and acted crazy even though nobody else was even close. USA beat Australia by almost five seconds. Ann leaned over and said that we should have been on that relay. I nodded, feeling a mixture of anger and sadness. When the awards ceremony started, I wanted to be with them atop the podium celebrating a victory. Instead, I cheered my regrets away as they presented the gold medals to the USA. At least I still had the freestyle relay, but Ann was finished.

I knew I would be on the freestyle relay because Friday morning George had set us up for a swim-off time trial: Molly Botkin, Shirley Stobs, Donna de Varona, Sylvia Ruuska, and me. Afterward, when

I'd beaten them all, Bob Burke told me that *certain parties* wanted me off the relay because I was a "head case."

"I fought like the dickens for you, baby doll. George had to do the time trial to get them off his back. You proved you belong."

"I didn't know that's why we had a time trial. I thought..." My voice drifted off because I hadn't really thought about it at all. It was just another race.

"You know what George said afterward?"

I shook my head.

"He said, 'Something like this happens to a real fighter and it's tougher than if it happens to a quitter who looks for condolences. Carolyn Wood is a fighter.'"

"He said that?"

"He did. I can't wait to see your split on the relay."

Bob made me feel determined.

By Saturday night Chris and I had swum six races in nine days—seven for me, counting the time trial. Joan Spillane had only raced the medley relay prelims, and Shirley hadn't had a single competition except the time trial on Friday. She did have an Italian boyfriend, though. Mom had written to me, *You haven't said anything about the recreation area. Is that where Shirley met her fella?* I didn't even know there was a recreation area. There were a lot of athletes at the Games following the creed, "It's more important to take part." If you were trying to win races, the Olympics were a whole different experience.

We grouped together in the dressing room waiting for our relay, the last event for swimming in 1960, scheduled after the men's 1500-meter freestyle. We'd already watched Lynn win her race and receive her second gold medal. When the band played "God Save the Queen" for John Konrads's win in the 1500 freestyle, I started singing "My Country, 'Tis of Thee." Shirley joined me softly, and then we all gathered volume so that by the end, our whole relay belted out, "From every mountainside, let freeeeedom ring!"

In 1956 Australia had won almost every gold medal in swimming. In Rome they only had one gold to our four. They wanted to beat us in the freestyle relay. Shirley Stobs led us off with a 1:03.3 against mighty Dawn Fraser, who was attempting another world record. When Joan Spillane took off, we were far behind, and she hardly gained on their second swimmer. Chris gave me a quick fist pound up and down my back before I stepped up on the block.

"Okay, Woody. Get me a lead." I looked over to see that Lorraine Crapp, the star of Melbourne, was Australia's number three swimmer.

Oh, Crapp. I'm going to crap on you. I made myself laugh. "Crap," I said out loud when she took off three or four seconds ahead of me. This felt like those races Tye used to set up—only this time I wasn't holding off the big kids racing after me. I was chasing the big kid.

By the fifty we were almost even. Bob told me later he feared I'd blown it all on the first lap, but I had a lot of mad to burn. I had a team, and we wanted the gold. At seventy-five meters I couldn't see anyone on either side. I gave Chris a one-meter lead for her last leg, and we smashed the world and Olympic records: 4:08.9.

Bob shouted something at me from the stands that sounded like, "Jesusjosephandmary, you head case, you had the fastest split."

When the little band stopped playing as the flag reached the top, we finished our national anthem singing it together. The presenters hung gold medals around our necks and gave us long white cases to store them in, as well as a bouquet of flowers for each of us. And that was it. The Olympics were over for swimmers.

A Japanese reporter interviewed me afterward. "You'll be back for Tokyo in 1964, won't you? You'll be back for that medal you lost?" I'd had lots of time to think about this question since the butterfly. Everybody said, "Oh, you'll have another chance. You're so young." But I remembered Nancy Ramey and Carin Cone. They'd trained for four years and planned to return for the gold medals they'd missed in Melbourne. Their parents had plane tickets and hotel reservations and everything. And then some fourteen-year-old beat them, and they didn't even make the team as alternates. I didn't want that to happen to me.

Olympic champions, world record holders in 400-meter freestyle relay: Chris von Saltza, Joan Spillane, me, and Shirley Stobs

"I won't be in Tokyo," I told the reporter. "I'll be in college. You can't really train after high school unless you don't go on to school. This is it for me. I'm really glad I got to be here. I'm proud to be on the team."

Even though it was after midnight when we got back to the Village, I had to call home. This time I got to talk to both Mom and Dad. Dad was so excited.

"You did it, sis. I knew you would. A gold medal!" He couldn't stop talking even at four dollars a second. "You're a real champion. You proved it when you swam to the end of the pool after that muggie. You finished that race. I'm so proud of you."

"You can learn a lot from losing," I told him, not completely sure what I meant.

"Here's Mother. Remember, you're going to be the best next year. Now have some fun." He handed off the phone. For Dad the future always had that promise of delight. The next pull on the slot might yield the pot; his dog in the next race might win. He told me once that when he got a nickel on the ranch for doing something extra, he could hardly wait to get to town and spend it. "I'd talk to Louis or Bertha all week long about what I could get—some penny candy or an orange. Ruth always said, 'If you save up, you could buy a baseball,' but I just couldn't ever do it. I'd think about that candy jar." Mom would have been worrying about cavities, probably. When she got on the phone, though, she was excited, too, until she asked if I was tired and started fretting about me in New York.

"When are you coming home?" she asked as I was hanging up.

In bed I couldn't sleep for the longest time. I'd won a gold medal, even if it was only for a relay. And I'd bombed a big race. What *had* I learned from losing the butterfly? Some people like you better when they feel sorry for you. They were different from the people who wanted to be friends or hang around you when you won. But it was more than that. Mostly you learned about yourself. That you can go on. It's not the end of the world if you lose. It's not *On the Beach*.

Once I started thinking, I couldn't stop. Maybe I'd made it happen when I listened to Chris and talked to Bob Burke, when I said out loud my biggest fear: choking with more than twenty-five meters to go. Maybe that postcard had jinxed me. But even though it had happened, even though I'd lost out on a chance for as many medals as Chris—as many as Wilma Rudolph—it didn't kill me. I still came back. Dad liked to say there's always another chance, just like in baseball. There's always another inning, or another game, or the next series. *He's right*, I thought, drifting off to sleep. That relay proved it.

30

BITTERSWEET

September 1960

FOR THE FIRST TIME IN over a year, two years, ever since I'd resolved to make the team, nothing lay ahead—no goal or test, no practice, meet, or trial. Only empty days. The Games of the XVII Olympiad had finished for swimmers. "You should expect a little letdown," my mother would have warned if she'd been there.

The girls whose races had been earlier in the week had already explored the city. They led the rest of us that Sunday on an expedition to the Rome flea markets where Molly knew the best stalls for bargains. Shopping would postpone the inevitable doldrums. One hundred dollars burned in my pocket. Along the way we passed a British woolen shop where I bought some fabric—Stewart Dress and a dark-green plaid that reminded me of Oregon forests. Grandma Green could make me kilts from real Scottish wool, and Mom would be happy that I'd chosen "something unique in clothes," as she'd suggested.

We ambled up the tree-shaded street toward the open-air markets. Ahead of us on the sidewalk, a legless man pulled himself along on a little rolling board. We separated and walked around him. "The war," Chris murmured when we were past. I fought the urge to turn back and look. Despite reading *Battle Cry* and *On the Beach*, or seeing *The Diary of Anne Frank* and *The Young Lions*, at the Olympics, caught up in cheering crowds and white doves, I forgot about wars until I swam in a pool that Mussolini had built for the 1940 war-canceled Games or saw the German team divided between East and West or avoided staring at a war-maimed veteran on the street.

People streamed toward the park where vendors had set up shops under tents. Lynn found a stall selling ski sweaters, and I bought three because I couldn't choose one, as well as linen tea towels and leather gloves for Mom, a vest for Dad, another sweater for Richard, and a little leather coin purse for Grandma Green. We rambled up and down the streets laughing and trying on clothes. Little clusters of boys followed. Sometimes they'd push one boy forward to try out his English, and then he'd back up and disappear into the group. A man recognized Chris and asked for her autograph; a crowd started to push around us, but as soon as she signed, we hurried away. Late in the day, rain clouds gathered, so we headed back to the Village.

On the way we spotted a group of gymnasts practicing routines on mats spread below a men's dormitory. A girl wearing a Soviet sweatshirt noticed us and came over, pulled a green pin with a gold silhouette out of her pocket, pointed at it, and to us. Most of our team who'd stayed in the Village had traded away their pins at the recreation center or at dances, but I still had all we'd been given. This would be my first trade. A couple more Russians came over with all sorts of pins—red with *CCCP* engraved in gold and one with Sputnik. I stopped trading after four pins because I wanted some from other countries too. Chris picked through my treasures and pointed to the green-and-gold pin. "Lenin," she said, "the father of Communism." I'd exchanged pins with Communists, and they weren't anything like what people thought back home. I felt a little puffed up, like some sort of goodwill ambassador fostering friendship.

When we finally got back in our dorm, Betty Baldwin had a message: All medal winners would go by train to Naples on Monday for a reception and banquet sponsored by the International Swimming Federation (FINA). We needed to be ready in parade-day uniform by 9:00 a.m.

Races over for Ann Warner, Lynn, me

We were to bring our tank suits because gold medalists would give an exhibition before dinner.

"This is our first night off in forever. I'm going out tonight," Lynn said. She had a date with a javelin thrower, and she'd even gotten a date for me with a boy from the men's team, someone she knew from Santa Clara. Shirley stepped next to Lynn and announced that she was going out and she'd stay out all night if she wanted to.

Donna and I whistled.

"We leave here at nine o'clock," Betty repeated, unwilling to tangle with them. She had her orders, though. "Nine a.m. Naples."

Outside, the temperature had risen, and hot, heavy clouds grew into thunderheads. A few of us lounged in a room that overlooked the interior quad when lightning struck the concrete next to the door of the balcony. Its white flash and the boom hit simultaneously, deafening us and leaving a black smudge on the deck.

"Oh my God," Molly screamed. "I could have been killed. I was just going outside. Oh my God." Others ran into the room to see.

"It was so loud," we repeated over and over.

"Like being right under fireworks," Donna said.

Bobby Burke's firecrackers! I dug them out of my suitcase and lay the first one on the edge of the balcony to light it. KAPOW. Echoes reverberated in the courtyard.

"Almost as loud as the lightning," Donna said.

"Where'd you get those?" Carolyn House asked in a voice that sounded like, *Naughty naughty!* I set off another one.

Outside, a few girls from the other dorms came onto their balconies and looked around.

"I'm going to throw one out in the center to see if it's louder." I pulled two off the string and twisted the fuses together like I'd seen Richard do, ducked out of the wind below the balcony, and lit the match, holding the double cracker in my left hand. When the flame caught and fizzed, I switched hands and hurled it up and out.

"You hit the Russians' balcony," Molly yelled as the bomb exploded.

From the stairwell we heard Betty Baldwin's voice. "What is going on up there?"

Everyone scattered. I plunged under the sheets, my face to the wall, all feelings of letdown vanished. Outside in the hall, I heard Molly explain that lightning had struck on her balcony. She showed Betty the mark. "It practically killed me. It's striking all over."

I imagined the Russians on their porches watching Betty and Molly as they inspected the concrete floor. Hopefully, this wouldn't become an international incident prompted by a lapsed goodwill ambassador.

In the early evening, Bob took Lynn and me to dinner at a fancy rooftop restaurant where an American singer he knew about was performing, someone grown-ups liked. Maybe Tony Martin. When the singer sang "Three Coins in the Fountain," Bob asked us if we'd tossed a coin into Trevi Fountain yet. Yes, we had, and according to the legend I would be returning to Rome for sure because when we went there, I'd thrown in all the coins in my pocket. Nestled into the dark, warm night up on that Roman roof with Bob drinking wine and retelling each race and Lynn laughing and adding details, I felt about as happy as I could imagine. Before we left, Bob sent a request for "Que Sera, Sera."

"It's true, isn't it, brat? 'What will be, will be?'"

Yes, I thought. I'd worked as hard as I could swimming lap after lap. I'd sacrificed sugar and sleepovers, football games and late nights, not that I really wanted those things. I'd eaten Irish moss and raw eggs and swallowed zillions of vitamins. I'd made a billion wishes and yet...

"You lost your gold, and you won your gold. *Que sera, sera.*" He grinned at me and reached over like my dad might have done and tousled my hair. I understood what bittersweet meant.

Some grumpy swimmers and divers climbed aboard the train for Naples the next morning. Each compartment sat about eight people, and before we went through the first tunnel, most of the team had fallen asleep. I dozed off and on, too, but after an hour or so, it got boring. I thought I saw Ilsa Konrads walk past our car, so I got up to follow her. We'd shaken hands after the relay, but now the races were over and I had a chance to talk with the famous Australians I'd read so much about.

I lurched along the corridor, balancing between the windows and the compartment doors. In one, Dawn Fraser looked up as I passed, and her face brightened as she motioned for me to come in. No Ilsa in there, but Lorraine Crapp and a couple other older swimmers from Australia and England sat with Dawn.

"Oy. Sit down with us, mate, and tell us your story." Dawn reached under her bag and pulled out a green bottle. "Have some vino, mate. 'Ow old are you, anyway?"

I sat on the edge of a seat. I wasn't going to drink anything. Geez. Even my parents didn't drink.

"Come on, then, be a sport. Just a nip. We'll drink to the Olympic spirits," and she handed me a paper cup with a little wine in it. "Cheers, mate." She reached her cup toward me and the other girls and laughed. They all said, "Cheers," and drained their cups. I looked her in the eye, took her dare, and drank what she'd given me. I liked Dawn Fraser, her rowdy spirit, her defiance of ladylike standards.

"Oy. You the one with the crackers?" she asked. "Boom, boom?"

How did she know? There didn't seem to be any secrets in the Olympic Village. Everybody knew that the track guys stayed up late at night dancing, that Wilma Rudolph wore Ray Norton's hat to the medal awards ceremony. They knew cyclists took drugs. Now I knew that the Aussies drank wine, and Dawn Fraser knew I had firecrackers.

"Be a luv and give me some. Just for fun." I didn't think I could say no to the fastest woman in the world.

Late that afternoon we swam our exhibition in an outdoor, mosaic-tiled pool. Each gold medalist did solo laps followed by each of our relays. The second- and third-place teams stood around and watched with the officials and guests. After the demonstration we sat together for dinner with our teams at tables set in a glass-walled, multileveled pavilion. Just as the waiters brought in dessert, a string of firecrackers erupted, dancing across the marble floor behind the FINA officials' table.

Everyone at our table looked up at me. I shrugged. "Not me." Betty Baldwin pushed her chair back, then scooted in, and smiled across the room at the hosts. The waiters continued serving the desserts as if nothing had happened. At the Australian table, Dawn Fraser looked up and winked before she bent over her gelato. With that wink she recognized and acknowledged me. We shared a secret. More than I knew at that time. Dawn Fraser would return to win more gold in the 1964 Olympics, get married, have a child, divorce, and live in a long-term relationship with a woman. But all that lay far ahead.

US Olympians didn't have chartered flights home. The USOC sent us back sport by sport as we finished our events. Only participants in the last week of competition would march in the Closing Ceremony. I wished we were staying because I wanted the chance to parade into that huge stadium as part of the whole team. It would've been sweet, but instead we were heading home.

Athletes had assigned seats like everybody else on the Pan American flight, mine a middle seat between two young men. When I tucked my medal case under the seat, the guy at the window looked over.

"Wad ya win?" he asked.

"Gold." I tried to sound nonchalant.

"Me too." He grinned. "Let's see yours." I pulled out the case and opened it. He touched the little plaque at the bottom and read, "*Nuoto*. What's that mean?"

"Swimming," I told him. "What was your event?"

"Boxing. Light heavy." He pumped his fists at the seatback in front of him.

"Where's your medal?"

"In my bag."

"What's your name?" I asked as he pulled out a pillow.

"Cassius Clay." He leaned against the window and slept all the way back to New York.

The long journey back began with that flight over the Atlantic. I'd be returning to school a couple of weeks late. Everyone would be ahead of me, familiar with the teachers, the expectations. They'd have solidified their social groups over the summer and be well into the poses of sophomore year. I wondered how long I'd have off before starting back training. Down at the MAC, Don, Patsy, and the rest of the team would want to hear all about Rome. The plane's engines droned while the letdown settled in.

I already knew the questions everyone would ask: What was it like being in the Olympics? What happened in the butterfly? What's it like to win gold? The questions seemed too big to answer. There wasn't really a story to tell about what it was like. Being in the Olympics had started long ago with a dream when I was eleven, when I'd first come to the MAC and seen Mo Murphy's picture. The possibility became real with Lynn as a training partner and after she made the Pan Am team. Being in the Olympics was all about the long winter and the summer training, being determined to make the team, and the endless trials in Detroit. And even then it wasn't over, merely another step along a rocky, dark path. It was like being all alone walking slowly down a steep trail and into a narrow tunnel where you saw no light and didn't know how far you'd have to go before you got out. Or it was like inching forward at a crowded subway station knowing you'd be late if you didn't get on, anxious that the doors would close and you'd be left alone in the dark on the platform. It was all that work and wait and worry. And it was over in a flash. Somehow I didn't think that would be the answer people wanted to hear when they asked what the Olympics were like.

I thought about home, how Mom would probably be narrating my stories before I ever arrived. She would already have told everyone about the Opening Ceremony and each race. Her versions would not be the way things really happened. She'd have the wrong people, or she'd say I said something I hadn't even thought. I remembered other times she'd told stories that never captured the way I felt. "Oh well," she'd sigh if I tried to correct her. "You tell it." She'd look at me patiently while the audience shifted. It would be too much effort to correct her, so after a pause, she'd go on while I pretended to listen.

On that long plane ride, my imagination ran down another dark road. She'd have retold the butterfly race a hundred times by now and related every phone call. I'd probably be a wreck in her story, but she'd consoled me, boosted my spirits, and I'd made a comeback. She'd become the hero of my story. Or else the martyr. "I should have been there with her, she's so young, but I just couldn't..." she'd say, her voice trailing off, suggesting something. By the time I got home, nobody would want to hear the real story.

I was already blaming Mom for something that hadn't even happened. I don't know why I made such a case against her. Maybe I still felt disappointed that she and Dad hadn't been there. Or perhaps it redirected my own disappointments, ones I didn't want to examine or admit. When Penny Pitou had apologized for getting second in her ski race in Squaw Valley, I scoffed. Back then I'd thought I'd be happy to make the Olympic team.

Multnomah Athletic Club bulletin board, September 1960

But now, I felt embarrassed for not marching in the Opening Ceremony, ashamed for finishing fourth in the freestyle. And I'd have to explain my colossal failure in the butterfly. I'd let Mom tell it for me, and blame her for telling it wrong. I felt vulnerable on the long return, unsure what lay ahead at home, at school, on the team. Would they be disappointed that I hadn't won all my races? What would they expect of me next?

When I got home, sure enough, Mom had shared her version of the Olympic Trials and Games. These many years later, I believe that she recognized my unexpressed doubts the year of the Games, and wanted to protect me from a disappointment we both feared. She told my stories because she wanted to have shared everything as it happened, taking pleasure from vicarious participation. By arranging the few details she had into a convincing and entertaining account, she could almost persuade herself she'd really been there.

Actually being there provided me with no such perspective. The whole experience had been so big, so long, so complicated, I could never boil it down to a single story or a clever answer to the repetitious question: What was it like? Even if I tried to answer, could anyone understand the experiences I'd had?

If I talked about dark trails and lonely subways, I wouldn't be giving the whole picture of it anyway. Because it was also like stepping into a swift mountain stream that sweeps your feet from under you and carries you downstream so fast, you can't grab a branch. When it finally lets you go, your heart pounds in your throat, your arms and legs feel numb. You're exhilarated, exhausted, bruised, and so happy, you twirl in a circle on the bank. It was all that and more.

Joy and Sadness

2012

AFTER THE MESETA, THE WAY winds into green hill country that looks like Yamhill or Hood River in Western Oregon, and waves of longing wash through me. Carmel-colored fields edged with cherry, fig, and prune trees alternate with vineyards that stretch across the rounded hills of Bierzo. Farther along, the trail climbs into strips of thin clouds that sweep over villages and streams. Holly trees, their berries bright red, nestle close to houses. Valleys shimmer yellow with poplars. The only sounds besides my boots on the road are hounds and hunters in the distance. For days the trails and roads, at times lined with ferns and evergreens, at others with giant rocks, have snaked through river canyons and up over low mountains.

The steep, rocky path cuts up through a chestnut forest angling toward the border between Castile and Galicia, the last section of the Camino. I swing along the uphill, my mind empty, until I hear rustling ahead, off to the side among ferns and leaf fall. An ancient couple, wicker basket between them, fumble through the underbrush on hands and knees searching for nuts or mushrooms. Their presence seems so unlikely, such a long climb from where I've been. But not much farther along, the forest gives way to a clearing. Ahead on the ridge, an old woman in a blue work dress, wearing wooden clogs and hand-knit green socks over tights, lifts a latch to let a horse out to pasture. Her husband limps across the field below, a young dog beside him. A bit farther along the cow-dunged path, two more old couples carrying woven baskets head toward the chestnut woods. I watch them and think of all the daily work and hardships they must share. In so many towns, the young are absent, the elderly left behind.

These old people who have been abandoned in the villages live in the same world and walk the same paths as I do now: who will care for them, I wonder, when they become too old, too sick? *But they're together*, I think, envy biting like a wasp. Rose still shadows me. I know that I am thinking about myself. Who will walk with me on the difficult paths ahead?

How easily I can slip back into self-pity and sadness, though the moments come less often. I kick at a rock but don't pick it up. Instead, I think about my last years teaching and my focus on noticing place and landscape in American literature, the role of season, weather, plants, terrain, sky, and water. Of course, we read Thoreau and Dillard. Every year I asked the students to design a personal experiment, one that would explore a question important to them, and to record their experiences and their findings. This trek is my Walden, an experiment in living alone and paying attention here in the real world. What have I noticed?

The first days hiking reminded me of early-fall workouts when we'd return to training after several weeks off, endless laps with kickboards and toe cramps, aching calves, days when I learned that my body could tolerate pain, that it could go on even when I wanted to quit. Now within the first hour of hiking, I get in the groove, a rhythm of arms and legs and a melody of leaves, poles, breath, gravel. On the uphills I feel loose and easy, like those training days when everything felt right and I could stroke on and on, burning through the laps. That easy stride, like the easy stroke, never lasts. Fatigue sets in at some point. Or something else: blisters, tendinitis, heat, rain, mud. The joy comes then in walking on through it. I've learned my capacity to cover distance. I might be tired, but I can summon up strength when I need it. *Finish hard to the wall*, I remember.

The path continues in and out of trees and then opens to fields that drop away on either side as clouds rise up through clefts below and dissolve into the blue sky. Heather, broom, gorse, berry vines, bracken fern, oak and acorn, chestnut and pine spread out and down from the ridge. Ravens chase after a hawk. Beside the trail autumn crocus blooms purple as it did more than thirty days ago in the Pyrenees. I yawp out loud in a joyous whoop. "Here I am."

Eventually, the path becomes a cobbled lane and winds into the tiny hilltop hamlet of O'Cebriero. Traditional stone structures, once part of an eleventh-century monastic community, trail westward from the church, one of the earliest buildings on the Camino. I'd expected gray clouds and mist atop the ridge, but wind has cleared the skies, and views sweep out and away to the far horizon. Outdoors at a cafe, I sit and greet walkers as they arrive.

The main event this Friday night is Mass in the ninth-century church with two celebrants and a beautiful contralto whose voice washes over the congregation and warms the walls. Afterward, the priest and many of the locals fill the small taverna in the hotel where I am staying. I sit alone, but soon an old man with Peter O'Toole eyes joins me and then his caregiver and another local man, too, men who had shaken my hand in church as a sign of peace. We talk a mix of Spanish and English, and they tell me a bit about themselves, their village, and the old man, Jesús. I understand some of what they say. Jesús, his hands cupped around his wine glass and staring out into the room, is ninety-two. His head doesn't work too well anymore, they tell me, but he knows the words to every song. After they finish their wine, the men look Jesús in the eye and begin to sing, first, "Bésame Mucho," and then old Gallegan folk songs, all three of them with beautiful tenor voices. Several villagers turn to listen, and a cook comes out of the kitchen, stands until they finish, and then kisses Jesús on both cheeks as he weeps at the table.

Here I am. Look. This is it, I think. *The tenderness. The communion. I'm part of this too.*

The caregiver wipes Jesús's face and helps him stand, and then both men turn and offer their hands. *"Buen Camino."* The old man's hand feels warm and papery, like my mother's felt toward the end.

I'd been frightened of her neediness when my father died, afraid she'd tighten a hold I'd never escape. Instead she'd lived independently for over twenty-five years, until a series of strokes and forgetfulness hobbled her. She'd supported me through the difficult year when I got divorced, came out, lost custody. She tried to understand how "such a thing could have happened," but she never stopped loving me. Every Tuesday and Friday, she picked up Michael from school and kept him until I finished work.

She could be both tender and fierce, with a strong will and intense competitive spirit that I hadn't recognized as a child. She'd seemed such a worrywart when I was swimming, but watching her with her grandchildren, I saw her differently. On Michael's third birthday, we played pin the tail on the donkey, the donkey taped to the dining-room door. Each of his cousins took her turn, and donkey tails ended up stuck all over the door. My mom went last, looked at the donkey, pulled on the blindfold, spun around, marched forward, and slapped the tail right on its ass.

"I won!" she exclaimed. "What's the prize?"

"But, Mom..." Nope. She was serious. She wanted the first-place prize.

I laugh to myself over my cider and remember another time at the beach. We were returning to the cabin, and the kids were dawdling, so she suggested a race between Michael and his older cousin, Robyn, the way she had set up contests between my brother and me. "Let's see who can get to the top of the hill first," she challenged.

Michael dug in. "No more beating games, Mommo."

Toward the end of her life, she flowed in and out of presence, saying, "Oh, hello, I didn't know you were here," and "I love you," before falling back into restless sleep. On her last day, I helped an aide bathe her, watched her relax and loosen when warm water poured over her forehead and through her hair. I gently toweled it dry and sat beside her. Outside, January cracked against the window. Inside, I watched her as

I had done for days, watched the pulse in her neck, like a leaf, tremble and then cease. Just like that. A flicker—then it stopped. It seemed like an act of love to share her last moments with me.

Jesús and his caregiver are long gone, and in the taverna the evening is winding down. Many of the pilgrims have left for the albergue, their tables now covered with green cloths for a card game. Villagers move away from the bar, the women to cluster in the kitchen, the men to sit and play before heading home together. Upstairs I check the guidebook: one hundred miles to Santiago, the official end of the Camino, and only fifty-four more to Finisterre on the coast. There's not enough time left for me to walk all the way to the waves, but I'm a day ahead of schedule. Why not take a bus from Santiago to Cee and walk the final fifteen miles to the ocean? It would be a more complete ending, like swimming all the way to the end of the pool, a finish at the edge of the world.

RIDING THE WAVES

September 1960

LYNN LED US TOWARD THE water where we found a spot close to the surf and spread our towels side by side, squeezed between a family with loud little kids and three teenagers listening to a transistor radio. The beach stretched long and flat in both directions, every inch occupied— towels, chairs, umbrellas, and thousands of people crowded next to each other. Hurricane Donna down in Florida was roiling the surf all along the Atlantic seaboard and drawing beachgoers to the shore.

We hadn't gone to Coney Island, my mother's fear, but to Jones Beach out on Long Island where Lynn promised the water would be perfect for bodysurfing. I'd never heard of that but was willing to try, although mostly I wondered how cold the water would be, having never ventured deeper than my knees at the Oregon coast. The waves that day seemed to swell up into towering mountains, bigger than any I'd seen in Oregon. They broke a long way from shore, pushing water far onto the beach. Hundreds of people waded in the shallows through foamy water up to their ankles or knees or thighs. Children screamed and tugged away from their mothers' grasps wanting to run free into the wild water.

Once in a while, one of the bodysurfers bobbing out beyond the breakers would suddenly sprint toward shore, head up, legs pounding. The incoming swell would lift her higher and higher as she raced to catch its peak before it broke. If she caught it just right, she'd ride with it, slicing across its face, one arm outstretched, body an elongated arrow as it carried her in, folding on itself behind her. It looked pretty cool and very scary.

"Perfect waves for surfing," Lynn yelled as she ran to the water, lifted her knees, and splashed into the foam. Chris stood on the sand with her hands on her hips, watching. Donna flung her shirt onto a towel and chased after Lynn. Seconds before a wave broke, they both dived under it and surfaced in the calm water beyond the breakers.

"Here goes," Chris said. "Are you coming?" We ran into the water almost together. I splashed forward watching a wave rise up, and just after Chris dove, I did too. The wave caught my arms, yanked them up and over my head, and somersaulted me flat onto my back in the sand. Water sucked out around me as I scrambled to my feet, disoriented. I was facing the beach. I turned around to see Lynn slice across a wave. From beyond the breakers, Chris called, "Come on. What happened?"

I didn't know what had happened except I'd had the wind knocked out of me. When Lynn's wave tapered out and her ride ended, she waded toward shore. "Dive into the base of the wave, right in the sweet spot. Watch me." She turned back to the ocean, studied a second, and sprang into the green just as the wave broke. In a second she popped up on the other side of it in the calm water beyond the breakers. I let one wave come in and focused on its base. When the next one rose, I aimed low.

I'd felt ready, but the wave scrambled me around like eggs in a blender. Sand swirled in yellow plumes so that I couldn't tell the bottom from the sky. A powerful tow pulled at me. *I'm drowning,* I thought, air gone from my lungs. My knees scraped across the bottom, my hands reached out, frantically trying to find the way up. When I felt someone's ankle, I held on. Then a hand tugged at my strap and lifted me to my knees, where I knelt in about two inches of receding water.

"Are you all right, honey?" asked a woman in a black bathing suit as big as a tent.

"I think so," I coughed. Sand filled the crotch of my suit so that it sagged down my thighs. I felt slightly nauseous. This felt worse than choking in the butterfly.

Without looking back, I walked to the dressing room and stripped off my Olympic suit, ashamed that people might have seen me practically drown in the ocean. I stood in the shower for a long time replaying what had happened before I put on a green Speedo, one an Australian had offered me in a trade after Naples.

Back on the beach, I lay on my towel, chin in hands, and watched for what seemed like hours as Lynn and Donna and Chris dived through the waves and rode them in. I watched until my body understood what to do, and then I got up, walked down the sandy slope and out through the kids and moms and grandpas until foam came up to my knees, all the time watching the waves rise and crest and crash, and when the next one came, I dived.

Out in the calm water, out beyond the breakers, I lay back and looked at the sky for a while, then kicked out even farther before righting myself. Colored specks shimmered and danced down the long white beach. I turned toward the horizon. *That's where I've been. Across that ocean.* For a while longer, I bobbed on the swells and then turned back to shore and swam all the way in.

THE END OF THE WORLD

2012

All across Galicia the trail stretches westward toward the Atlantic, rising and falling over undulating hills forested in oak groves and chestnut, birch and pine, bordered by green pastures and fields lined with black rock fences. Gray stone houses, roofed with huge rounded slate tiles, support slumping sheds that groan with cows. The low morning sun beats through corn rows like an animated film as I walk along.

Thinking has mostly stopped; the cloudy waves of emotion and memories that have pummeled me these past years are calming. I feel awake and present, as if I've swum beyond the breakers again. For a while I trail an old woman who drives her three cows with an umbrella. In a far field, a mule rolls over and over in the bracken ferns snorting with pleasure. Farther along, a young mother and her daughter clamor through leaves, filling their sacks with chestnuts. Around a bend I startle another gleaner, her hair a white halo, her face an instant smile. I could have been following Walt Whitman along the open road, "afoot and light-hearted... healthy, free, the world before me, the long brown path before me."

The next day the trail climbs out of the village through low-lying fog and up along country roads. The fields and forest are shielded by clouds until ten thirty, when the sun breaks through or the road climbs high enough, yet still below, thin clouds drift and rise. In the afternoon

I follow two small herds of white cows driven to pasture by an old man in the lead, an old woman at the rear, each carrying sticks and hollering the slow cows onward. Their shouts urge me on, too, through the afternoon fatigue.

In those last days, I contemplate how the journey is changing, winding down and also opening up. The end might come before I want or feel ready for it. I could rest a day, turn around, and walk back like the pilgrim and his dog headed to Rome. Why not? I laugh at the thought of another forty days in the same gray pants and wool shirt. It will be enough to finish.

Time's grip returns with the tick of white stone markers every five hundred meters indicating the distance remaining to Santiago. The broad horizon narrows to a dirty road. More walkers, school groups, couples, day hikers with transistor radios and clean clothes, join the pilgrimage for the final one hundred kilometers, just far enough to earn a Compostela, or Credencial del Peregrino. The way itself changes, with fewer remote trails and more roadways, the land filled with farms and villages. The world pushes in all around—cars, airplanes, protest marches, PRO-LIFE graffiti spray-painted on sheds and rocks every mile or so. The third time I see the red scrawl, I swear out loud. When I hear the schoolkids' chatter coming close behind me, I speed up, caught by my competitive spirit. A few kids pass, but when they stop for a snack, I smugly walk on, amused and slightly embarrassed by my behavior.

To remain mindful with what lies ahead will require effort. When the restless eucalyptus trees give way to a native oak grove, the road noise lessens, and my thoughts return to the Camino. *One step at a time. Pay attention.* In the sun an old man naps, two canes leaning against his knees. Behind him in a cowshed doorway, a rope of yellow corn sways. Down the cobbled lane, his wife—perhaps—shades her eyes as she sits listening to two younger women in jodhpurs and rubber boots who lean on their brooms and tell stories of yesterday or make plans for tomorrow. No one looks up as I pass.

In the morning, vapors lie across the meadows and on the backs of cows as I follow Venus through the darkness to the top of Monte do Gozo looming above Santiago. Sunrise changes the sky from dark to pink to salmon. Somewhere below the clouds lies the city. By ten o'clock I walk through the ancient Gate of the Way and find the cathedral, filled with incense and the songs of morning Mass. When I kneel, tears begin without thoughts. My body softens and exhales with a sigh.

Outside, a French girl I recognize from last week in an albergue walks toward me, arms outstretched. "Congratulations. You're here!" In the Pilgrims' Office, Michel, the old Quebecois, stands waiting for his Compostela. Another traveler from weeks before waves from across the Plaza de la Quintana, and up from its stone steps rise the New Hampshire mother and two daughters who have walked from Le Puy, the ones who "got smarter" or "got stronger" depending on how their trail finding went. They passed me over thirty-five days ago, arrived in Santiago on Obama's victory day, and walked on to Muxía and Finisterre, the end of the world. Tonight they'll leave for home.

A group of pilgrims, all French speakers, who have zigzagged the route with me over the final weeks, sits together in the sunny Quintana courtyard sipping beer. They wave me to join them, and we sit mostly in silence listening to a musician whose electric guitar fills the empty plaza with slow jazz variations.

The Camino has ended just as it began for me. I feel alone, separate, an observer, an outsider who connects only with a few and even then only for a short time—Monica and Gordon, Jesús, the mother and daughters, Silvia. *It is how I am*, I admit. Over these weeks I've begun to recognize the difference between solitude and loneliness. I feel comfortable with one and less afraid of the other.

Sometimes in the early morning or late evening when you're walking on summer roads, you suddenly encounter a pool of cooler air that you feel on your bare arms or along your legs. Memories and emotions have been like that all along the Camino; they arise without source, as if waiting for me, and I walk right into them. Pale light would fall through rain along a dark street, and suddenly I'd be waiting for my father to pick me up after swim practice. Ladies would walk side by side with brown and black umbrellas outside the train station in Santiago, and Rose and I would be arriving there in 1987. Knitting needles would punctuate a boisterous conversation in a country inn, and I'd see my mother, her hand reaching to pull red yarn from her basket, leaning in to hear Marthadent's news. Memories brushed against me. I felt them and walked on through.

All along the journey, Rose has traveled with me. How could she not when half my life's memories include her? They will not go away, these memories, but they don't need to catch and hold like burrs on a sweater or cheatgrass in socks. They can flow past like weather, like the clouds I've watched fill a valley, then rise and disperse. Or I can move through them, the way I swam through the surf.

On the far western reach of the Iberian Peninsula lies Finisterre, a sacred site for ancient Celts, where offshore stones mark the tomb of Orcabella, a version of Cailleach Bheara, crone goddess of winter and wilderness, mother of all gods and goddesses. It seems a fitting end to this long journey.

Don't worry, I tell myself now that it's the last day. *One foot after the other on down the road. On down the road to the end of the world.* From high on the path, I see a long stretch of white sand appear. Black-bottomed rain clouds obscure the headlands to the south, but where I stand a shred of sunshine breaks through. Even before I hear the surf or reach the sand, I see the glassy gray-green waters that stretch all the way to New York, to the New World, and I sit on the trail and cry. I have walked from Saint-Jean-Pied-de-Port in the Pyrenees to the Atlantic Ocean alone. I feel so grateful to be alive.

Around the curve of the beach, Finisterre clings to the isthmus and crawls across the headland in faded terra-cotta and apricot. Even this late in the season, kumquats and figs hang over fences and oranges turn from green. *All the world is turning, spinning, and I am part of it. Here I am.*

Endings happen slowly over time, just like beginnings. When did this journey end? Seeing Santiago from Monte do Gozo on Friday morning? Or entering the cathedral and kneeling behind the altar? Receiving the Compostela filled out in Latin, stamped, and dated? Or sitting in the sun in Plaza de la Quintana with fellow travelers greeting new arrivals? Or did it end when I hiked in the late afternoon out past the port of Finisterre to the far point, the *faro*, the lighthouse, under threatening skies and howling wind, where I finally reached "the end of the known world," where Roman soldiers had fallen to their knees and wept when they thought the sun was drowning and the end of the world had come? Did this journey end when I gazed west to the horizon, out over the same ocean I'd studied more than fifty years before when I'd returned from Rome?

On my final day in Spain, a storm blows in and rain drenches the city. It is late November and time to return home. The long walk has altered my perspective and given hints of a possible future. But unlike the girl who came home from Lansing determined to make the Olympic team, I have no specific goal other than to stay awake, pay attention, and wait for the lessons of the Camino. *You don't take your feet off the bottom, swim dock to dock, race, and win all in one summer*, I remind myself. *It's all practice.*

WHAT CAME NEXT

1960–1963

"WEAR YOUR UNIFORM," MOM SAID when I called from the Burkes' to tell her the flight plan: New York to San Francisco and then a second plane to carry me home. Portland's mayor, Terry Shrunk, had no trouble finding me on the connecting flight up from San Francisco. He congratulated me, asked a few questions, and told me to wait on board until everyone got off and to be sure to wear the gold medal around my neck. I guessed there'd be a celebration when we landed.

Photographers stood on the tarmac, cameras aimed and flashing, as Mr. Shrunk and I stepped to the door. My whole family—Mom, Dad, Grandma Green, and Richard—grinned as the mayor presented me with a key to the city. Then Maureen Murphy and a Royal Rosarian in full uniform and the president of the Multnomah Club each took turns shaking my hand and posing for photos. By the time I got off the runway, my arms were laden with bouquets of roses and the city key. Ahead the waiting area teemed with celebrants—Stevie and Mary and other neighborhood playmates, Donnie and teammates from the Club, the Beaverton High swim team, Gretchen and Gretchen in rally uniforms, classmates, our minister and church friends, my parents' friends from all my life. Cheers and laughter, jostling and hugs welcomed me home as a police officer nudged us through the concourse and out the front doors. We drove from the airport through downtown in an impromptu, horn-honking, celebratory parade, my own Portland closing ceremony.

Sophomore year began on the following Monday. Everything felt different without the intense anxiety and focus of the previous year. I still wanted to swim faster, break records, win championships, but I also wanted to excel in school and have fun with my classmates, ride the rooter bus to football games, cheer in the stands at Tuesday-night basketball games. Life beyond the pool seemed available now that the Olympics were over. A group of girls—we called ourselves Wicked Sophomore Women, or WSWs—began sitting together at games and shouting out our own wild cheers. When the oldest among us got her driver's license, we packed her car, turned up the radio, and sang our way to games in Hillsboro and Milwaukie and across town to Central Catholic. I felt independent and defiant on those nights, like I had playing as a child.

At the Club, however, my swim world seemed confusing and disappointing. Swimmers who had come to Portland to train with Coach, hoping for an Olympic berth, returned to their families in New York and Florida; older girls quit, and boys went off to college. A younger group of kids was coming up, but Coach seemed distant and distracted. Our workouts became repetitious and boring and were often presented on typed sheets taped to his office window. He seemed to neglect some swimmers and to favor others, and parents, dissatisfied with his methods, his attitude, began to openly criticize. The competition between Nancy Kanaby and me felt even more uncomfortable than it had the previous year, especially after Marthadent told us that Coach was giving her extra workouts during the day while we were in school. Confronted, he explained that he wanted her times to drop to improve our relay, but I felt cheated, bitten by jealousy and a sense of injustice. Why couldn't I swim for a coach who would help me be the best even if I weren't going to try out for the '64 Olympics? Someone like Rod Harman, the high school coach, or George Haines, Lynn and Chris's coach. These thoughts and questions recurred throughout the year as we trained and raced and trained some more.

Maureen Murphy greeting me at Portland International Airport

Mom, Richard, Grandma Green, and Dad welcoming me home

Airport welcome from neighbors, teammates, classmates, and friends

Our MAC relays won at indoor nationals in Florida, and my individual times were good enough to place, but if I was going to continue to train hard, I wanted more: I wanted a goal as clear as the one Lynn had set out for us in 1959, the one that carried me through the year after she left. I wanted a coach who would help me find a new purpose after the Olympics.

In New York after Rome, Lynn turned professional. Soon her photo appeared in *Look* magazine advertising RC Cola, and at nationals she provided color commentary and interviews for *Wide World of Sports*. Other Olympians quit after Rome: Shirley Stobs, Joan Spillane, Carolyn Schuler, Molly Botkin, and Sylvia Ruuska. But Chris and Donna de Varona swam on, and in August 1961, we all earned places on the first American women's traveling team to Europe for a series of meets in Holland, England, and Germany. These were friendly competitions in unheated pools interspersed with sightseeing tours of lowland dairies, highland lakes, and German beer halls. I roomed with Chris often, and she tutored me in shopping for antiques, linens, sheepskin gloves, and skiwear. In Blackpool she nursed me and the rest of the team stricken with food poisoning, and there I tied a world record in the butterfly. In Germany she took over as coach since our AAU chaperone knew nothing about swim training.

Our last scheduled meet of the tour, planned for Berlin, had been relocated to Munich. We heard snatches of news reports on an English-broadcast radio station about a wall being built and felt the tension of the adults who smothered us in oppressive fellowship. Tired of being marched around from luncheon to dinner, tired of listening to speeches about friendship, reconciliation, reunification, I begged off practice one day and the subsequent sightseeing to stay behind in the hotel and read. From the window I looked out over the ruined upper stories of buildings that, from the street, seemed whole. *We bombed them*, I thought, and for a moment I imagined the planes and noise, and then I thought of Anne Frank, whose diary I'd read that summer, and the tanks we'd seen rumbling through the countryside in Holland two weeks before. The world seemed vast and complicated, and I was beginning to want to understand it.

After the summer nationals in Philadelphia and before we left for the European tour, I had asked Chris if she thought George would take me on his team, and she said she would talk to him. I gave no thought to what my parents might think but simply told them I'd decided to move to California and swim for Santa Clara when I got back from Europe. Chris would be off to Stanford, and maybe I could room at her house as Lynn had done. It seemed reasonable. Did I really think that was all I had to do, tell my parents and they'd arrange it or even allow it? When the team returned in September, I spent a few extra days in New York with the Burkes. At home, a surprise awaited.

Coach Schlueter had been fired. He and Nancy were gone. A new coach, the Club's swim instructor, a kind but inexperienced woman, took over the team. What happened in those weeks between the Philadelphia nationals and my return to Portland, I don't know, but the results included Donnie's departure for Santa Clara to swim for George and my sense of obligation to stay at the Club. I somehow felt responsible for the upheaval because I'd wanted to change teams and now felt duty bound to give the new coach a chance. I would not move to California or swim for George, but Don had years of swimming ahead. The Tokyo Olympics, college, even Mexico City in 1968 seemed possible for him.

At school, the WSWs were now Wicked Junior Women, and we ripped around the neighborhoods on game nights, wore cut-off jeans and sweatshirts flouting the dress code, and defied the administration by sneaking into the school and painting a belly button on our school mascot, a giant Beaver who loomed over the basketball court. At an after-game dance, a few of us were kicked out for defying the principal's ban on dancing the twist. Childish pranks from swim days grew into gentle rebellions after school. In class, however, I worked hard to achieve, especially in English.

A beautiful, challenging first-year teacher taught our advanced American literature class. I fell in love with her the first day, and with the novels and poems we read. Her lectures—which came straight from Dr. Nolte's American Novel course, as I would discover three years later when I sat in his class at University of Oregon—opened the literary world to me, and her teaching techniques I would use in my own classrooms for over thirty years. Literature and writing became as important as swimming that year as I found characters who felt as deeply as I and whose stories and emotions seemed familiar.

I loved the sprawl of *Moby-Dick* and our class discussions as we tried to make sense of difficult chapters. I admired Hester Prynne's courage and identified with her secret and forbidden love, keenly aware of how "normal" society labels and punishes a deviant. I recognized Holden Caulfield's alienation and Stephen Crane's experiments in observation. Over vacation I struggled through *The Sound and the Fury*, excited by the challenge of being inside someone else's mind as it drifted through thoughts, sensations, memories. An intellectual classmate introduced me to Caffe Espresso, a beatnik coffeehouse near Portland State, where we sipped cappuccinos and tried to interpret Quentin's suicide and Benjy's ramblings. That year I began buying books our teacher mentioned, tried writing in stream of consciousness, and submitted poems to our literary magazine. I was waking up to a life of the mind. Swimming had opened doors to people and countries far beyond Oregon, but literature would take me further.

In late August after the 1962 national championships in Chicago, I made the decision to quit training for national and international competition. I'd swim out the high school season, I reasoned, but after the state championships, I'd turn professional. In those days, any paid work related to your competitive sport meant losing amateur status. My job, which paid a little over a dollar an hour, was lifeguarding and assisting Coach Harman with his age-group team. For spring vacation I spent all my earnings on a plane ticket east to visit Lynn and the Burkes in New York and then up to New Haven to cheer Donnie at the men's nationals at Yale. When the week ended, I called home wanting to stay longer to visit Philadelphia, an easy train ride away.

I was seventeen, a senior in high school, already a world traveler, happy to be out on an adventure. Ahead lay college and the ever-unfolding future—teaching English, a year with the Robert Kennedy family, marriage, motherhood, divorce and the complications of coming out, finding a life partner and losing her. But in that moment in early-spring New York at Penn Station, all I had to do was get on the train, find my seat, and settle in for the ride.

Epilogue: Here I Am

2013

THE TGV TRAIN SPEEDS THROUGH the French countryside on its way to Le Puy, and I am on board full of questions. The euphoria from completing the Camino lasted well into the new year, and under its spell I declared my intention to walk the French section, the Chemin, from Le Puy to Saint-Jean-Pied-de-Port, another five hundred miles. It seemed important to keep working on my state of mind. Setting a new goal to work toward would focus me, I reasoned. Meanwhile, yoga, meditation, books and plays, first-year French and films, but most of all friends, helped me through the winter storms and spring rains. Throughout the year, I practiced noticing techniques I'd learned on the Camino and found I could often step aside and watch as gloomy thoughts built, cycled, and dispersed. For moments, my feet danced off the bottom as they had decades before when I'd learned to swim. But like learning any new skill, it required discipline and dedication to the process. Humor and forgiveness helped too.

By April I was back in Forest Park getting my feet ready to hike. *But do I need to go to France and walk another forty days?* I wondered as I hauled a weighted backpack up and down the Wildwood Trail. It was such a long time to be gone, and it would be hard to leave late-summer Portland. Did I really need a second test to prove I could swim from dock to dock over dark waters?

Now, outside the train window, yellow, buttery light streams over low, tree-covered hills and reflects off the Loire, which runs below the tracks in a narrow, rocky gorge. The late-September trees give no hint of fall. Questions disrupt the tranquil setting, the hushed railcar. *Why am I here? What am I doing? Who is this for?* One answer is obvious: I am walking again because the breakup still haunts me. For all my work, I still need more practice letting go.

When the train arrives in Le Puy, I step off alone into unknown territory, hoist my backpack on, and find my way to a hotel. The next morning, fog rises from the river, winds through the twisting, cobbled streets, and shrouds the hilltop Cathédrale Notre Dame. I wade through it searching for the route out of town, preparing for tomorrow's beginning. Stone steps lead down from the cathedral, and I note where the red-and-white painted trail markers point pilgrims onto a wayside track. *In the morning I'll be able to find it again,* I assure myself.

Past experiences create expectation. The night before starting the walk, I catalogue what I know lies ahead: long days, shin splints, fatigue and pain, the dread of rain, wet boots and socks, steamy rooms, mud. I can also expect aching solitude and the recurring fear that I will not love or be loved again. In the afternoon when the kind lady who runs the hotel kitchen tried to understand my fractured French, I broke into tears and retreated to my room, overcome by feelings of helplessness. But in the morning, excitement and curiosity awaken with me.

If experience ferries us between two places or states of being, then this journey begins with sadness and doubt much as it did last year. *Where will I be at the end?* I wonder. Within an hour of striding along the path, I feel the old joy of being outdoors, moving, sensing: the vast sky dotted with clouds, ground birds flying up, a red button on the trail, wildflowers and escaped domestics: carnations, scabiosas, geraniums. Fields of grain, corn, cabbage. Peat smoke and cow dung, a hawk's scream, a lost lamb's cry, dogs in a courtyard, a distant tractor. Encouraging thoughts arise: *I'm walking alone because I can find the joy in life even if I can't share*

it. And when the pain begins, the physical pain, I can stand it. I can walk
through it just as I swam through it.

By the end of the first week, the differences from the previous year emerge. Of course, the trails and culture in France differ from Spain, but I am a different pilgrim, more open to sensing moments, to noticing detail, to engaging. Memories triggered by scents and light range from childhood swimming to the innkeeper I met two days ago. They flow like river currents unblocked from the debris of breakup.

Last year's experience on the Camino may have prepared me for the physical labor of the walk but not for the difference in camaraderie. Among the trekkers and pilgrims along the Chemin, I find laughter and story, kindness and company, as if we are a team, ever shifting and changing. On any given day, we come together at the end of one long workout to complain, tease, recover, and share. In Rome I was too young to seek out others' stories, too busy to sit and listen, too absorbed in the task of racing. Last year I carried pain like a shield and savored my isolation. But this year from the very beginning, bands of us share dinner and a night or two or more along the way.

One day begins in dusky morning twilight along the Lot River, the air so still, I can hear fish jumping and the morning songs of countless birds. When the clouds descend and foggy scarves clog the streambeds and drape around gnarled trees, muting all colors, I feel as if I am walking through a fairy-tale engraving. Right after noon, light showers become torrents, raindrops splatting against chestnut leaves. The limestone trails run ankle deep in milky torrents, and the dell's streams over-swell their banks. Just outside a hamlet, lightning strikes nearby, and thunder rolls through the storm-battered village. I hurry onward following a steep track cut across an open field and down into a small wood. Suddenly, a tiny man scurries and leaps from under a grassy fringe on one side of the trail to a small opening on the other—a small, long-legged leprechaun or elf. A frog. I laugh with delight and want to tell someone the story.

Before dusk, soaked to the skin, I arrive at a *gîte* and join five other "wet dogs" from the trail: a man from Marseilles, a German from a previous gîte, the Swiss father and daughter I met at an Ursuline convent and hiked with for one afternoon, a young Parisian who'd been an exchange student to St. Louis. We pool our sad supplies and cook up dinner together: vegetable soup, lentils with onions and sausage, apples and cheese, a bottle of wine, and canned peaches for dessert. We entertain each other with stories from our rainy day and then food fantasies about cookies, Christmas baking traditions in Germany, Paris, Switzerland.

For several days the trail passes south of the Dordogne, an area where Rose and I had rented a farmhouse from an old French woman three different summers. The names of the tiny towns the Chemin passes through remind me of those near Montferrand where we stayed. We visited Pech Merle—a prehistoric cave with a wall painting of two beautiful spotted ponies and the handprints of a woman and child in the sandstone—which is now only a day's hike off the Chemin. I think back to the day a year ago when I crossed the Pyrenees and encountered two ponies beside the trail standing almost in the pose of the cave painting. I wished Rose were with me to tell her. I missed the Rose who had shared adventures in Ireland, Wales, Spain, and Portugal, who explored cave paintings and local brasseries in France. I missed that companion of adventure and discovery.

But I've learned from the first walk and in the intervening year what I hadn't been sure of—how I would bear the sadness and loneliness of life without my partner. I have done it just as I've walked, step by step, day after day. Silvia, the Basque separatist from the Camino, had told me that the real meaning or lesson of the pilgrimage would come after the walk was over, at some unexpected, unplanned time. They need to keep walking, those experiences and thoughts and feelings, she'd told me. One of its lessons has emerged: a person can find joy in solitude or in company by paying attention and being present.

To move deliberately through a region, across a country, to watch it change in both place and time, to watch yourself, to see and feel the difference in trail, topography, people, the difference in emotion and reaction, to experience the villages, the ones that feel good and the ones that feel sad or mean or deserted, to do all this is a gift and a privilege, not to be squandered. What rich variety to walk through landscape, through time, a whole day, from sunrise to noon and on into dusk, a whole season day by day.

As the Chemin comes to an end, climbing back into the Pyrenees to the village of Saint-Jean, I slow down a bit, not ready for it to be over. Some things should not be a sprint to the finish. This might be a good time to drop my feet to the bottom and wade in, head up, eyes open.

I know where I've been. I don't need to look back.

This is it.

Here I am.

MAP OF THE

CAMINO DE SANTIAGO

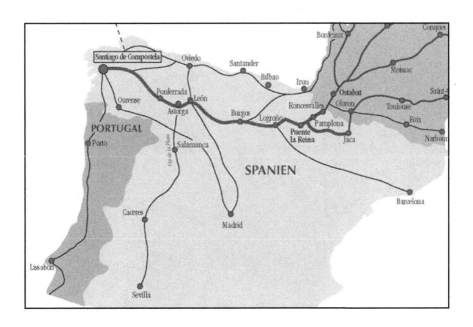

ACKNOWLEDGMENTS

THIS BOOK IS MUCH ABOUT teaching and learning—how to swim, how to compete, yes, but also how to prepare and journey through a life. Our parents are our first teachers, and I thank mine for their steady support and love, for the hours they spent driving me to and from practices, for the days away from home and work at swim meets. Many details in the book are possible because of my mother's careful tending to scrapbooks and my father's friendships with *Oregon Journal* photographers and writers.

Every child deserves the opportunity to learn to swim, and I want to acknowledge Portland Parks & Recreation and Tualatin Hills Park & Recreation District's long commitment to providing year-round pools and instruction, essential for children's safety and enjoyment.

The Multnomah Athletic Club has offered its members fine coaches and teachers for over 125 years. When my family first joined, it provided me with a team, friendships, and a home away from home. After the Olympics, I was granted a lifetime membership, for which I am very appreciative.

In an Oregon Writing Project summer workshop, Linda Christensen advised us to write along with our students, and this book emerged from a series of vignettes begun in various classes over the years. My students inspired me with their curiosity, honesty, and courage in writing, but it was Tom Hallman's question in a class at the Multnomah Club, "What do you want your granddaughter to know about you?" that launched my exploration and subsequent answers. We find many teachers along the road.

I'm especially grateful to Fishtrap's Imnaha Writers' Retreat and Tom and Priscilla Turner, who offered quiet, remote places to write.

For several years, Andrea Carlisle, coach and editor, provided provocative questions, careful readings, and useful and encouraging conversations, essential to my growth as a writer. Thank you.

Editor Ali McCart Shaw has guided me through the final drafts, and I am grateful for her belief in and encouragement for the project. Others on her Indigo Editing & Publications team have been essential to me in completing this project: Olivia Croom, Susan DeFreitas, Kristen Hall-Geisler, and Vinnie Kinsella. Melissa Flamson of With Permission helped locate necessary consents for lyrics and photographs. Thank you all.

Many others have kindled the writing fire and helped along the way by listening, reading, advising, and encouraging: Leigh Coffey, Judith Barrington, Erika Ricordon, Tom and Woesha Hampson, David Oates, Chris de Vallet, Sherrie Barger, Jane Comerford, Connie Soper, Anita Bigelow, and George Vogt. A special thanks to Kate Rood and Donna Darm.

Most of all, Michael, thank you for a lifetime of love.

About the Author

Carolyn Wood, born and raised in Portland, Oregon, still lives in her family home. She is a retired English teacher who spent over thirty years encouraging students to write and is now taking her own advice, although often she'd rather be practicing yoga, or outdoors tending her bees and garden, or hiking back roads and mountain trails. Ms. Wood's work has appeared in *Teachers as Writers* and *Elohi Gadugi Journal*. This is her first book.

CPSIA information can be obtained
at www.ICGtesting.com
Printed in the USA
FSOW03n1352220816
24049FS